The Disney Musical on Stage and Screen

Related titles from Bloomsbury Methuen Drama

British Musical Theatre since 1950
Robert Gordon, Olaf Jubin and Millie Taylor
ISBN 978-1-4725-8436-6

Clowning as Social Performance in Colombia
Barnaby King
ISBN 978-1-4742-4927-0

Critical Companion to the American Stage Musical
Elizabeth L. Wollman
ISBN 978-1-4725-1325-0

Contemporary Adaptations of Greek Tragedy:
Auteurship and Directorial Visions
Edited by George Rodosthenous
ISBN 978-1-4725-9152-4

Popular Performance
Edited by Adam Ainsworth, Oliver Double and Louise Peacock
ISBN 978-1-4742-4734-4

Scenography Expanded:
An Introduction to Contemporary Performance Design
Edited by Joslin McKinney and Scott Palmer
ISBN 978-1-4742-4439-8

Script Analysis for Theatre
Robert Knopf
ISBN 978-1-4081-8430-1

The Disney Musical on Stage and Screen

Critical Approaches from 'Snow White' to 'Frozen'

Edited by
George Rodosthenous

Bloomsbury Methuen Drama
An imprint of Bloomsbury Publishing Plc

BLOOMSBURY

LONDON · OXFORD · NEW YORK · NEW DELHI · SYDNEY

Bloomsbury Methuen Drama

An imprint of Bloomsbury Publishing Plc

Imprint previously known as Methuen Drama

50 Bedford Square	1385 Broadway
London	New York
WC1B 3DP	NY 10018
UK	USA

www.bloomsbury.com

BLOOMSBURY, METHUEN DRAMA and the Diana logo are trademarks of Bloomsbury Publishing Plc

First published 2017
Reprinted 2017

791.
436
578
DIS

British Library Cataloguing-in-Publication Data
A catalogue record for this book is available from the British Library.

ISBN:	HB:	978-1-4742-3417-7
	PB:	978-1-4742-3416-0
	ePDF:	978-1-4742-3419-1
	ePub:	978-1-4742-3418-4

Library of Congress Cataloging-in-Publication Data
Names: Rodosthenous, George, 1973- editor.
Title: The Disney musical on stage and screen : critical approaches from "Snow White" to "Frozen" / edited by George Rodosthenous.
Description: London ; New York : Bloomsbury Methuen Drama, 2017. | Includes bibliographical references.
Identifiers: LCCN 2016045323| ISBN 9781474234160 (pbk.) | ISBN 9781474234177
(hardback) | ISBN 9781474234191 (ePDF) | ISBN 9781474234184 (ePub)
Subjects: LCSH: Walt Disney Company. | Motion pictures–United States–History and criticism. | Musicals–United States–History and criticism.
Classification: LCC PN1999.W27 D576 2017 | DDC 384/.80979494–dc23 LC record available at https://lccn.loc.gov/2016045323

Cover image © JTB MEDIA CREATION, Inc. / Alamy Stock Photo

Typeset by Fakenham Prepress Solutions, Fakenham, Norfolk NR21 8NN
Printed and bound in Great Britain

Contents

List of Tables and Figures

Biographical Note and Notes on Contributors

George Rodosthenous is Associate Professor in Theatre Directing at the School of Performance and Cultural Industries of the University of Leeds, UK.

Sam Baltimore is an independent scholar in Washington, DC.

Geoffrey Block is Distinguished Professor of Music History at the University of Puget Sound, USA.

Emily Clark is Visiting Instructor of Theatre Arts at Marymount Manhattan College, USA.

Donatella Galella is Assistant Professor of Theatre at the University of California, Riverside, USA.

Barbara Wallace Grossman is Professor of Drama at Tufts University, USA.

Stefanie A. Jones is an Adjunct Lecturer at New York University, USA, and the City University of New York (CUNY), USA.

Olaf Jubin is Reader in Media Studies and Musical Theatre at Regent's University London, UK.

Raymond Knapp is Professor of Musicology at the University of California, Los Angeles, USA.

Paul R. Laird is Professor of Musicology at the University of Kansas, USA.

Tim Stephenson is Senior Lecturer at the School of Performance and Cultural Industries, University of Leeds, UK.

Dominic Symonds is Reader at the University of Lincoln, UK.

Aaron C. Thomas is Assistant Professor of Theatre History and Literature in the School of Performing Arts at the University of Central Florida, USA.

Elizabeth Randell Upton is Associate Professor of Musicology at the University of California, Los Angeles, USA.

Sarah Whitfield is Senior Lecturer in Musical Theatre at the University of Wolverhampton, UK.

Stacy E. Wolf is Professor of Theater, Director of the Program in Music Theater, and Director of the Princeton Art Fellows in the Lewis Center for the Arts at Princeton University, USA.

Catherine Young is a Communication Fellow at the Bernard L. Schwartz Communication Institute, Baruch College, City University of New York (CUNY), USA.

Acknowledgements

I would like to thank Mark Dudgeon at Bloomsbury Methuen Drama for his immediate interest in my research proposal. Also many thanks to Susan Furber and the editorial team at Bloomsbury Methuen Drama for all their help and guidance towards the final steps of the process, the anonymous reader for his or her constructive feedback and insightful suggestions, Jill Morris and Kim Storry at Fakenham Prepress Solutions. I am grateful to all the contributors to the volume for their excellent contributions and working together to ensure its smooth publication.

Many thanks to the editors of *Studies in Musical Theatre* Dr Dominic Symonds and Dr George Burrows and the members of the International Federation of Theatre Research: Music Theatre Working Group for all their feedback, discussions and encouragement throughout the years. Also, sincere thanks to Dr Olaf Jobin for sharing his expert knowledge on the Disney corporation and his comments on my Introduction, Arthur Pritchard, Jordan James Taylor, Professor Stacy E. Wolf, Dr Duška Radosavljević, Dr Scott Palmer, Professor Alice O'Grady, Dr Joslin McKinney, Ms Susan Daniels, Professor Jonathan Pitches, Professor Robert Gordon, Dr Nektarios Rodosthenous, Dr Demetris Zavros, Dr Tim Stephenson, Kelli Zezulka, Sophie Massa and all my students for the fruitful debates on the Disney musical.

Special thanks to Ken Cerniglia, Dramaturg and Literary Manager at the Disney Theatrical Group, for his invaluable help and support.

Dr George Rodosthenous
Associate Professor in Theatre Directing
University of Leeds

Introduction

George Rodosthenous

> The US Marines are respected around the world for their formidable fighting reputation. But their ability to strike fear into the hearts of America's enemies may have been somewhat dented by a hilarious video that has emerged online. The footage shows a group of them, with trademarks shaved heads and khaki t-shirts, singing along ecstatically to the song 'Let It Go' from the Disney animation. They become particularly excited at the moment the character of Elsa delivers an exuberant hair flick, cheering and grunting in a manner that, barring the context, would not be out of place in Full Metal Jacket. (Anon. 2014)[1]

Undeniably, Disney's impact on society has been and remains tremendous: its animated and live-action films, television and stage shows, as well as its related products (cruise lines, theme parks and merchandise) have an incalculable importance in our lives. They have influenced the way in which we grew up and shaped the creation of our collective memories of childhood. This intricate relationship between childhood and memory can perhaps explain the moment described above, in which tomorrow's Marines let their hair down and celebrated this moment of carefree distraction. For the cynics, this incident can be read as a paradox. We have a group of alpha-males rejoicing in a song from a Disney film musical that is usually enjoyed predominantly by young girls: Marines singing Disney songs was never part of the homosocial activities agenda in the barracks. The power ballad about 'letting go' has become a universal mantra not just for young girls, but also for people who are in need of a personal moment of liberation, a moment with which they can empathize and which makes them feel empowered and free. For these Marines, at this specific time in their lives, that moment arrived courtesy of Disney's highly successful animated film *Frozen* (2013).

Walt and Roy Disney started their company in 1923 and Walt introduced music into animated storytelling in 1928, with *Steamboat Willie*. Music, and particularly songs, became an increasingly important and integral part of the company's output. According to Byrne and McQuillan, 'Far from being mere adjuncts to the animated narrative, musical interludes between anthropomorphic action, the[se] songs represent some of the decisive indices in which the Disney ideology is most securely embedded' (1999: 8). This volume is an edited collection of 13 essays about the Disney musical, featuring the work of eminent academics working in the field of musical theatre in the US and Europe today. The chapters open with *Snow White* (1937), Disney's first animated full-length feature film, based on the Brothers Grimm's homonymous fairy tale (1812), and conclude with *Frozen* (2013), a 3D, computer-animated musical fantasy film (the 53rd in the Animated Classics series), inspired by another fairy tale – *The Snow Queen*, by Hans Christian Andersen (1844).

This short introduction will establish three main frameworks for reading the Disney musical in its stage and film incarnations. I will suggest that we revisit musicals not only as popular entertainment (Dyer, Taylor) or as a globalized commercial product (Savran, Rebellato), but firstly as a political tool for enhancing our understanding of race, sexuality and gender, secondly as an educational tool for younger children and thirdly as a place for artistic innovation.

The chapters that follow address these three aspects of the Disney musical and offer new critical readings of a vast range of important works from the Disney musical cannon, including *Enchanted, Mary Poppins, The Hunchback of Notre Dame, The Lion King, Newsies, High School Musical, The Jungle Book, Aladdin* and versions of Broadway musicals for television in the early 1990s and 2000s. The critical readings are detailed and open-minded and come to surprising conclusions about the nature and impact of the Disney musical. The present book is the first to explore the Disney musical in such an extensive manner. Its chapters open up new territories in the critical discussion of the Disney mega-musical, its gender, sexual and racial politics, its outreach, and the impact of stage, film and television adaptations.

The Disney Musical as a Political Tool

Mark Van Doren, a leading intellectual figure of the 1950s, insisted that Disney 'lives somewhere near the human center and knows innumerable truths that cannot be taught.' In fact, though, those truths can be taught. Not to [Walt] Disney, who sensed it in his soul without any need for advanced 'tutoring,' like other intuitive geniuses from Shakespeare to John Lennon. But *by* Disney, to *us*, through his work. No truths contained in Disney films are more significant than the teaching of tolerance and acceptance through a heightened understanding for the full range of diversity among members of the human race. (Brode 2005: 17)

Musical theatre can incorporate political messages in, what might superficially seem to be, simple entertainment. There is a dearth of academic writing when it comes to the Disney musical, something that this volume aims to address, particularly when it comes to gender politics in musical theatre (Stephenson, Knapp, Laird, Jubin, Whitfield) and on Disney's handling of sexuality (Baltimore) or race (Clark, Galella, Jones and Young).

In the Disney musicals, the continuous presence of Disney princesses (for example Ariel, Belle, Elsa and Anna) offers a range of opportunities for discussing representations of gender including, in certain cases, the political message of women being strong role models (see also Brocklebank 2000; England et al. 2001). This follows Stover's concern that

> it is possible to make profound, quality narratives for children, and still produce iconic, marketable images ... [But u]ntil Disney develops and markets its heroines in this fashion, these females will never truly champion the progressive ideals of equality that inspired the women's movement for decades. (2013: 8)

Disney's creative teams are conscious that the princesses are one of their strongest merchandise branches. Thus, when they adapt them to the stage, they make adjustments that speak for our time. For example, in the stage production of *The Little Mermaid*, Ariel confronts the villain Ursula directly, and saves herself. Do Rosario's study on 'The Princess and the Magic Kingdom: Beyond Nostalgia, the Function of the Disney Princess' re-asserts that the Princess (referring to Pocahontas, Ariel and Jasmine) 'still exists ostensibly in a patriarchy in which her father has vested power, but where once it was the role of the *femme fatale* to disrupt patriarchal continuity, under Team Disney, the princess herself has taken an active role in the disruption' (2004: 57).

There are several studies addressing the impact of Disney on society (in the form of Disney merchandise and theme parks), such as *The Disneyization of Society*, where Bryman claims that Disneyization and McDonaldization can be viewed as 'signals of globalization, the sense that the world is becoming one place in which national boundaries become less significant' (2004: 158). Furthermore, in *Multiculturalism and the Mouse*, Brode tackles the issues of 'race, gender, sexual orientation, ideology, or spirituality' (Brode 2005: 270).

The Disney Musical as an Educational Tool

Our willingness to challenge the status quo and embrace change is one of our greatest strengths, especially in a media market rapidly transforming with each new technology or consumer trend. We're inspired and energized by the opportunities in this dynamic era, especially given our unparalleled pipeline of creative content and collection of worldclass media brands – ABC, Disney, and ESPN – which allow us to navigate the changing landscape strategically and effectively.

Robert A. Iger Chairman and Chief Executive Officer of
The Walt Disney Company (Iger 2015: 1)

Disney has a significant role to play in children's moral education (Ward 2002: 3) and how children form values and understand society and its members. For this reason, it has received (and still does) a lot of criticism for its role as principal educator considering the creative link between education and entertainment. *Mouse Morality* (Ward 2002) addresses how moral behaviour is represented in Disney's film adaptations and how these can shape children's perceptions. And in fact, Pinsky suggests that Disney's animated films 'were always designed to be "message" films in the broadest sense, and especially for children' (Pinsky 2004: 2). The one cautiously critical voice has been Giroux, who insists that we need to view Disney as an educator responsible for national identity:

> Rather than being viewed as a commercial venture innocently distributing pleasure to young people, the Disney empire must be seen as a pedagogical and policymaking enterprise actively engaged in the cultural landscaping of national identity[2] and the 'schooling' of the minds of young children [...] Disney needs to be held accountable, which will require that parents, educators, and others challenge and disrupt both the institutional power and the images, representations, and values offered by Disney's teaching machine. (Giroux 1999: 114)

In addition to these criticisms, Wonderly (2009) suggests that we need to properly educate children in order for them to think independently about ethical issues, and educate people about their responses to certain emotions. She stresses the importance of children films, and in extension children's musical films, in shaping the children's moral instruction (1).

One in 68 children is diagnosed with autism (Animated Language Learning 2015). In what is yet another aspect of Disney's contribution on society, studies have shown that Disney films can help children with autism (for a moving account of how Owen Suskind leaned to speak and interact after watching Disney films, see Suskind 2015). Animated Language Learning suggest that Disney movies make children more positive, can help them bond with the characters, can teach manners, assist with speech skills and help children not to worry (Animated Language Learning 2015).

When it comes to musical theatre, there is an empathetic relationship between the audience and the spectacle on stage, and music plays a defining role in that emotional release. Millie Taylor explains that:

> voice and song in musical theatre have the capacity to move audiences through pre-motor responses and mirror neurons that create a mimetic response to the portrayal of emotion in the voice and body of the performer. This is amplified by the musical stimulation and a physically embodied witnessing of the performance events. In other words the presence of music and the response to song has the capacity to elicit a greater emotional release than performance without those elements. (Taylor 2010: 53)

Disney's mission is to create theatre for the widest possible audience, and most of their shows appeal to families, as consistent with the Disney brand. Therefore, the company pays attention to the messages that its shows communicate. In addition to Broadway productions, Disney has developed over twenty musicals for young performers and has extensive outreach activities that build theatre programmes in disadvantaged elementary schools (for more information see www.disneytheatricallicensing.com and www. disneymusicalsinschools.com).

As Giroux clarifies, 'Disney is more than a corporate giant; it is also a cultural institution that fiercely protects its legacy status as [a] purveyor of innocence and moral virtue' (1999: 86). Musicals can develop and shape young children's understanding of society and life around them (also see Wolf, Thomas and Symonds in this volume). In this way, it is crucial that the messages represented are up-to-date reflections of contemporary society so that young people can feel part of the world, and thus stage and film representations may be able to affect change. It is evident that

> [i]f we imagine the Disney Company as a teaching machine whose power and influence can, in part, be measured by the number of people who come in contact with its goods, messages, values, and ideas, it becomes clear that Disney wields enormous influence on the cultural life of the nation, especially with regard to the culture of children. (Giroux 1999: 19)

The Disney Musical as a Place for Innovation

The New York opening of the Walt Disney Company's first Broadway show, *Beauty and the Beast*, came hard on the heels of the news that Disney would also be renovating and occupying the historic and long-vacant New Amsterdam Theatre on 42nd street [...] Disney's action is expected to accelerate interest in the other theatres on 42nd street, which the city and state hope to revive as part of an overall plan to redevelop the area as a theatrical and entertainment district. (Nelson 1995: 71)

With *Beauty and the Beast*, Disney secured a permanent place on Broadway. The company's next venture was the stage adaptation of *The Lion King*; here, Disney took a risk, embarking on a new direction with a production that included puppets. This was a new, innovative way of telling the story, since the stage machinery was exposed, but the risk paid off, and still does, making *The Lion King* one of the boldest stage adaptions of any musical. Julie Taymor's production was hailed as an 'Electric Shock of Excitement' (Anon. 2007).

Disney values 'creativity and innovation as well as financial performance. For the fifth year in a row [in 2015], The Walt Disney Company delivered record results with revenue, net income and earnings per share' (Iger 2015: 1). With each new Disney project, risks are taken and inventive elements are incorporated in the production; Disney lets each project and its creative team experiment as needed to find the best possible way to tell a story on stage. Hence, innovations create a sense of adventure, as opposed to the musical being a complete stage replica of the film version.

In 2003, Disney was strongly criticized for the way it represented the traditional 'nuclear family'.

Unfortunately, families with gay, lesbian, bisexual, or transgender members are not represented in the Disney animated film. Consequently, children in these families are not able to benefit from the variety of family forms presented in the same way other children can, in that they are not able to see a reflection of their family in any of the animated films. (Tanner 2003: 367)

However, this was partly addressed in *Frozen*, by including the first same-sex family in a Disney musical (see Luttrell 2014 and Whitfield in this volume). Also, in 'an episode of Disney Channel's *Good Luck Charlie*, one of Charlie's friends had two mums' (Contera 2016), and in *Finding Dory* (2016) there is a female couple with a baby. These innovations and cultural developments reflect Disney's awareness of societal changes and market demographics. As Mackenzie re-affirms, 'Disney films were made in different eras, different times, and we celebrate them all for different reasons but this one was made in 2013 and it's going to have a 2013 point of view' (Mackenzie 2014). According to Carmenita Higginbotham, 'Until you have a broad audience that will welcome alternative presentations [...] Disney won't go there' (quoted in Contera 2016).

Even after nine decades, Disney still searches for new ways to engage audiences (see Upton, Grossman, Block). Paul Dergarabedian of Rentrak states that '[i]t makes perfect sense for Disney to sift through their vault and repurpose, reimagine and retool the classic tales that audiences know and love' (in Walker 2015). Yet, Disney can still surprise us with some radical decisions about casting, narrative plotline developments and use of music. This has the potential to redefine audience expectations about gender and can challenge some of preconceptions in relation to semiotics and visual readings when it comes to educating a (young) audience.

The Structure of this Book

This book is divided into three parts. The first deals with Disney musicals on film, the second with Disney adaptations on stage and beyond, and the third on gender and race in Disney musicals. The volume starts with Elizabeth Randell Upton's examination of Disney's first feature-length animated film, *Snow White and the Seven Dwarfs* (1937). The author reflects on Disney's approach to animating human characters, what Mori called the 'Uncanny Valley' (MacDorman and Kageki 2012: 99), and explains how the juxtaposition of songs and characters contribute to the film's stylization and realism, offering 'an unanticipated element that enhanced the aura of reality for audiences'.

Raymond Knapp's contribution centres on *Sleeping Beauty* and focuses on how Tchaikovsky's music is used, together with new lyrics, to ensure drama-turgical consistency. He elaborates on how romantic agency is expressed in specific songs and provides a close, critical reading of the use of song as a structural device. Knapp reminds us that 'song can indeed have such power is a well-established fact that has long provided a familiar trope for musicals. But there is more involved in this case than the film simply adapting its narrative to familiar contours of romantic inspiration.'

Tim Stephenson's study of *Mary Poppins* engages with the notion of the representation of women in film musicals and applies genre-specific approaches to gender analysis. He associates the film musical as a utopian paradox and identifies how the importance of the character of Mary Poppins shifts away from the traditional heteronormative romance. The author offers a different understanding of dystopian mythologies and reads this work as 'a wonderful joyous, anachronistic, concoction'.

The final chapter of the first part of this book reflects on the tradition of Disney princesses in the film musical genre *Enchanted* and demonstrates how this is inverted through self-reflexivity and pastiche. Paul R. Laird's analysis of the music and computer graphics illuminates how the film rethinks the role of 'magical transformation' and the place of Disney princesses in contemporary society.

Part Two opens with an investigation of 'Disney Versions of Broadway Musicals for Television in the Late 1990s and Early 2000s'. Geoffrey Block concentrates on four television adaptations: *Cinderella*, *Annie*, *The Music Man* and *Once Upon a Mattress*, highlighting the role of the creative auteur and making connections to the original stage productions. In examining non-traditional casting, this chapter explores casting stereotypes and ways to approach colour-blind casting.

Olaf Jubin offers a historical overview of *The Hunchback of Notre Dame* and by doing raises questions of the 'Disneyfication of the character', Quasimodo as the *other* and the role of the church within the narrative. His critical comparison of the 1999 and the 2014/15 stage versions further explores how the artistic team operated within the constraint of the Disney brand and shows which adaptation of the Hugo novel will be licensed for regional and amateur theatres.

In Chapter 7 Barbara Wallace Grossman crystallizes the technical and aesthetic path of *The Lion King*'s journey from a hugely successful animated film to the highest-grossing Broadway production to date. She celebrates the innovations of the stage adaptations directed by Julie Taymor and scrutinizes the use of music both on stage and screen. Grossman concludes by investigating how the stage version engaged the audience by creating a work that is not merely a two-dimensional film on stage, but an imaginative production that doesn't hide its stage mechanics.

Disney's education and outreach in encapsulated in Stacy E. Wolf's chapter and presents 'Disney's twenty-first-century tripartite of projects for children – licensable kid-friendly musical theatre adaptations of Disney movies and shows, supplementary production materials and teachers'/ directors' guides, and public school outreach programs across the US – transform child consumers into producers'. Wolf argues that Disney's outreach work is important in the Disney Theatrical Group's agenda and she references productions of *Aladdin KIDS* and *The Little Mermaid JR.* as case studies to demonstrate the impact of amateur productions on child development, engagement and participation.

The chapters in the third part problematize race and gender in the Disney musical canon. Issues of masculinity, male dancing and maleness are interrogated in the ninth chapter. Aaron C. Thomas's study of *Newsies* juxtaposes feminine power and masculinity and touches upon the third sex in the adult work of *1899*. He engages with questions of presenting new masculinities on stage and allows the dancing body to be his guiding influence in reading the work.

In evaluating the impact of *High School Musical* (both on screen and stage), Dominic Symonds considers in some detail the gender politics of the Disney films. He turns his attentions to re-imagining heteronormative relationships and in combining singing and school life within a high school environment. Symonds explains that *High School Musical* has become 'more globally circulated that any other Disney product to date' and links it to two other teen-centred musicals, the film *Grease* and the TV series *Glee*. He postulates that 'girls can achieve, can have a voice and can gain independence (we are told); but the only way they will achieve access to those rewards is if they conform to the "inhibitions" of their gender'.

The third section continues with a chapter on race, racism and orientalism in *The Jungle Book*, authored by the quartet of Emily Clark, Donatella Galella, Stefanie A. Jones and Catherine Young. The focus of their argument is that white supremacy is still evident in racial hierarchies and that the film's diversity, tolerance and cultural mix allow new critical readings. The four authors employ critical frameworks from Omi and Winant, Swartz and Davis, and extend them in order to contextualize the creation, distribution and consumption of cultural products.

In the penultimate chapter, Sam Baltimore proposes that *Aladdin* can be perceived as an analogy that goes beyond musical comedy and extends to the queer orientalist tradition. The author indicates how *Aladdin* has queer foundations in other homoerotic musicals, which resonates with the idea that 'this queerness has often expressed itself through an orientalist lens that, while opening the stage to many queer performers of colour, nonetheless reinscribes notions of the static, exotic and sexually perverse East on the bodies of those performers'. His final remarks shift from contribution of lyricist Howard Ashman to James Monroe Igelhart's interpretation of the genie as a show-stopping character.

Sarah Whitfield's chapter concludes the volume by challenging the notion that *Frozen* is a feminist musical. The author sums up the heated debate of whether *Frozen* is 'feminist enough' and establishes links to constructions and re-enactments of gender on stage. Whitfield believes that *Frozen* 'may be a problematic feminist text, incomplete and unrepresentative, but it rewards the hope of more'. She bases her analysis of the work on structural and dramaturgical considerations and proposes that 'it reflects a certain progress in attempting to balance a 'similar' double duty. It has achieved this by turning to the Broadway musical for a model that supports more comprehensive character development and permits women characters to enact the resolution to their own dramatic conflict.'

The Disney Musical: Impact on Notions of Childhood

After the unprecedented success of *Frozen* in 2013, with its positive implications on merchandise development and sales, Disney continues to work at full speed on creating further projects to build on this hit. *Frozen* the musical has been planned to open on a pre-Broadway engagement in the summer of 2017. It is expected to be joining *The Lion King* and *Aladdin* on Broadway in spring 2018. Disney continues to exploit creative and artistic innovations by building on existing successes and is developing *Frozen 2*, initially as a film animation, but also by providing a filmed stage version of *Newsies* and a live-action remake of *Beauty and the Beast* to follow *Cinderella* and *The Jungle Book* amongst others.

It is easy to be always critical of an organization that has such a huge responsibility when it comes to children's entertainment, both as a role model and providing ethical paradigms for children to follow. Robert Iger states that:

> The world certainly looks a lot different than it did when Walt Disney first opened shop in 1923, and so does the company that bears his name. Our company continues to evolve with each generation, mixing beloved characters and storytelling traditions with grand new experiences that are relevant to our growing global audience. (Iger 2015: 1)

As times change, policies on equality and diversity are expanding and the 'nuclear family' is becoming more inclusive in nature, so Disney has to adapt and reflect these changes. It is apparent that Disney is catching up with the politics of inclusivity, whether these concern racial, sexual or gender imbalance. After all, inclusivity is a priority for casting directors, and this also affects their casting decisions. Disney Theatrical Group has been at the forefront of diverse casting and won a Casting Society of America award for the casting of *The Little Mermaid* in 2008 (and has employed hundreds of performers of diverse backgrounds through productions such as *AIDA*, *The Lion King* etc.). The company strives to cast its shows to reflect the diversity of their audiences, feeling feel it is important for children to see people on stage who look like them.

For Disney, theatre is always a 'local' event, even if the base production is a replica. Disney spends a lot of time and effort not only in translating their shows well but also in localizing them for each international production. And thus, the Disney musical becomes a political tool to reflect and change the world around us. As a company, it has the ability to 'adapt and anticipate demands. It is particularly flexible and reveals an aptitude to transplant narratives from one region to another and to diffuse them to the general public' (Bohas 2015: 40). The artistic impulse is always their priority and there is a strong need to create great stories on stage. 'It's an impressive winning streak that speaks to our continued leadership in the entertainment industry, the incredible demand for our brands and franchises, and the special place our storytelling has in the hearts and lives of millions of people around the world' (Iger 2015: 1). Once a story worth telling is found, Disney then tries to open it up to the widest possible audience for each particular work. This translates to financial success (let us not forget that *The Lion King* has earned $6.5 billion worldwide), which maintains Disney's reputation as a monumental part of the film and theatre industry.

When we watch theatre, mirror neurons allow us to empathize with the material on stage (see Carr 2006; Taylor 2010; Upright 2002; Taylor and Symonds 2014). 'Since brain and body are connected, autonomic and somatic responses are triggered and the observer actually experiences the actions and feels the emotions of the performers and can become passionately connected to song, dance and characters' (Taylor and Symonds 2014: 243). This is especially significant for young audiences whose first live experiences of musical theatre can shape their future enjoyment, understanding and interaction with the art form. Elsewhere I investigate the impact of the various adaptations of stage musicals and in specific their journey from stage to screen: 'The[se] film adaptations provide new contexts, layers and dimensions of meaning' (Rodosthenous 2017: 1). Our sensory experiencing of the Disney musical alters between the different media and forms of entertainment: a theatre performance is live – which offers close proximity, an embodied physical experience and a more direct form of involvement. The film musical is projected onto the big screen in the dark, allowing us a different kind of immersion in the narrative and identification with the characters. And when watching the Disney Musical on a DVD at home 'without the possibility of witnessing other audience member's responses [...] the urge to empathize with the material and its dynamic energies is stimulated by direct address' (Rodosthenous 2014: 46).

Educational philosopher Kieran Egan acutely observes that Disney's 'typical products try to recapture a kind of paradisal quality, suggesting nostalgia for the world before the Fall, providing a sense of the Garden of

Eden' (Egan n.d.). The Disney musical with its utopian fantasy attributes allows song and dance to be part of these heightened worlds, which then 'structure collective imagination' (Bohas 2015: 23). Disney has been around for over ninety years, so it is possible that some audiences associate watching a Disney musical with how they felt when they (or their parents, or grandparents, or great grandparents) first encountered the source material. This creates an invaluable dynamic: the nostalgia of reimagining one's childhood.

References

Animated Language Learning (2015). *Disney Helps Fight Autism*. Available online: http://animatedlanguagelearning.com/disney-autism-language/ (accessed 22 August 2016).

Anon. (1997). 'The Best Theater of 1997.' *Time Magazine*. Available online: http://content.time.com/time/magazine/article/0,9171,987618,00.html (accessed 22 August 2016).

Anon. (2014). 'Marines Let Their Hair Down with *Frozen*'s "Let it Go".' *Telegraph*, 2 May. Available online: http://www.telegraph.co.uk/news/worldnews/northamerica/usa/10802990/US-Marines-let-their-hair-down-with-Frozens-Let-It-Go-rendition.html (accessed 22 August 2016).

Anon. (2016). 'The Walt Disney Company Reports Record Quarterly Earnings.' 9 February. Available online: https://thewaltdisneycompany.com/the-walt-disney-company-reports-record-quarterly-earnings-for-the-first-quarter-of-fiscal-2016/ (accessed 22 August 2016).

Bell, E., L. Haas and L. Sells (1995). *From Mouse to Mermaid*. Bloomington: Indiana University Press.

Bispo, Ashley (2014). 'Fairy Tale Dreams: Disney Princesses' Effect on Young Girls' Self-Images.' *Dialogues Journal* 9: 1–15.

Bohas, Alexandre (2015). 'Transnational Firms and the Knowledge Structure: The Case of the Walt Disney Company.' *Global Society* 29 (1). Available online: http://www.tandfonline.com/doi/abs/10.1080/13600826.2014.961126 (accessed 20 October 2016).

Brocklebank, Lisa (2000). 'Disney's *Mulan* – the True Deconstructed Heroine?' *Marvels and Tales: Journal of Fairy-Tale Studies* 14 (2): 268–83

Brode, D. (2005). *Multiculturalism and the Mouse*. Austin: University of Texas Press.

Bryman, A. (2004). *The Disneyization of Society*. London: Sage.

Byrne, Eleanor and Martin McQuillan (1999). *Deconstructing Disney*. London and Sterling, VA: Pluto Press.

Carr, David (2006). 'Moral Education at the Movies: On the Cinematic Treatment of Morally Significant Story and Narrative.' *Journal of Moral Education* 35 (3): 319–33.

Cheu, Johnson (2013). *Diversity in Disney Films: Critical Essays on Race, Ethnicity, Gender, Sexuality and Disability.* Jefferson, NC and London: McFarland & Co.

Contera, Jessica (2016) 'Frozen 2: Is the World Ready for a Gay Disney Princess?' *Independent*, 12 May. Available online: http://www.independent.co.uk/arts-entertainment/art/frozen-2-elsa-disney-is-the-world-ready-for-a-gay-lgbt-princess-a7025351.html (accessed 22 August 2016).

Davis, Amy (2006). *Good Girls and Wicked Witches: Women in Disney's Feature Animation.* New Barnet: John Libbey.

Do Rozario, Rebecca-Anne C. (2004). 'The Princess and the Magic Kingdom: Beyond Nostalgia, the Function of the Disney Princess.' *Women's Studies in Communication* 27 (1): 34–59.

Egan, Kieran (n.d.). 'Fantasy and Reality in Children's Stories.' Available online: https://www.sfu.ca/~egan/FantasyReality.html (accessed 22 August 2016).

England, D., L. Descartes and M. Collier-Meek (2011). 'Gender Role Portrayal and the Disney Princesses.' *Sex Roles* 64 (7–8): 555–67.

Giroux, Henry (1999). *The Mouse That Roared: Disney and the End of Innocence.* New York and Oxford: Rowman & Littlefield.

Giroux, Henry (2004). 'Are Disney Movies Good for Your Kids?' In Shirley Steinberg and Joe Kincheloe (eds), *Kinder Culture: The Corporate Construction of Childhood*, 2nd edn. Colorado and Oxford: Westview Press, 164–80.

Giroux, Henry (2011). 'How Disney Magic and the Corporate Media Shape Youth Identity in the Digital Age.' *Truthout*, 21 August. Available online: http://www.truth-out.org/opinion/item/2808:how-disney-magic-and-the-corporate-media-shape-youth-identity-in-the-digital-age (accessed 22 August 2016).

Iger, Robert A. (2015). 'Fiscal Year 2015 Annual Financial Report and Shareholder Letter.' Available online: https://ditm-twdc-us.storage.googleapis.com/2015-Annual-Report.pdf (accessed 22 August 2016).

Luttrell, G. (2014). '7 Moments That Made *Frozen* the Most Progressive Disney Movie Ever.' Available online: http://mic.com/articles/79455/7-moments-that-made-frozen-the-most-progressive-disney-movie-ever (accessed 22 August 2016).

Mackenzie, S. (2014). '*Frozen*: Disney's Icebreaker.' Available online: http://www.bigissue.com/features/3593/frozen-disney-s-icebreaker (accessed: 22 August 2016).

Nelson, S. (1995). 'Broadway and the Beast: Disney Comes to Times Square.' *The Drama Review* 39 (2): 71–85. Available online: http://www.jstor.org/stable/1146445 (accessed: 22 August 2016).

Pinsky, Mark L. (2004). *The Gospel According to Disney.* Louisville, KY: Westminster John Knox Press.

Rodosthenous, George (ed.) (2017). *Twenty-First Century Musicals: From Stage to Screen.* Abingdon and New York Routledge.

Rodosthenous, G. (2014). 'Relocating the Song: Julie Taymor's Jukebox Musical *Across the Universe* (2007)'. In D. Symonds and M. Taylor (eds), Gestures of

Music Theater: The Performativity of Song and Dance. New York: Oxford University Press, 41–53.

Smith, K. (2014). 'The 7 Wackiest Hidden Meanings in Disney's *Frozen*.' *New York Post*, 5 February. Available online: http://nypost.com/2014/02/05/the-7-wackiest-hidden-meanings-in-disneys-frozen/ (accessed 22 August 2016).

Stover, C. (2013). 'Damsels and Heroines: The Conundrum of the Post-Feminist Disney Princess.' *LUX: A Journal of Transdisciplinary Writing and Research from Claremont Graduate University* 2 (1), Article 29: 1–10. Available online: http://scholarship.claremont.edu/cgi/viewcontent.cgi?article=1028&context=lux] (accessed 22 August 2016).

Suddath, Claire (2015). 'The $500 Million Battle Over Disney's Princesses.' Available online: http://www.bloomberg.com/features/2015-disney-princess-hasbro/ (accessed 22 August 2016).

Tanner, L. (2003). 'Images of Couples and Families in Disney Feature-Length Animated Films.' *The American Journal of Family Therapy* 31 (5): 355–73.

Tavin, Kevin and David Anderson (2003). 'Teaching (Popular) Visual Culture: Deconstructing Disney in the Elementary Art Classroom.' *Art Education* 56 (3): 21–4, 33–5.

Taylor, Millie (2010). 'Experiencing Live Musical Theatre Performance: *La Cage Aux Folles* and *Priscilla, Queen of the Desert*.' *Popular Entertainment Studies* 1 (1): 44–58.

Taylor, Millie and Dominic Symonds (2014). *Studying Musical Theatre: Theory and Practice*. London and New York; Palgrave Macmillan.

Upright, Richard (2002). 'To Tell a Tale: The Use of Moral Dilemmas to Increase Empathy in the Elementary School Child'. *Early Childhood Education Journal* 30 (1): 15–20.

Walker, T. (2015). 'Disney's Mega Money-making Formula: "Human" Remakes of Cartoon Classics Are Part of a Lucrative, Long Term Creative Plan.' Available online: http://www.independent.co.uk/arts-entertainment/films/features/disneys-mega-money-making-formula-human-remakes-of-cartoon-classics-are-part-of-a-lucrative-long-10137215.html (accessed on 22 August 2016).

Ward, Analee (2002). *Mouse Morality: The Rhetoric of Disney Animated Film*. Austin: University of Texas Press.

Wasko, Janet (2001). *Understanding Disney: The Manufacture of Fantasy*. Oxford and Malden, NY: Blackwell.

Wasko, Janet, Mark Phillips and Eileen Meehan (eds) (2001). *Dazzled by Disney? The Global Disney Audiences Project*. London and New York: Leicester University Press.

Whelan, Bridget (2014). 'Power to the Princess: Disney and the Creation of the Twentieth-Century Princess Narrative.' In Alexander Howe and Wynn Yarbrough (eds), *Kidding Around: The Child in Film and Media*. New York and London: Bloomsbury, 167–92.

Wonderly, Monique (2009). 'Children's Film as an Instrument of Moral Education.' *Journal of Moral Education* 38 (1): 1–15.

Part One

Disney Musicals:
On Film

Music and the Aura of Reality in Walt Disney's *Snow White and the Seven Dwarfs* (1937)

Elizabeth Randell Upton

The association between Disney heroines and singing is very strong, dating back to 1937 and *Snow White and the Seven Dwarfs*, the first feature-length animated Disney film.[1] But in 1937 there was no tradition of singing heroines in animation for the character of Snow White to emulate. Why, then, is Snow White made to sing? The film was in production for three years, with two years of preparation leading up to approximately a year of animation work.[2] With such an elaborate production (the film ended up costing close to $1.5 million[3]), every element had to be deliberately planned, deliberately chosen to help ensure the success of what some in Hollywood had been calling 'Disney's folly'.[4] So, if Snow White sings, her creators must have had a good reason for it.

One obvious reason is the widespread connection between fairy tale material and musical theatre, and indeed Walt Disney had seen the film of a Broadway musical theatre dramatization of the fairy tale as a boy of fifteen.[5] The *Kansas City Star* newspaper sponsored five free showings of *Snow White* (Paramount 1916) on 27 and 28 January 1917 in Kansas City's enormous Convention Hall. A four-sided screen was suspended in the centre of the hall, with four projectionists, and a thirty-five-piece orchestra accompanied the film from directly below. Walt, who had worked as a *Star* paperboy since he was nine years old, attended one of the showings; in 1938, he wrote 'My impression of the picture has stayed with me through the years and I know it played a big part in selecting *Snow White* for my first feature production' (Gabler 2006: 216). A second and more immediate inspiration was the Disney studio's successful series of musical shorts, the *Silly Symphonies*. 'Action came first in the Mickey shorts and sound was tightly matched to it. In the companion series of *Silly Symphonies*, it was the other way around: Music took the lead and action and story were built around it' (Canemaker

1999: 187). Several of these shorts married fairy tales with peppy new songs, including the award-winning *The Three Little Pigs* (1933), which featured the hit song 'Who's Afraid of the Big Bad Wolf?' Disney shorts had been famous for their marriage of animation and music since *Steamboat Willie*, the first sound cartoon, in 1928.[6]

There is no evidence to suggest that Disney ever considered a non-musical version; the decision to have Snow White sing seems to have been made early, and never questioned. While it wasn't necessary to make Snow White sing, that she sings affected the audience in ways that help to explain why the film was so successful. *Snow White and the Seven Dwarfs* draws on audience familiarity with stage musicals and the suspension of belief that allows singing characters to be perceived as 'real'. This perception strengthens the aura of reality for the animated character of Snow White, enhancing the audience's emotional identification with her.[7]

In this chapter I will explore the creative decisions Walt Disney and his team made in their pursuit of cinematic realism and the significance of music in this process. First, I discuss the structure of the finished film, and especially the placement of songs. Next, I discuss how Walt Disney's concern for the realistic animation of human characters led to a serious problem, one that would not be named until 1970, when Japanese robotics expert Masahiro Mori dubbed it the 'Uncanny Valley'. I show how Disney's animators solved their problem of the Uncanny Valley, establishing stylistic design paradigms that would characterize Disney animation for fifty years. Finally, I return to music, discussing how the songs the characters sing participate in the artists' solution of combining stylization and realism.

Structure of the Film: Songs and Characters

The film strongly associates the title characters, and especially Snow White, with singing. There are eight songs in the 84-minute film. Four are sung by Snow White herself ('I'm Wishing', 'With a Smile and a Song', 'Whistle While You Work' and 'Some Day My Prince Will Come'), three by the dwarfs (the magnificent 'Heigh-Ho', begun in the mine and then sung as they make their way home from work, 'Bluddle-Uddle-Um-Dum', sung as they wash up for dinner, and 'The Dwarfs' Yodel Song', sung to entertain Snow White after dinner), and one, titled 'One Song', sung by the Prince immediately following Snow White's 'I'm Wishing' and featured prominently in the opening credits. One song for the dwarfs, 'Music in Your Soup', was partially animated but deleted from the film for reasons of length and pacing; another, 'You're Never Too Old to be Young', was recorded but dropped in favour of 'The Dwarfs'

Table 1.1 Animation Sequences for *Snow White and the Seven Dwarfs*

1A	Credits and storybook
1B	First Queen and mirror sequence
2A	Snow White and the Prince in the garden
2B	Queen orders Snow White's death
3A	Snow White and Huntsman; Snow White into woods
3B	Snow White meets animals
3C	Snow White discovers dwarfs' house
3D	Snow White and animals clean house
4A	Dwarfs at mine
4B	Dwarfs march home from the mine
4C	Snow White discovers bedroom
4D	Spooks
5A	Bedroom
5B	Snow White tells dwarfs to wash
6A	Dwarfs at tub washing
6B	Soup sequence [cut from the film]
7A	Queen leaves mirror, prepares disguise
8A	Entertainment
8B	Story telling
8C	Going to bed
9A	Witch at cauldron; prepares apple
10A	Dwarfs leave for mine
10B	Queen on way to dwarfs' house
11A	Lodge meeting [cut from the film]
11B	Bed building [cut from the film]
[12	Originally a link between scenes 11 and 14; some material reused in 14E
13A	Snow White making pies; Witch enters house
[14A	Linking material cut with scene 11]
14B	Dwarfs at mine; animals warn them
14C	Witch urges Snow White to make wish
[14D	Comedy with dwarfs, cut to tighten the dramatic chase]
14E	Dwarfs start for house to rescue Snow White; meet turtle
14F	Snow White starts wish
14G	Dwarfs on way to house
14H	Snow White Dies
[14I	Doc and Grumpy were to stay with Snow White while the others chased the Queen; scene deleted during development, for pacing]
14J	Dwarfs chase the Queen
15A	Snow White dead
15B	Titles
16A	Snow White in coffin; back to life; away with the Prince

Table 1.2 Songs in *Snow White and the Seven Dwarfs*

1B	Snow White: 'I'm Wishing'; the Prince: 'One Song'
3B	Snow White: 'With a Smile and a Song'
3D	Snow White: 'Whistle While You Work'
4A	Dwarfs: 'Heigh Ho'
4B	Dwarfs: 'Heigh Ho' continued
6A	Dwarfs: 'Bluddle-Uddle-Um-Dum' ('The Dwarfs' Washing Song')
[6B	Dwarfs: 'Music in Your Soup' (not used in film)]
8A	Dwarfs: 'The Dwarfs' Yodel Song' ('The Silly Song')
8B	Snow White: 'Some Day My Prince Will Come'

Yodel Song' before animation. Music fills most of the 84 minutes of the film,[8] and songs make up almost 25 minutes, about 30 per cent of the total time.

The eight songs are not distributed evenly throughout the film; instead, the film is front-loaded with singing. Table 1.1 above lists the animation sequences, numbered according to Kaufman (2012),[9] while Table 1.2 lists the film's songs. Five of the songs are placed in the first third of the film, with the remaining three appearing in the second third; there are none at all in the last third of the film.[10]

For roughly the first third of the film (up through Sequence 4A), the introduction of the Dwarfs' singing 'Heigh-Ho' at the mine, almost half the time is taken up with songs and singing: 13 minutes and 16 seconds of song versus 13 minutes and 51 seconds without singing. Snow White herself sings far more than she speaks, and when she does speak she frequently speaks in rhyme, as in her first words, the introduction to her first song, 'I'm Wishing':

> **Snow White** (*speaking*)   Wanna know a secret? Promise not to <u>tell</u>?
> (*singing*)   We are standing by a wishing <u>well</u>
> Make a wish into the well,
> that's all you have to <u>do</u>
> And if you hear it echoing,
> the wish will soon come <u>true</u>.
> (*chorus*)   I'm Wishing ... (etc.)[11]

Snow White speaks short, non-rhyming lines to the baby bird while outside in the meadow (Sequence 3A), but finishes the encounter by delivering two rhyming couplets:

> **Snow White**   Your Mama and Papa can't be <u>far</u>,
> (*bird chirps*) There they <u>are</u>!
> Can you <u>fly</u>?
> Good-<u>bye</u>, good-<u>bye</u>!

While running through the scary forest, Snow White screams and cries wordlessly, but when she reaches the sun-filled clearing she speaks to the woodland creatures in rhyme again, as the introduction to her next song, 'With a Song and a Smile'. At the end of the song she returns to simple rhymed dialogue in asking the animals if they know somewhere she can stay the night.

Snow White   I really feel quite happy now.
                 I'm sure I'll get along somehow.
                 Everything's going to be all right.
                 But I do need a place to sleep, at night.

                 I can't sleep in the ground like you,
                 Or in a tree, the way you do.
                 And I'm sure no nest would possibly
                 Be big enough for me.

                 Maybe you know where I can stay,
                 in the woods somewhere?
                 (*birds twittering*) You do? (*twittering*)
                 Will you take me there?

Snow White begins speaking using non-rhyming, prose lines only when she enters the dwarfs' cottage, commenting on how dusty and untidy the place is. She quickly returns to rhymed dialogue for the spoken introduction to 'Whistle While you Work'. Snow White doesn't appear in a scene without singing until the dwarfs come home to find her asleep in Sequence 4D, around the middle of the film.[12]

Similarly, the Wicked Queen's first speech, speaking the incantation that summons the Spirit in her Magic Mirror, is in rhyme, and her line 'Alas for her! Reveal her name' while not rhyming is patterned rhythmically as in poetry or song:

Queen   Slave in the Magic Mirror
             Come from the farthest space
             Through wind and darkness I summon thee
             Speak! (thunderclap) Let me see thy face!
Mirror   What wouldst thou know, my Queen?
Queen   Magic Mirror on the Wall, who is the fairest one of all?
Mirror   Famed is thy beauty, Majesty,
             But hold! A lovely maid I see.
             Rags cannot hide her gentle grace.
             Alas, she is more fair than thee.

Queen	Alas for her! Reveal her name.
Mirror	Lips red as the rose. Hair black as ebony. Skin white as snow…
Queen	(*gasps*) Snow White!

The Queen doesn't speak completely in prose until her second scene (Sequence 2B), with the Huntsman:

Queen	Take her far into the forest. Find some secluded glade where she can pick wildflowers.
Huntsman	Yes, Your Majesty.
Queen	And there, my faithful Huntsman, you will kill her!
Huntsman	But Your Majesty! The little princess!
Queen	Silence! You know the penalty if you fail.
Huntsman	Yes, Your Majesty.
Queen	But to make doubly sure you do *not* fail, bring back her heart … in this!

By this time the audience has already heard the film's first two songs, the first sung by Snow White and the second by the Prince.

The final characters to be introduced, the Dwarfs, do not speak at all in their first scene; rather, during Sequences 4A (at the mine) and 4B (on the way home) they sing their marching song, 'Heigh-Ho', for almost three minutes, with no spoken dialogue at all. Only in Sequence 4D, when the dwarfs discover that someone has been in their cottage, do we hear an extended sequence of prose dialogue.

In their 1981 book *Disney Animation: The Illusion of Life*, animators Frank Thomas and Ollie Johnston (young animators working on *Snow White*, later two of Disney's lead animators, the famous 'Nine Old Men') describe the central challenge the animators faced in creating *Snow White*:

> A feature film would have to have tender moments, sincere moments, quiet moments. There would be a need for drawings with great appeal, characters with life and believability, and personalities that could hold an audience for well over an hour. Gags, funny actions, and visual tricks would not do it. If the audience were to be drawn into this film, this world of fantasy would have to be a real world, with real people doing real things. This would not be a cartoon. It would be theatre. (Thomas and Johnston 1981: 90)

Walt Disney's concern with realism, with having the characters, especially Snow White herself, look and move as realistically human as possible, is palpable throughout published accounts of the *Snow White* story conferences and production notes. As a trial run for animating a human character,

Disney had produced *The Goddess of Spring* (1934), a retelling of the Persephone myth as an extended short (it runs about nine minutes) in the *Silly Symphony* series. Thomas and Johnston describe animators Hamilton Luske and Clark as being 'stumped' when asked to draw a believable, pretty girl. Thomas and Johnston report that, when viewing Ham Luske's first attempt, 'Walt was not pleased with the animation, feeling it was too rubbery and flexible.' Les Clark speculated on his own results, which he describes as 'miserable': 'I think the reason it didn't come off, the character wasn't designed to be animated. To me, the key to character animation is the design quality of the figure that you can use. I had a hard time with the figure, not that I didn't know how to draw it, but to animate it' (Thomas and Johnston 1981: 109). The animators worked with live models, analysing how the body moves. Describing their final results, Thomas and Johnston conclude:

> The animators occasionally got the grace, the rhythm, the relationship that distinguished the leading lady of *The Goddess of Spring* as a lady; they even got the weight and balance and perspective accurate enough

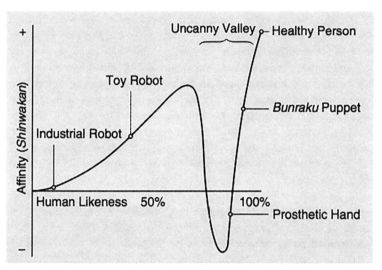

Figure 1.1 'The graph depicts the uncanny valley, the proposed relation between the human likeness of an entity and the perceiver's affinity for it. [Translators' note: *Bunraku* is a traditional Japanese form of musical puppet theatre dating to the seventeenth century. The puppets range in size but are typically a meter in height, dressed in elaborate costumes, and controlled by three puppeteers obscured only by their black robes ....]' (Mori, trans. MacDorman and Kageki 2012: 99)

so that in some scenes she moved convincingly. But, exhausted by the effort, they relied on a 'pretty girl' formula for the face that not only looked as if she were wearing a mask, but defeated the total effect by giving her a zombie look. She certainly was not alive and was totally devoid of personality or feelings. (Thomas and Johnston 1989: 109)

A zombie look. Not alive. It would not be theorized for another forty years, but in their attempts to make the Goddess of Spring both pretty and as lifelike as possible, the Disney animators had fallen into what is now known as the 'Uncanny Valley'. In the 1970s, Japanese roboticist Masahiro Mori (b. 1927), then on the faculty of the Tokyo Institute of Technology, conducted psychological investigations into human emotional response to robots. He discovered that the more similar robots become to humans in their appearance and motion, the more emotionally appealing they become to us. But, paradoxically, as the anthropomorphic robots approach the fullest similarity to actual humans, their appeal collapses and they are seen as repulsive. The 'Uncanny Valley' represents the point of greatest repulsion (see Figure 1.1). Interestingly, Mori found the effect more strongly produced by movement than by mere appearance (see Figure 1.2).

The 'Uncanny Valley' on these graphs marks the place of the corpse – a dead body looks fully human, but it is not alive, and the absence of life, the greatest possible discrepancy between normal human appearance and abnormal human movement, produces horror.[13] The phenomenon is easily explained: if a robot or other non-human creature looks or moves only somewhat like a human, we notice the resemblance to us, emphasizing its similarity while downplaying the differences we notice. But if a robot or other non-human creature looks almost perfectly human, the small differences that can be perceived between its appearance and movement and 'real' human qualities stand out as obviously strange or wrong, and can become unbearable to see.

Mori's theory has been discounted by some robotics experts, based on criticism of his experimental design, but it has been widely accepted by computer scientists, graphics engineers and animators. Film critics noted a particularly strong demonstration of the phenomenon in two contrasting Computer Graphics (CG) films both released in late 2004. For Pixar's *The Incredibles*, the human characters were stylized in their design even as the physics of their movements and the detailing of surface textures were made as realistic as possible. In contrast, the character designs in Robert Zemeckis's *The Polar Express*, based closely on motion-captured images of the actors (it was the first completely motion-capture, 'mo-cap', film), were realistic, not stylized at all. Critics and audiences noted that the *Incredibles*

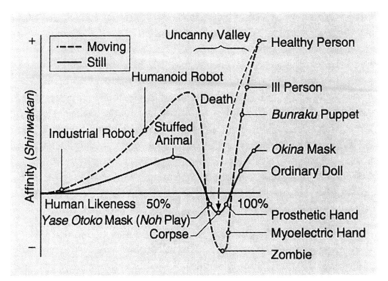

Figure 1.2 'The presence of movement steepens the slopes of the Uncanny Valley. The arrow's path represents the sudden death of a healthy person. [Translators' note: *Noh* is a traditional Japanese form of musical theater dating to the fourteenth century in which actors commonly wear masks. The *yase otoko* mask bears the face of an emaciated man and represents a ghost from hell. The *okina* mask represents an old man.]' (Mori, trans. MacDorman and Kageki 2012: 99)

characters were appealing and believable, while those in *The Polar Express* were disturbing – many described them as 'corpselike'.[14]

The Mechanics of the Animation: Facial Characteristics and Other Design Elements

It was animator Hamilton Luske who solved the problem of making Snow White look like a girl instead of an animated corpse. He realized that to avoid a mask-like face the artists and animators would have to pay a lot more attention to the character's facial movements. The size of Snow White's eyes was increased, to allow for a greater range of expression, and she was given mobile eyebrows.[15] The Wicked Queen was remodelled as well and given larger eyes that flash as she tells the Huntsman he must kill the princess.

Further expressive emphasis was created by drawing both Snow White and the Queen to look as if they were wearing theatrical makeup: heavy eyeshadow, mascara and lipstick. Snow White was even given 'blush' through the use of transparent red dye, applied to the front (ink) side of each cel by the 'Ink and Paint girls', to Walt Disney's astonishment.[16] Finally, Snow White's body was stylized in its proportions: her head is a little larger than a real fourteen-year-old girl's, her hands and feet a little smaller, she is a bit thinner through the torso and more short-waisted and long-legged than any real girl would be. These are the kinds of details that Les Clark meant when he talks of a character 'designed to be animated'. With a more stylized body and face, the animators could create graceful movement that looked all the more realistic for being slightly exaggerated. Luske also determined how to make the woodland creatures more believable. Thomas and Johnston write:

> Ham Luske felt that the rabbits we were drawing were thin and bony instead of soft and furry. The more artists tried to draw a rabbit's anatomy, the less the drawing looked like soft fur. Ham realized that an absence of lines and fullness of shape would make the drawings look soft … we were told by Ham to think of 'Dr. Dentons', the sleep suits young kids wore that hid the anatomy under a thick, soft flannel covering …
> (Thomas and Johnston 1989: 112)

So, large eyes, childlike faces, cuddly bunnies – all these familiar adorable qualities of Disney characters were originally state-of-the-art design solutions to the problem of realistic movement and appearance. By making the characters more stylized and cute, their movements could be made more realistic and believable without producing any 'Uncanny Valley'-style revulsion.

Colour and Music as Elements of Verisimilitude

Other design elements were also manipulated so as to enhance the audience's perception of realism while providing stylization necessary for animation. Particularly in the first part of the film, the (human) characters – Snow White, the Prince, the Queen and the Huntsman – are presented realistically, in realistically detailed settings. The goal was not photographic realism, but rather the effect of a realistic storybook illustration style familiar to audiences from artists such as N. C. Wyeth 'come to life' (Allan 1999: 59–60).

After the titles, the film begins with a live shot, not animation. We see a prop book with an elaborately tooled white and gold cover lying on a rich blue cloth next to what presumably is the brass base of a candlestick or lamp. An unseen hand opens the book to reveal close-up shots of two successive pages of text, with medieval-esque black-letter calligraphy illuminated with red, blue and gold letters and historiated initials. The text begins appropriately with the words 'Once upon a time' and goes on to introduce the princess Snow White, forced to work as a scullery maid by her vain and wicked stepmother, the Queen, who possesses a Magic Mirror that reassures her as to her beauty.

The animation proper begins with an establishing shot, just as a live-action film would.[17] The gleaming stone castle atop a cliff, bright blue sky and leafy green foliage looks very much like a storybook colour plate. The newly invented multiplane camera allows for independently moving clouds and water as the camera slowly zooms closer.[18] This first shot dissolves to show a closer view of the castle walls, centred on the leaded glass window of what we will soon discover is the Queen's chamber. This view of the castle looks very much like a stage backdrop, with its subdued colour palette adding to a more realistic design than previously seen in cartoons.[19]

After a slow zoom towards the window, the third shot moves us into the Queen's chamber. The Wicked Queen in her throne room is vividly coloured: she wears a gown of deep purple with a black, fur-trimmed velvet cloak, and her golden peacock throne gleams amid deep red velvet hangings. But when we see Snow White for the first time, scrubbing the stairs in the castle courtyard, the colour palette is again more subdued and the backgrounds more highly detailed.

Once this sense of verisimilitude has been established, the visual style for characters and the colour palette slowly changes. When the Huntsman takes Snow White to pick wildflowers in Sequence 3A, Snow White has changed from her drab and shabby work clothes into her more brightly coloured 'princess' dress. Only the light yellow colour of her skirt mitigates the brightness of the primary colours of red and blue employed for her costume. Similarly, the doves around the wishing well in Sequence 1B, with their small eyes and realistic proportions, are succeeded by the cartoony baby bluebird in this scene. One of the wishing-well doves had been shown to blush and pantomime embarrassment, not normal behaviour for doves, but the baby bluebird, with its larger eyes and unrealistic body shape, is exaggerated in design and demonstrates a much more anthropomorphic character. Snow White's terrifying passage through the woods, in the conclusion to Sequence 3A, is realistic in specific observed detail while stylized in design for the fantasy 'scary trees'. When she recovers in Sequence 3B's sun-filled glade and meets the woodland creatures, the continued use of highly detailed backgrounds allows the audience to accept the softer, cartoon-like animals while maintaining the established sense of realism.[20] From the woodland creatures it is a short step to the entirely exaggerated dwarfs themselves. Their character design would have been unimaginably jarring if seen in the context of the Prince and Snow White in the castle's courtyard, but once we have followed Snow White on her passage through the woods their new level of unreality is easier for the audience to accept.

Similarly, the songs themselves take us through a progression from an establishing ideal to a style that is more congruent with contemporary Disney practices. The first two songs, 'I'm Wishing' and 'One Song', are both scored for accompanying strings alone, while the next two, 'With a Smile and a Song' and 'Whistle While You Work', add percussion and brass – muted brass, but brass nonetheless. In their melodic style the first two songs are closer to older operetta numbers while 'Whistle While You Work' and 'Heigh-Ho' are much more jazzy, or at the least modern and peppy.[21] 'With a Smile and a Song', sung by Snow White as the woodland creatures take her to the dwarfs' cottage, is transitional: a more old-fashioned melody combined with more contemporary scoring. 'The Dwarfs' Yodel Song' and 'Someday My Prince Will Come' are the most self-consciously European and theatrical of the songs, appropriate to their setting in which the dwarfs and Snow White take turns performing for each other.

Conclusions

Besides displaying the continuum of register evoked by older and contemporary styles, the songs in *Snow White and the Seven Dwarfs* literally underscore the move from reality, or at the least theatrical reality, to animated fantasy. And this theatricality itself provided an unanticipated element that enhanced the aura of reality for audiences and allowed them to believe that Snow White was 'real'. By recourse to theatricality, to the stylized artificiality of stage conventions featuring singing heroines, Disney and his team were able to push Snow White to look more realistic than cartoony but without seeming uncanny. That is, Snow White's singing added a significant element of stylized unreality to counteract problems with her realistic animation. Even though real people almost never break into song in real life, audiences have no problem believing that actors in musicals are real people even while portraying fictional characters.[22]

Raymond Knapp states the principle: 'The addition of music to staged, spoken drama thus does not simply heighten emotions; rather, it also imposes, through its obvious and conventional artificiality, a kind of mask that both conceals and calls attention to the performer behind the persona' (Knapp 2005: 12).[23] By the strategy of having the characters communicate almost exclusively through singing, something that never happens in real life but always does in musical theatre, Disney convinces the audience to accept painted drawings as genuinely sympathetic characters at least as real as any others portrayed on stage or screen by human actors. When Snow White sings, and sings, and sings, she can be seen not just as a cartoon character, but rather as a real person in a theatrical performance. Thus for Disney's first heroine, the artifice of musical performance paradoxically enhances the aura of reality for her, for her story and for her world.

References

Allan, R. (1999). *Walt Disney and Europe: European Influences on the Animated Feature Films of Walt Disney*. Bloomington and Indianapolis: Indiana University Press.

Barber, P. (1988). *Vampires, Burial, and Death: Folklore and Reality*, 2nd edn. New Haven: Yale University Press.

Barrier, M. (1999). *Hollywood Cartoons: American Animation in its Golden Age*. New York and Oxford: Oxford University Press.

Canemaker, J. (1999). *Paper Dreams: The Art and Artists of Disney Storyboards*. New York: Hyperion.

Gabler, N. (2006). *Walt Disney: The Triumph of the American Imagination*. New York: Borzoi.

Harmetz, A. (1989). *The Making of the Wizard of Oz*, 2nd edn. New York: Dell.

Johnson, D. (1988). 'Not Rouge, Mr. Thomas!' *Animation Artist Magazine*. Available online: http://www.animationartist.com/columns/DJohnson/Not_Rouge/not_rouge.html (accessed 30 August 2015).

Kaufman, J. B. (2012). *The Fairest One of All: The Making of Walt Disney's Snow White and the Seven Dwarfs*. San Francisco: The Walt Disney Family Foundation Press, LLC.

Knapp, R. (2005). *The American Musical and the Formation of National Identity*. Princeton and Oxford: Princeton University Press.

Knapp, R. (2006). *The American Musical and the Performance of Personal Identity*. Princeton and Oxford: Princeton University Press.

Knapp, R. (2012). 'Getting off the Trolley: Musicals *Contra* Cinematic Reality'. In M. Sala (ed.), *From Stage to Screen: Musical Films in Europe and the United States (1927–1961)*. Tournhout, Belgium: Brepols, 157–72.

Krause, M. and L. Witkowski (1995). *Walt Disney's Snow White and the Seven Dwarfs: An Art in its Making*. New York: Hyperion.

Looser, C. E. and T. Wheatley (2010). 'The Tipping Point of Animacy: How, When, and Where We Perceive Life in a Face.' *Psychological Science* 21 (12): 1854–62.

Martin, P. (1956). 'Diane Disney Miller: My Dad, Walt Disney'. *Saturday Evening Post*, 22 December 1956, 24, 80–2.

McCloud, S. (1993). *Understanding Comics: The Invisible Art*. Northampton, MA: Tundra.

Mori, M. (1970). 'Bukimi No Tani' [The Uncanny Valley]. *Energy* 7 (4): 33–5. English translation K. F. MacDorman and N. Kageki (2012). *IEEE Robotics and Automation Magazine* 19: 98–100.

Pavlus, J. (2011). 'Did the "Uncanny Valley" Kill Disney's CGI Company?' *Fast Company*, 31 March. Available online: http://www.fastcodesign. com/1663530/did-the-uncanny-valley-kill-disneys-cgi-company (accessed 30 August 2015).

Thomas, B. (1994). *Walt Disney: An American Original*, 2nd edn. New York: Disney Editions.

Thomas, F. and O. Johnston (1981). *The Illusion of Life: Disney Animation*. New York: Disney Editions.

Medieval 'Beauty' and Romantic 'Song' in Animated Technirama: Pageantry, Tableau and Action in Disney's *Sleeping Beauty*

Raymond Knapp

Flora *Little Princess, my gift shall be the gift of beauty.*
Fauna *Tiny Princess, my gift shall be the gift of song.*[1]

Disney's *Sleeping Beauty* (1959) was the studio's sixteenth animated feature and the third entry in its classic fairy tale trilogy, which also includes *Snow White and the Seven Dwarfs* (1937) and *Cinderella* (1950). Yet it marks a striking departure from both the others in the trilogy and from most of the longer series in being filmed in a widescreen format (Technirama).[2] It also incorporates Disney's avowed attempt to create a more consistent look and sound, deriving specifically from Eyvind Earle's medievalist background illustrations and style design on the one hand and from Tchaikovsky's 1889 ballet *The Sleeping Beauty* on the other.[3] Six years in the making (nearly eight, counting back to a 1951 plot outline) (Allan 1999: 232) and costing the studio over six million dollars, *Sleeping Beauty* failed to turn a profit during its first run, although it has long since recouped its initial losses through multiple rereleases. Despite its later public acceptance, however, most commentary has endorsed the earlier tepid response, finding its laudable artistic aspirations at best only sporadically realized, especially in the visual realm.

Blame for the film's artistic failures has been placed on both Walt Disney's lack of sufficient oversight, owing to his deep involvement with the development of Disneyland during the film's gestation, and on Earle's relative inexperience with the specific needs of animated film, which to succeed requires a stronger coordination between background and foregrounded action than his evocative, highly detailed illustrations tend to facilitate. Thus, arguing from acute observation confirmed by interviews with those involved, John Canemaker and Robin Allan both note that Earle's persuasive early illustrations for the project, which led Disney to install him as the chief architect of the film's 'look', were later overlaid and elaborated with so much detail that they did not provide sufficient 'space' for the animated foreground, nor provide that foreground with a compelling focal point.[4] Indeed, one might imagine a different visual outcome if this accrual of fussy background detail, which may well have seemed necessary within the more static visual realm where Earle worked most comfortably, had simply been replaced by the film's central ongoing action. In addition to noting this lack of visual coordination, Allan deems the human characters (Aurora and Prince Phillip) 'cardboard', with a 'spiky contemporary' look he sees as a response to Earle's backgrounds, and finds the more caricatured characters too derivative, with the three good fairies in particular 'no substitute for seven individual dwarfs'.[5]

Importantly, neither Allan nor Canemaker – nor any other serious commentators before Cari McDonnell in her 2015 dissertation – discuss the deployment of music in a similarly critical way, or take the full measure of the difficulties the film has with its use of Technirama. Even on the face of it, *Sleeping Beauty* presents an uneasy blend of elements within its 70mm widescreen format: imitation medieval painting, musical-comedy songs and background scoring deriving from Tchaikovsky's ballet *The Sleeping Beauty*, and the kind of comic byplay among an assortment of secondary characters already well known to Disney's audiences from (among others in the extended series) the earlier entrants in the fairy tale trilogy. Partly because some of these elements do not blend easily, however, what should seem the least mutually congenial among them – medievalist visuals, late nineteenth-century ballet music and the widescreen format – form a striking alliance. Against this alliance, it is the extended scenes of comic byplay that seem out of place, as if the characters do not quite know how to fill the wide screen, self-consciously uneasy in their medievalist accoutrement and somewhat at odds with the scoring. Tellingly, these elements of discomfiture are mostly absent from the film's more memorable sequences of pageantry, tableau and action.

In this chapter I limn the medievalist–balletic–widescreen alliance and probe the film's many moments of awkward disjuncture before considering how song, in tying the balletic and leitmotivic dimension of Tchaikovsky's music to styles and tropes then prevalent in musical theatre, helps hold the film together by making us believe, at least some of the time, in the consistency and oneness of the world the film presents to us.

The Gift of Beauty: Managing the Visual Realm

In reducing its good fairies from Charles Perrault's seven to three, Disney's *Sleeping Beauty* also reduces their initial blessings for Princess Aurora to two; in each case, it is left to the final fairy to partially counter the evil fairy's curse, commuting the princess's death sentence to a sleep from which she may be awakened with true love's kiss. Thus, Disney's Flora and Fauna bequeath Aurora beauty and song, leaving aside the wit, grace, dance and musical prowess with which Perrault's additional fairies blessed her. While Disney's Aurora, as Briar Rose, will exhibit some wit along with her considerable grace and dancing abilities, it is precisely the film's pretensions to her two specified gifts that set it apart from its siblings.[6]

As noted, the film's visual realm has received the most critical attention, with its perceived flaws located mostly in the fold between the different requirements of static and animated art. Yet there is another, related fold: between various kinds of visual beauty and the sensibilities supported by Disney's brand of generally good-natured, asexual, frumpily folksy characters, frequently ineffectual (or seeming so). The latter sensibility is exemplified in the film by the three good fairies, some of the woodland creatures (the owl in particular) and Prince Phillip's plump father, King Hubert. Yet the film stakes a significant claim for beauty well before this sensibility takes over, in the process employing the widescreen frame to full advantage. To begin with, there are the richly textured backgrounds for the opening credits, followed by the ornately bejewelled and elaborately illustrated storybook, framed by candles and tapestries, that appears and falls open as the narration begins (filmed using an actual book made just for the production).[7] The action then commences with an extended scene of processional pageantry that – however much it tends to resemble moving flats on a stage instead of a fully textured three-dimensionality – finds varied and often compelling ways to fill the full screen with opulent colour, carrying forward this resplendent processional grandeur into the presentation of gifts by the young Prince Phillip and the first two good fairies, with each of the latter accompanied by 'visualizations' within a starry realm. When the third fairy's gift is dramatically interrupted by the appearance of Maleficent, suffused with a green glow against darkened backgrounds, her commanding confrontation with the now-darkened court temporarily disrupts its colourful grandeur, which is then restored through the intervention of Merryweather (the third fairy), whose blessing is also visualized. Offering a frame to the film's first chapter – corresponding roughly to the Prologue in Tchaikovsky's ballet – the action then takes us back outside, where the flames from the conflagration of spinning wheels stand as starkly against a darkened courtyard as had Maleficent just before in the darkened throne room of the castle, each visual providing a vertical gash in the same segment of the screen's subdued lighting. All of this takes place in the first 12 minutes of the 75-minute film, with each described sequence filling the screen with rich tapestries of colour, accompanied continuously by leitmotivic elaborations of no fewer than eight separate numbers from Tchaikovsky's ballet score, including three that are rewritten as choral songs, and with the orchestral sections rendered in state-of-the-art recordings by a first-rate orchestra.[8]

Particularly effective in this opening sequence is the dramatic shaping achieved by shifting from the perspectival linear movements of the processions and ceremonial entrances to the circular motion introduced with the element of fairy magic. The latter including not only the galaxy-like visualizations that accompany the good fairies' bestowals of gifts, but also Maleficent's circular stroking of the green spherical crystal atop her staff and, arising from that, the circular visualization of her own 'gift', which resolves into the image of a spinning wheel, presented as the future agent of Aurora's death. This circular visual motif will return, more spectacularly, when she conjures the encirclement of the castle by a forest of thorns late in the film. This visual differentiation between the realms of fairy magic and mortals (which has a parallel in the deployment of music, discussed below) reaches a more immediate climax as the screen fills with spinning wheels, to be put to the flame in a futile attempt by the mortal realm to dispel Maleficent's evil magic.

This dramatic shaping closes off the opening sequence and its imaginative exploration of a widescreen colour palette, reaching with some success for a kind of medievalist sublime, buoyed by music that had originally been written to support an otherworldly beauty of a different if similarly arcane sort (that is, ballet). But in so doing it also opens the door to the film's lurking good-natured frumpery. By this point we have seen, but not yet heard, the bumbling King Hubert, and the three good fairies have only begun to show that side of their personalities. King Stefan, Aurora's father, will eventually reveal a similar sensibility in his interactions with King Hubert, but his tall, stately appearance affords him a regal dignity early on, consistent with the courtly beauty on display. Yet, in the film's next chapter, when the wings come off the fairies and they enter into a domestic sphere that renders them spectacularly ineffectual, beauty has no place, not even that of the eponymous Beauty, now named Briar Rose, who is summarily sent outdoors. And even before this symbolic event, although the film has managed to keep the widescreen well occupied for a time, other frumpish characters have made their appearance, as Maleficent's squat hench-toads are themselves revealed to be utterly hapless, in Maleficent's words, 'a disgrace to the forces of evil'. By the time we finally enter fully into the domestic space of the cottage

(18:50 into the film), we can palpably feel the widescreen giving way to a more comfortable 3/4 ratio as the grouping of the colourfully dressed good fairies, now transformed into peasant women, tends to define a separate, more limited space against their increasingly neutral-coloured backgrounds. While a certain beauty may be seen to lurk in that background's detail-work, the emphasis has moved from the sublime to the earthly – specifically, the domestic – defining the terms that will govern, if fitfully, the main action of the film until its final climactic battle.

To be sure, beauty still has its place in the film, if mainly within the traditional divide between the beautiful and the sublime, each of which tends, in its turn, to occupy the full screen effectively. But now both stand in opposition to the domestic spheres where Disney's animated films seem most comfortable, which from this point on will include not only the cottage but also the castle's interior spaces. In each case, when action in the domestic sphere does fill the screen, it seems often at the expense of the vertical dimension, which frequently appears foreshortened, as if the top and/or bottom has been lopped off. Within the realms more comfortably occupying the wider screen, the sublime and the beautiful, Maleficent represents the fearsome former and Briar Rose the latter, beautifully at one with nature – indeed, as she leaves the cottage, she plays true to her birth name, Aurora, as the future 'Sleeping Beauty' awakens a sleepy nature with the antiphonal music of dawn, foreshadowing her own later rescue (beginning 22:58).

Acknowledging that the beautiful and sublime dimensions of the film constitute its most compelling use of its most individuated resources – that is, its widescreen format, medievalist art and romantic ballet music – and that these were the result of fundamental choices made in its design, two less-than-plausible readings of the film present themselves. We may, somewhat perversely, see these resources deployed as a kind of anti-Disney force, implicitly pointing up the inadequacy of the studio's habitual recourse to bumbling, frumpy, domesticized niceness (and occasionally evil) as a means to create its emblems of the true, the good and the valuable (and occasionally their opposites). Indeed, the film may be seen to make this implicit reading explicitly structural in two broad concluding strokes. First, Prince Phillip's capture, taunting, flight, battle and eventual triumph efface the domestic (indeed, this process begins in the transformed domestic space of the cottage) with Maleficent's version of the sublime. And second, the sublime is itself then duly vanquished in favour of the beautiful, while putting Tchaikovsky and Technirama to good use and, in the end, leaving the good fairies on the sidelines and King Hubert befuddled. We may even extend this reading of the film to explain its eventual acceptance within an emergent age of animated film that extends more easily into these more daring realms than Disney's golden age generally allowed.

But these readings are, as indicated, implausible, not least because Disney's animated feature films always already had recourse to the sublime, especially the scary sublime, which was a cardinal feature of *The Three Little Pigs* (1933), *The Goddess of Spring* (1934) and – most famously – *Snow White and the Seven Dwarfs*, with its frightening, even trauma-inducing glimpses into the corruption of beauty through evil. This is not to say that readings along these lines have nothing to say to *Sleeping Beauty*'s internal dynamic, its eventual acceptance by audiences or even the later development of a less sentimentalized aesthetic for animation. Yet, they do not do full justice to the film's internal logic, which is much more accepting of the domestic realm than they suggest. That internal logic, however, is not fundamentally visual, but musical.

The Gift of Song: From Tchaikovsky to Musical Comedy

In adapting *Sleeping Beauty*, the Disney studio drew from a number of sources. While the basic story returned to Perrault, with modifications, Perrault's anonymous beauty became Aurora,[9] as in the ballet (borrowing the name of her firstborn child in Perrault), whereas her 'peasant' name, Briar Rose, was adapted from the Brothers Grimm, who end their version, with its echoes of Brünnhilde, upon her awakening. But despite the ballyhooed claim that Disney had gone back to something more original than the ballet, the film's basic structure comes mainly from the latter, which moves from the Prologue directly to the fateful day, years later, when celebration turns to tragedy (Act I), followed by princely vision and rescue (Act II) and concluding with marriage (Act III). Gone is the generational plotting of Perrault, whose Part II, sometime after the awakening and marriage, has the Prince returning home with his wife and two young children only to endure having his ogress of a mother – the Mother of all evil mothers-in-law – attempt to do the interlopers in and to feed them to her son, each in turn, prepared with *sauce Robert*. Nor is there any shadow of an even creepier earlier version, by Giambattista Basile, in which the sleeping beauty (named Talia) is raped and impregnated, gives birth to twins while asleep and is awakened by one of her babies who, by suckling on her fingers, removes the poisoned barb.

The Disney version (story adaptation by Erdman Penner, with several other writers credited) thus keeps the basic structure of Tchaikovsky's ballet (scenario by I. A. Vsevolozhsky and Marius Petipa), while restoring the spinning wheel as the specific agent of death/sleep, eliminating the parade of fairy-tale guests at the culminating wedding and renaming most of the characters. The ballet's evil fairy, for example, was named Carabosse, after a character in Madame d'Aulnoy's *The Princess Mayblossom*. But, significantly, Disney adds a further wrinkle not present in any earlier models by recasting the story within a single generation, which drastically shortens the length of Aurora's enchanted sleep and so eliminates a core element of the familiar tale. Plausibly, this was done so as to build into the story a mutual basis for the 'true love' whose kiss will awaken Aurora, echoing a recurrent concern of Disney to question the awakening power of 'love's first kiss', a concern that had already led in *Snow White and the Seven Dwarfs* to the interpolation of an early meeting between the future couple. In recent years, similar concerns have led the studio to introduce new takes on the premise, in *Enchanted* (2007), *Frozen* (2013) and *Maleficent* (2014).[10] Whatever its motivation, in *Sleeping Beauty*, the newly formulated plot provides the basis for the musical organization in two ways.

Most fundamentally, the reworked story offers a plot well in line with those of many musicals, allowing it to incorporate a common trope in which the song that marks the awakening of love between the central couple returns, as a reprise, when that love has fully blossomed at the end of the story, after whatever obstacles that have stood in the way of its consummation have been overcome. This familiar device gives considerable agency to the central couple in musicals, who must in some sense earn the love they initially feel, which, early on, they perhaps deny or do not fully recognize. Typically, as in Disney's *Sleeping Beauty*, it is the woman who is the primary architect of the romance, although it is then usually the man whose actions allow that romance to blossom. But the replotting of the story also offers a particular way for the film to engage the music of Tchaikovsky's ballet score, consistent in important ways with Tchaikovsky's own method, while at the same time frequently departing from the score's specific associations, or putting those associations to new purposes.

Tchaikovsky's music for *The Sleeping Beauty* works on two basic levels apart from its specific capacity to support balletic dance (itself not really relevant for the film). Most evidently, it establishes character, employing, for example, different types of music for humans and fairies, and giving particular character types an appropriate musical profile. But his music also participates in telling the story, both in terms of gesture, for interactive and dramatic sequences, and in shaping individual numbers, using variations and developments of given material to set out related events. In particular cases, these techniques approach the level of leitmotiv, as when Carabosse's music and the 'counterspell' music of the Fée des Lilas, which together frame the Introduction to the ballet, return at key moments in the narrative.

A more subtle example – perhaps not quite leitmotivic, or at least in the same sense – concerns the celebratory waltz near the beginning of Act I (No. 6), whose head-motive returns later in the act in subdued form (and on the mediant rather than the tonic) to head the main melody in the Coda of the 'Dance of the Maids of Honour and the Page Boys' that follows the famous 'Rose Adagio' (No. 8). On a broad level, the events marked by the shared motive relate to each other in accompanying group expressions of celebration, but their assonance also frames the central action of the act – the courtship of Aurora by her four suitors – which occurs as a kind of insert between the looming threat established near the beginning of the act and its execution near the end. Thus, the famous waltz celebrates the King's clemency regarding the knitting women who appear in the opening Scène (No. 5), while the recollection occurs just before the Finale (No. 9), when the threat that the women's needles represent returns and Carabosse exacts her vengeance.[11]

All of these strategies – and, indeed, all of these musical passages – are used in Disney's *Sleeping Beauty*, where they are coordinated much differently. The famous waltz and its echo in the Coda of No. 8 become the basis for three separate but linked songs, 'Once Upon a Dream', 'I Wonder' and 'One Gift – Sleeping Beauty', all in a sense framing the action of the film, but in entirely different ways from how they frame the action in Act I of the ballet. The Lilac Fairy's music, which offers sleep instead of death in the ballet, in the film establishes the 'Once Upon a Time' feeling near the beginning, then returns with perverse irony as Maleficent describes to a captive Prince Phillip how he will ride off as an old man to rescue his sleeping princess and, finally, marks the awakenings near the film's end. And Carabosse's distinctive music provides not the basis for malevolent action but heroic action against such forces, since it becomes, in the film, sometimes with extensive rewriting, associated with the fairies and Prince Phillip as they take action to save Aurora and restore her kingdom.[12] Thus, the music of group celebration becomes the basis for the core love story, its echo becomes the basis for the key interventions of the good fairies, the music of sleep becomes the music of fantasy and reawakening, and the distinctive and powerful music with which Tchaikovsky endowed his evil fairy is repurposed to support the principal forces for good in the film. As for Maleficent, her music in the film is mostly derived from one of the novelty numbers in Act III of the ballet, a 'Pas de caractère' for Puss in Boots and the White Cat, fairy-tale guests at the royal wedding, whose meowing and scratching (the latter in the form of 'stinger' chords) transmute into the evil fairy's menace and wanton cruelty.[13]

Table 2.1 Derivation and Deployment of Music from Tchaikovsky's *The Sleeping Beauty* in Disney's *Sleeping Beauty*

A. **Derivation of Songs and Other Leitmotivic Music from Tchaikovsky's *The Sleeping Beauty***

Songs:	Derivation from Tchaikovsky's *The Sleeping Beauty*:
1. 'Once upon a Dream'	principal melody of No. 6. 'Valse', in Act I
2. 'Hail to the Princess Aurora'	opening of No. 1. 'Marche', in Prologue
3. 'One Gift' / 'Sleeping Beauty'	Coda of No. 8. 'Pas d'action', in Act I
4. 'I Wonder'	trio of No. 6. 'Valse', in Act I
5. Briar Rose's Vocalise	first part of No. 25. 'Pas de quatre,' in Act III (Cendrillon, Prince Fortuné, L'Oiseau Bleu, La Princesse Florine)
[6. 'The Skumps Song'	uncredited; not from Tchaikovsky's *The Sleeping Beauty*]

Other Leitmotivic Music: A. The three good fairies	Derivation from Tchaikovsky's *The Sleeping Beauty*:
i. pre-materialization	opening of variation iv (Canari qui chante) in No. 3. 'Pas de six [Les six Fées]', in Prologue
ii. routine magic	from variation ii (La Fée-Argent) in No. 23. 'Pas de quatre', in Act III (La Fée-Or, La Fée-Argent, La Fée-Saphir, La Fée-Diamant)
iii. domestic	'Danse des demoiselles d'honneur et des pages', part 6 of No. 8. 'Pas d'action', in Act I
iv. to action	from the opening section of No. 9. 'Finale', in Act I
v. sneaking	from variation 1 (Candide) of No. 3. 'Pas de six [Les six Fées]', in Prologue
B. Maleficent	
i. menace	No. 24. 'Pas de caractère: Le chat botte et la chatte blanc he', in Act III
ii. Forbidden Mountain	No. 19. 'Entr'acte symphonique (Le Sommeil) et Scène', in Act II, Sc. 2 (also Lilac Fairy's forest spell in No. 9. 'Finale', in Act I)
C. Prince Phillip (ceremonial)	beginning of 10. 'Entr'acte et Scéne', in Act II, Sc. i
D. Storybook	Fée des Lilas's 'counterspell' music, first heard as the principal counterweight to Carabosse's music in the 'Introduction', then elaborated anew in: No. 4. 'Finale', in Prologue; in No. 9. 'Finale', in Act I No. 14. 'Scène (Désiré et la Fée des Lilas', in Act II, sc. i No. 19. 'Entr'acte symphonique (Le Sommeil) et Scène', in Act II, sc. ii (again as counterweight to Carabosse's music)
E. Heroic Engagement	initially from Aurora's sleeping death in No. 9. 'Finale', in Act I (derived from Carabosse's *leitmotiv*), but subsequently drawing more generally on Carabosse's music (e.g., opening section of 'Introduction', and, *passim*, in No. 4. ' Finale,' in Prologue, and in No. 9. 'Finale', in Act I)
F. Apotheosis	from No. 30. 'Finale et Apothéose', in Act III

Table 2.1 continued

B. **Deployment within Disney's *Sleeping Beauty* of the Derived Songs and Leitmotivic Music Detailed in A.**

NB: Following the labelling in A, the six songs are given by number, and the leitmotivic scoring by letter and sub-numeral. Songs, when used only instrumentally, are given in Italics.

Opening Credits:

Vocal: 1 `00:28`

Instrumental: Aii- Aiii `01:08  01:23`

Curse trajectory:

`03:11  06:38  10:45` `18:38  22:58 25:58  30:10  38:51 41:02  45:19`

2   3   3   4   5-4   1   (1) [6]   (1)

D   Ai-Aii   Bi   Aii- Aiv // Bi   5-Aiii   4-5   Aiii-Aii   *1*   C   *1* / Av / Bi

`01:56  05:26 06:00  08:17  13:08 14:52  16:11  19:22 20:00  27:35 28:02  33:26 34:54  39:16  44:35  45:45 46:51 48:46`

Storybook; celebrating   //   ~16 years later: critters & courtship; cake & dress;
Aurora; fairy gifts & curses //   back to magic; back to the castle; pricked; sunset

Aftermath:

`53:54  56:23  56:54` `74:27`

3 – (1)   (1)   1

2   Aiv   *1* - Bi - Aiv- E - Bii- E - Bi- D - E- D- *2* - F- *1-4*

`52:20   56:30  57:12  57:42  58:15 58:47  59:05 59:30  02:38  02:52  65:21  71:40  73:28 73:50  74:15`

Celebrations and sleep; capturing, taunting, and rescuing Prince
Phillip; heroic flight and battle; kiss; awakenings; waltz

Table 2.1 gives an account of the most salient derivation of the film's music from Tchaikovsky's score, in terms of song and leitmotiv, followed by a chart detailing when that derived music appears in the film.[14] As shown, the film relies heavily, although not exclusively, on leitmotivic associations, generally establishing new associations for the borrowed music, as when the Lilac Fairy's interventionist music sets the Forbidden Mountain (Bii). Yet, despite a strong tendency to repurpose Tchaikovsky's music, the filmmakers (led by George Bruns, responsible for the musical adaptation) frame the film's action by borrowing as literally as feasible from the ballet's own framing music, using the Prologue's opening 'Marche' for their extended opening procession, cast as the choral number, 'Hail to the Princess Aurora' with instrumental variations (3:12), and introducing the film's apotheosis with the head music for the ballet's 'Finale et Apothéose' (73:00). As well, its 'good fairy' derivations, while borrowing 'action' music from Aurora's somewhat frantic bravado early in the Finale to Act I (Aiv), otherwise stay true to the ballet's fairy music (Ai, Aii, and Av in Table 2.1.A) except when they forego magic, at which point they resort to second-tier mortal music (Aiii); that this represents a deliberate strategy may be inferred from the leitmotivic shift that occurs when the fairies return to magic during the second extended cottage sequence (from Aiii to Aii, at 34:54).

But in the critical choice to build the drama around the Act I 'Valse' (No. 6) and its later echo (Coda of No. 8), Bruns, with the help of lyricists Tom Adair, Winston Hibler, Ted Sears, Sammy Fain and Jack Lawrence, fashion a separate musical drama that embraces both Beauty and her various 'domestics'. In so doing, they discard the original basis for the specific associ-ations of the borrowed music, while forging new relationships that, in their way, remain true to the musical relationships established in the ballet and manage, as well, to refashion other elements of the balletic drama according to more modern sensibilities, as derived from musical comedy.[15]

'Once Upon a Dream': Song, Visionary Desire and Agency

The central event of Tchaikovsky's ballet is Prince Désiré's vision of Princess Aurora in Act II, after the Lilac Fairy chooses him as the one to break Carabosse's spell, and after which she leads him to the princess so that he can awaken her with a kiss. Similarly central are the visions that motivate the central love affair in the Disney film: Briar Rose's recounted dream of a prince ('Once Upon a Dream') and Prince Phillip's enchantment with her vocalizing, which he determines is 'too beautiful to be real' (29:13). But while the ballet's 'vision' sequence undoubtedly inspired the film's, the latter's constructions are as different, and those differences are as telling, as with the different shapes of their denouements, in which the ballet's ceremonial progress to an inevitable conclusion becomes, in the animated film, a series of confrontations in which each outcome is contested, to be decided by heroic action. If heroic agency is the key difference in the film's denouement, the key difference with the vision scenes themselves centres on *romantic agency*, and on how this is expressed in the shared song 'Once Upon a Dream'. Indeed, this song not only culminates the film's vision sequence, but also thereafter maintains an important diegetic musical presence that crucially informs the rest of the action. In this way, it propels the background leitmotivic scoring into the foreground, where it drives the dramatic plotting of the film in a way consistent with how song functions more broadly, not only in musicals, but also in real life.

To recount the song's deployment in the film: 'Once Upon a Dream' not only opens and closes the film, but also provides the basis for the lovers' first meeting (30:10) and, through brief reprises, provides the means through which the good fairies learn Briar Rose is in love (38:51), through which King Hubert learns of his son's betrothal (45:19) and through which the good fairies learn, at once, that it is Prince Phillip with whom their princess has fallen in love, and that he is in danger (56:23). Moreover, Maleficent's interruption of this song, as it fades from the prince's whistling into romantic background music when he arrives at the cottage expecting to meet Aurora (56:54/57:12), virtually compels the song's final return, as consummation, at the end of the film.

Before considering the song's musical deployment as a full song, it is worth considering the many ways its continued presence, as a fragment, matters to the success of the film. Especially when Aurora and Prince Phillip sing or whistle a phrase or two, it creates a natural afterglow of their encounter, instantly recognizable as such not only to us but also to those in the story, reminding us as well of their romantic agency, something almost entirely denied to their counterparts in other versions of the story. The repeated words, 'Once upon a dream', remind us of the vision-centred basis for their love and of the conduit between dreams and reality that song can provide, or at least seem to provide. King Hubert's repetition and Flora's recognition of the song also give these characters agency, demonstrating their active engagement in determining what happens, rather than simply playing out their roles within a predetermined plotline. And, together, these repetitions provide a narrative thread that keeps the romance at the centre while the familiar fairy tale events unfold around that centre, with those given events in the end answerable to the romance instead of the reverse. Because song makes the characters in the story matter in these ways, we feel their dramatic impact more vitally, which helps both to mitigate the sometimes unfortunate visual disjunctures discussed above and to efface the ineffectual domestic realm to which the three fairies had previously consigned themselves. Thus, with a courage specifically fuelled by the romance that rests in the balance, they are led instead to take effective action against Maleficent. Especially through 'Once Upon a Dream', song itself thus becomes a central actor in the film's unfolding action, as a force that leads from the realm of the imagination to the realm of action in the real world.

That song can indeed have such power is a well-established fact that has long provided a familiar trope for musicals. But there is more involved in this case than the film simply adapting its narrative to familiar contours of romantic inspiration. 'Once upon a Dream' functions, within the film, as part of a network of songs that both make Briar Rose a well-defined character (despite her oft-noted relative lack of spoken lines) and demonstrate a particularly savvy use of Tchaikovsky's music.

We are first introduced to the (nearly) adult Briar Rose as she opens an upper window of the cottage to vocalize (18:38). As with her later 'Vocalise', which will entrance Prince Phillip, she directs her singing outward, to the world beyond her confining cottage, and draws on a part of Tchaikovsky's score that is set antiphonally. Her vocalizing is thus not merely an indulgence in her 'gift of song', but acts from the beginning as an invitation for a responding voice to join her. Her first vocalized melody will provide the basis for her first texted song, 'I Wonder' (25:58), an 'I wish' song that makes it explicit that the responding voice she longs for is that of a romantic partner, although only birds and orchestra provide an echoing response. The song's dynamic thus follows that of her Vocalise, where she just before also found a responding voice in nature; thus, in 'Vocalise' (22:58), which is based on the antiphonal flute melody of the 'Pas de quatre' in Tchaikovsky's Act III, she assumes the role of Aurora (that is, Dawn) in awakening nature, as I described earlier. Then, in her follow-up song, 'Once Upon a Dream', she brings her wished-for romance closer and closer, first with the help of the forest creatures and Prince Phillip's cloak and boots, but then face to face with her dream prince, as Phillip takes the place of his surrogate, singing and then dancing with her.

This sequence draws implicitly on relationships already existing in Tchaikovsky's score. As already noted, the earlier 'One Gift', which in its second verse bequeaths Aurora the gift of song, shares an opening motive with 'Once Upon a Dream', a linkage that will be reinforced with the continuation of this song in 'Sleeping Beauty' (53:54), just before King Hubert's brief reprise of 'Once Upon a Dream' alerts Flora to Prince Phillip's situation. More subtly, the melody for 'I Wonder' derives directly from the trio of the same waltz that provides the melody for 'Once Upon a Dream' so that – especially for those who know the original – it will seem only natural that this particular 'I wish' song should yield to this particular subjunctive love song.[16] Indeed, the setup could not have been better planned for the final sequence from instrumental music to song, when the final waltz – now a full strain of Tchaikovsky's original waltz, leading directly to the 'I Wonder' trio – sets up the final choral version of 'Once Upon a Dream' as the couple dances up into the clouds and we return to the opening fairy-tale book with their concluding kiss.

Conclusions

One of the most remarkable features in the effectiveness of this interlocking deployment of song is that its linchpin, 'Once Upon a Dream', is not fully adequate either as a song or as a placeholder for Tchaikovsky's waltz. As a song, it is rather short (as Disney songs tend to be, and which arguably is appropriate to the animated format), consisting of a single chorus in waltz tempo. A more serious flaw is verbal and derives from what is itself a good structural conceit: ending the first phrase and the song itself with the title phrase, which at the end incorporates a return to the opening three-note motive (thus 'I know you' becomes '[Up]on a dream'). But the realization of this conceit ends up rhyming 'once' with 'once'. To be fair, this apparent lack of inspiration was perhaps unavoidable: 'dunce', the only common word that rhymes with 'once', just wouldn't have worked here. Yet, even if we are inclined to forgive this verbal infelicity, the song's flaws are also musical. While the second half of Tchaikovsky's melody, which we hear in the lead-up to the final reprise, does need to be rewritten to work as a song melody and to implement the song's structural conceit, the result manages to suggest something of Tchaikovsky's contour without retaining an ounce of the original's excitement.

We might thus, wryly, take considerable solace in the fact that most of the reprises of the song, as traced here, make do with a phrase or two. Or, perhaps, we may choose to recall, ruefully, Amanda's observation from Noel Coward's *Private Lives* (1930): 'Extraordinary how potent cheap music is.'[17] But it seems more satisfactory to point out how effectively it all works *despite* these flaws, and that its success – as with the insistent tune in *Private Lives* – depends on repetition, planning and timing, and ultimately on the potency of song as such.

References

Allan, Robin (1999). *Walt Disney and Europe: European Influences on the Animated Feature Films of Walt Disney*. Bloomington and Indianapolis: Indiana University Press.

Canemaker, John (1996). *Before the Animation Begins: The Art and Lives of Disney Inspirational Sketch Artists*. New York: Hyperion.

McDonnell, Cari Elizabeth (2015). 'Genre in Context: Toward a Reexamination of the Film Musical in Classical Hollywood.' PhD dissertation, University of Texas at Austin.

Sleeping Beauty (2003). 2-Disc DVD Special Edition. Burbank, CA: Walt Disney Video.

Tchaikovsky, Peter Ilyich (1974). *The Sleeping Beauty: Complete Ballet Music.* Foreword by Roger Fiske. New York, London, Zürich and Mainz: Edition Eulenburg.

3

Mary Poppins: A Precursor of the Feminist Musical?

Tim Stephenson

The patriarchal dominance of the metonymic Disney in the 1960s gave precious little opportunity for filmic representations of female protagonists that confront the male gaze, let alone address the verisimilitude of the missing female spectator. What was it that drove the purportedly sexist, even misogynist, Walt Disney to a fifteen-year pursuit of the rights to a set of stories about a patriarchy-disrupting closet feminist called Mary Poppins? What was it about the 'stern, dependable, businesslike, magical and yet eternally loveable' (Picardie 2008) character that so attracted him, and then went on to captivate the familial audience? And how, from a vitriolic melange of conflict and antagonism between P. L. Travers and Walt Disney, did the 'most wonderful, cheering movie' (Crowther 1964) that is *Mary Poppins* emerge?

For today's audience who manage to cast off the intoxicating nostalgia of the film and peek beneath the Disneyfied glitz and glamour, a more interesting narrative emerges. Fifty years after Julie Andrews brought the character to life, *Time Magazine* proclaimed 'Mary Poppins was the Original Disney Feminist' and 'a role model for young women' (Begley 2014) to boot. Can a film with a subtext of first-wave feminism, produced during the turmoil of second-wave gender inequality, now be seen as an ideological 'provocateur' (Grilli 2007: xx) for a generation steeped in the complexities of third-wave feminism and beyond? *Mary Poppins* is a film that both confirms and challenges cultural, familial and heterosexual conformity. It is a musical where the narrative is dictated by a female 'outsider', anticipating the erosion of the dominant heterosexual masculinities of most Hollywood film musicals, and pointing the way to recent contemporary critiques that recognize the centrality of matriarchal and feminist themes for the continuing health of the genre.

Musicals may be capable of creating 'wonderfully evocative worlds [...] but those worlds have relationships with the real world' (Taylor and

Symonds 2014: 2). On the surface, they might appear as 'frothy concoctions of song, dance, extravagant design and inconsequential stories' (Hiller and Pye 2011: 5), yet artists, performers, directors, producers and the organizations responsible for their production are by their very nature ideological. Thus, the narratives and subtexts within the stories, the unconventional philosophies of author Travers and the beliefs of the deeply flawed entrepreneurial genius who was Walt Disney all provide insights into the socio-political context from which the film emerged. Similarly, by applying genre-specific approaches to gender analysis, I shall demonstrate that a series of children's stories set in Edwardian London, written in the 1930s by a displaced Anglicized Australian (Travers) and turned into a classic film by the son of an Irish-Canadian and German-American couple in California in the 1960s (Disney) can still speak to a contemporary audience, because 'the performed, embodied, and envoiced difference between women and men is foundational to the very genre of musical theatre' (Wolf 2011: 6).

The Disney Musical: A Utopian Paradox?

Historically, the film musical has served as a, 'social barometer that both reflect(s) and shape(s) the national zeitgeist' (Johnson 2012: iv), despite, rather than because of, the hegemonic patriarchal ideology it reinforces. The film musical genre is inherently conservative and, as one of its chief exponents, Disney represents 'a distinctive moral and political order [...] in which social strife and conflict are always seen as temporary and abnormal; and an order in which every day must be a "Zippidy-doo-dah-day!"' (Rojek 1993: 121). This mediatized worldview perpetuates a Western cultural hegemony through the acquiescence of a complicit audience eager to buy into the utopian fantasies Disney projects. We recognize the ideological anachronism of their narratives for today's society, yet still enjoy submerging ourselves in nostalgic Disneyfied memories, comforted in our indulgence by a 'mythical past that was exciting, happy, and safe – a past in which the good guys always win' (Dholakia and Schroeder 2001: 12). Disney is able to 'tap into the lost hopes, abortive dreams, and utopian potential of popular culture' (Giroux and Pollock: 8), understanding that these worlds exist to reinforce 'the patriarchal symbolic order based on rigid notions of sexuality and gender' (Zipes 1992: 26). We excuse our perfunctory criticality and rationalize our complicity in this deception because 'the paradox is that social criticism is simultaneously implied and denied by the idea of a realized utopia' (Simons and Billig: 150). But this paradox extends far beyond the musical's ability to provide social commentary as the genre itself is inherently enigmatic, contradictory and, at times, even absurd. So what are these 'paradoxes', and how are they manifest in *Mary Poppins*?

Musicals may express socio-political ideals within their narratives, but that is not their purpose: musicals are meant to be 'flossy and flimsy; wonderful but lightweight' (Taylor and Symonds 2014: 1), aren't they? Dyer notes that the film musical 'does not simply give the people what they want', nor does it 'simply reproduce unproblematically patriarchal–capitalistic ideology' (Dyer 2002: 20). Thus within the utopian world Disney created we expect a fantasy abounding with clichéd stereotypes, false histories, parodied social structures and stereotypical familial, gender and class ideologies. We then bolster that fantasy through genre specific techniques 'built from the stuff in musical theatre's toolbox' (Wolf 2011: 5), which allow us to suspend further our disbelief as swathes of chimney sweeps balletically dance on rooftops, diegetic robins burst into whistling counterpoint, aged parents dance in the townhouse hallway cavorting with the domestic staff and metaphorical universal happiness prevails for all through the simple act of flying a kite, albeit one with an ideologically discarded suffragette sash as a tail. Then, finally, we add to this heady utopian mix a magical, no-nonsense nanny who flies, removes hat stands from an empty carpet bag, slides up bannisters, reorders clutter with a click of her fingers, communicates with animals and jumps in and out of chalk drawings on the pavement.

The utopia of *Mary Poppins* is therefore straight from the mould of all of the manufactured, idealized Disney worlds we have come to know and love. We accept the fantasy as we have been indoctrinated into their codes and mythologies since birth. So we know that 17 Cherry Lane never really existed; we understand that the Edwardian setting is a selective roman-ticized historical reinterpretation, and we know that Mary, Bert and the Banks family are figments of Travers' vivid imagination, simplified for child readers. Or were they? Travers had the luxury of eight books in which to develop the nuances of her characters. The medium of film is less accom-modating. Her archetypal figures (already moderated by a pseudo-magical realism) were interpreted by Walsh and DaGradi (the screenwriters) into quintessential stereotypes, then reinterpreted by professional actors through the imagination of Robert Stevenson, the director. Thus, the ridiculed, confused and ultimately enlightened Mr Banks is the ineffective patriarch of a household of sanitized, smiling and grateful Edwardian servitude. His scatter-brained, domestically incompetent wife's rationale for the neglect of her children is justified by her burgeoning feminist activities, despite the fact that these immediately dissipate at the end when Mary gifts Mrs Banks a new model of domestic bliss. The children transform from angelic-looking nanny terrorists into perfectly behaved, immaculately groomed and socially considerate model siblings. Bert, the impoverished but cheerful, heel-clicking cockney and grateful working-class sop, is a class victim who always knows his place. And finally there is the disturbingly forceful yet strangely asexual Mary, who transforms all of their lives, reinvents their world, then disappears as suddenly as she appeared: a 'practically perfect' catalyst who creates a 'practically perfect' utopian world, just as Walt Disney intended.

Baudrillard reminds us that 'a realized utopia is [in itself] a paradoxical idea' (1988: 79) and the ultimate paradox is therefore that Walt Disney's 'perfect' world can never quite escape the social, political and ideological context from which it emerged, nor the critiques that have subsequently been applied to its narrative, structures and symbolism.

Mary Poppins: A Patriarchal Feminist?

The conservative patriarchal conventions of Travers' stories, reinforced through their Disneyfication in the 1964 film, clash with the modest domestic feminism of the character creating a definitional tautology reflecting transition in the film musical genre commensurate with the socio-political upheavals of the period. Travers was never an overt supporter of feminism, yet 'feminist awareness' permeates all aspects of her writing, which, 'venerat(es) the feminine principle in myth' (Smulders 2014: 171). So, despite her unconventional and often misguided views on parenthood, the family and maternalism, she was still able to create Mary as a quintessential nanny, the apotheosis of the civilizing feminine, this despite the fact that one of the essential feminist determinants, namely the disaggregation of gender and sexuality, is missing. Mary is obviously gendered: Travis describes her as being in her twenties, 'thin, with large feet and hands, and small, rather peering blue eyes' (1934: 7). But other than Mary's vanity of self-objectification through looking at herself in the mirror, she is not overtly sexualized in either the novels or the film. The book illustrations, so obsessively controlled by Travis, 'made her look like a stiff, ugly Dutch doll' (Hughes 2005), hardly the porcelain-skinned, rosy-cheeked, practically perfect image of the Disney film.

Whilst Mary was formulaically 'sweetened' by Disney's commercially driven adherence to the golden age musical genre, Walt Disney deliberately chose to ignore the usual casting of major studio stars in the lead roles. Rather, in casting Julie Andrews and Dick Van Dyke, Disney chose established Broadway stars with limited film experience. Travers may have considered Andrews 'too pretty' for the role, yet the cinematic conventions of close-up shots, the exaggerated perfection of the Disney screen aesthetic and the need for someone with critically acclaimed acting and singing abilities made her choice inevitable. The fact that her career was defined by the roles of Mary and Maria (in *The Sound of Music*) is remarkable because of their similarities. Both are young, opinionated, independent, feisty, child-nurturing, maternal nanny figures who reform and re-establish the broken patriarchies into which they have been parachuted. The main difference is that Maria *is* sexualized and marries to fulfil heteronormative convention whilst Mary's burgeoning feminist credentials means she disappears on the West wind, leaving a wistful Bert looking longingly skywards: 'Mary Poppins exemplifies a kind of feminist hero who lives out ideals of women's equality by being completely assertive and autonomous [...] Mary Poppins values herself and is not male-defined' (Bell et al. 1995: 214–15).

It seems unlikely that Walt Disney, who was hardly renowned for his egalitarian views on gender equality, knowingly produced a film that created a 'feminist hero'. He usually wore his sexist, even misogynist, views on his sleeve, as evidenced by his support for the creation of the ludicrous suffragette Winifred Banks. Her bumbling feminist inventions never appeared in the books, so when Disney deliberately lampoons the 'errant mother, who cares more for feminism than for her mother-role' (McCleer 2002: 85) it is with the sole intention of ridiculing all feminist beliefs through her instantaneous patriarchy-reaffirming abandonment of the suffragette cause in the final scene.

Mary Poppins and Dyadic Maternalism

The maternal paradox in *Mary Poppins* is that in order to demonstrate the central importance of domestic motherhood for the nuclear family the narrative has to open by demonstrating its collapse. Ever since *Bambi* was abandoned by his father and then witnessed the murder of his mother, the studio's output was predicated on absent or problem parents and dysfunctional and broken families. In *Mary Poppins* we are presented with a family in crisis: a wittering, incapable mother, a ridiculous, blundering, domineering father, out-of-control children, openly critical domestic staff and a brow-beaten departing nanny who won't 'stay in this house another minute'. This sets the scene for the extended maternal transformation that is the substance of the narrative, with Mary at its centre as the model 'of self-sacrificing motherhood (that) is key to the maternal melodrama [...] and its inscription of women in patriarchy' (Bilbao 2011: 5). Yet Mary operates within the patriarchal constraints of the Edwardian family whilst deliberately undermining it – this domestic nanny 'interviews' Mr Banks for her position, concluding 'I'll give you one week. I'll know by then.'

The inter-relationship between the subservient expectations of the role of nanny, Mary's 'masterful' manipulation of Mr Banks and her contrasting, nurturing-yet-controlling relationship with the children represents 'one side of a dyadic split in a contemporary notion of womanhood, her counterpart being the absent mother Winifred Banks' (McCleer 2002: 85). Yet Mary's healing of the clichéd rift between womanhood and motherhood in Winifred is complicated. Disney may have literally emasculated aspects of Mary's maternalism by removing the darker aspects of her magical persona, softening her disciplinarian nature and limiting her obfuscation, but the essence of Travis' complex witch remains.

Travers' ideology was shaped by her indoctrination into the beliefs of Armenian philosopher and mystic George Gurdjieff. She developed a certainty that motherhood was one of the immutable human realities, enabling her to develop within her stories maternal motifs based on 'meaning, symbolism, and function [reinforcing] the myth of most mother goddesses – her disappearance and reappearance' (*Encyclopædia Britannica* 2015). Mary synthesized her beliefs in the 'mother goddess' role – a Kali-like figure, a re-creator of time and space who communes with nature – whilst displaying Shakti-like feminine dynamism manifesting itself in 'power, strength, force, and capacity' (McDaniel 2011), providing a contrary rational to patriarchy for those outwardly masculine traits. Thus, 'the omniscient nanny [...] was the embodiment of Gurdieff's off-beat teachings [and] related to the Mother of God' (Brown 2013).

To further complicate these pseudo-religious maternal ideologies woven into her belief system, were the mythologies of the Neopagan triple goddess, expounded by Robert Graves in *The White Goddess*. Graves' explanation of the transformation from the enchantment and enthusiasms of Maidenhood, through the fulfilment and power of Motherhood to the wisdom and repose of the Crone, concurred with Travers' bi-fold interest in mythology and poetry. Whether this was integral to the development of her nannying witch or retrospectively applied to agree with her changing philosophy is debatable: 'Poppins is a maiden because she is young and still has a spark in her life. Poppins is also a Mother, taking excellent care of her charges. And last but not least, she is a Crone, full of the wisdom of the ancients' (Brody 2013: 18). The dyadic split in the maternal role between nanny and mother is further exacerbated by the necessity to compensate for the incompetence and inconsistency in both the paternal and maternal roles in the Banks household. At times, Mary is the disciplinarian, organizing and controlling the children's behaviour with

Edwardian draconianism and refuting any suggestions that allude to the more feminine side of her character.

Jane   Don't you remember? You won the horse race.
Mary   A respectable person like me in a horse race?
           How dare you suggest such a thing? (Walsh and DaGradi 1963)

Thus, throughout the film, Mary alternates between more masculine traits – the whistling sergeant-major-like march to the park or the enforced parade at the start of the rooftop ballet – and her feminine primping and preening in front of the mirror, where her vanity is exaggerated by her magical reflection's failure to conform. Yet in other parts of the film traditional maternal values emerge when she sings the children to sleep and when we witness her tearful gaze as the children skip away, immediately prior to her solitary departure. These Disneyfied maternal inventions are hardly concordant with Edwardian values; they are 1960s ideology, straight from the pages of Dr Spock. For example, Mary creates games to persuade the children to tidy up and to drink their medicine – 'spit spot!' – and fills their days with play, encouraging them into scurrilous inappropriate behaviour such as giggling flying tea parties and dancing on the rooftops covered in soot.

Mary's complex maternalism is also moderated by the adult sensibilities of her character – the surreptitious hiccup following her spoonful of rum punch and the calculated exchanges with Bert, which ensure his ardour is always cooled, yet hints at a twinkle in her eye and a rather less constrained affability outside the thraldom of Cherry Tree Lane. Bilbao observes that the traditional maternal melodrama normally fails to 'help the woman gain agency in patriarchy' (Bilbao 2011: 14), but Mary usurps this. Her matriarchy is defined not only in relation to the absent mother, but also through the inclusion of characteristics from the 'absent' father. Through this assertive mix, she controls the patriarch, his spouse and the children: 'She is not a stereotypically nurturant caregiver, and she attends to the needs of the children without becoming a sacrificial, self-deprecating mother' (Bell et al. 1995: 214).

Despite Disney's concluding sentimental affirmation of the traditional family unit, we are left feeling that the reformed Mr Banks is only being allowed to masquerade temporarily as the patriarch – well, at least until the wind changes once again.

Mary Poppins: Usurping the Genre?

The almost monotheistic formulaic success of the Rogers and Hammerstein era, stretching from *Oklahoma* (1943) through to the film of *The Sound of Music* (1965), was largely responsible for defining the modern book musical. Their oeuvre confirmed the complex codices of the musical, which still govern the interactions between narrative, song, dance, acting, music, orchestration, design and production, and educated the audience into acceptance of its inherent conventions. The 1960s and 1970s saw the production of numerous musicals that reaffirmed their model, but which also saw a shift towards more progressive themes and more female-focussed narratives. Whilst some of these film musicals attempted to address a female spectator, the industry was still male-dominated, which consequently had the effect of 'reinscribing women into their roles in patriarchy' (Bilbao 2011: 9).

Mary Poppins appeared on the cusp of this formulaic transition, so within the overtly conservative form of the film musical the screenwriters Walsh and DaGradi, abetted by the Sherman brothers in their music and lyrics, unwittingly embedded a matriarchal feminist icon in the heart of Disney's patriarchy. Musicals of this period relied on a number of basic conventions:

> They alternated between spoken word and singing, their storylines were easy to follow, songs were sung from a specific character's point of view, there was aesthetic unity among the various elements of the production, and a heterosexual love story as a narrative force in the story. (Wolf, in Scherb 2014)

Most of these apply to *Mary Poppins*. The degree to which a musical confirms or denies such characteristics identifies the degree of radicalism within the output. By the 1960s, a dichotomy had emerged between golden-age musicals, which 'champion[ed] the mainstream ideology, and the "anti-musical", and "counter-mythology", which challenge[d] the social and aesthetic status quo' (Johnson 2012: iv). But this rather oversimplifies the changes in the genre at a time when the musical's ideological and narrative development was more radical and nuanced than the conservative commercial considerations supporting it. Therefore, it is more accurate to consider these binary positions as being either end of a spectrum of developmental potency in which *Mary Poppins* occupies the middle ground of largely conforming to the genre's historical roots whilst also challenging some aspects of its formulaic certitude.

The first challenge is that *Mary Poppins* predicates a genre shift away from the heteronormative romances of the previous decades. Previously, gender stereotypes confirmed patriarchalism through the 'reinforcement of the habits of social conformity' (Hall, in Bell et al. 1995: 86). The basic formula of boy meets girl, boy loses girl, girl modifies boy sufficiently to give in to his demands, thereby allowing them to ride off into the sunset together, was seldom challenged. The medium was dominated by female protagonists who relied on the male lead for her definition. There were few female leads who didn't slot readily into the antonymic 'Madonna or whore' stereotypes, and all were defined by the male gaze. As Wolf stated, 'the musicals I adored [...] featured women who only seemed to sing about love, who needed men to fulfill their dreams, and who hardly seemed like good role models for my growing feminist sensibilities' (2002: vii). Thus, the outcome was seldom in doubt (Laurey was always going to marry Curly – Jud never had a chance) and audiences simply went to watch the journey along the way.

But by the 1960s the very success of the Rogers and Hammerstein formula seemed to stifle the creativity of musical theatre, appearing out of kilter with the radicalism of the age. The post-war politics of the nuclear family also seemed ill at ease with the 'simmering pot of gender and race frustrations that exploded' (Wolf 2011: 51). The transition was heralded by a few minor female-empowered incursions into the rigidity of the formula, like Anita's control of her sexuality or Anybody's disaggregation of sex and gender in *West Side Story,* but these normative deviations were the exception rather than the rule. However, by the middle of the decade, Broadway was filled with complex, contradictory female protagonists who challenged the subservient trope, like Sally Bowles in *Cabaret* (1966) and Charity Valentine in *Sweet Charity* (1966).

In the middle of this transition appeared *Mary Poppins*, ostensibly another patriarchy-conforming, historicized, deferential woman, and yet her character not only challenged traditional views but arguably established a new standard for female representation in the musical. The outward normality of the familiar architecture of a children's fantasy narrative is challenged by the placement of Travis's mysterious, disenfranchised, gendered yet strangely asexual nanny into the heart of an exaggerated stereo-typical patriarchal-yet-dysfunctional household. Here, Mary is free to wreak her magical transformations, to upset and challenge the constructed reality, yet ultimately to reassert the dominance of the parent–child relationship by sacrificing her own happiness. Although heterosexual normalcy is confirmed through Mary's reconstruction of the Banks family, we are starkly aware throughout that she will never agree to Bert's subtle persistence. She even reminds him of the pointlessness of his advances in 'Jolly Holiday':

Mary   You'd never think of pressing your advantage,
Forbearance is the hallmark of your creed,
A lady needn't fear when you are near,
Your sweet gentility is crystal clear! (Sherman and Sherman 1963)

Thus, Bert's relationship with Mary is doomed to remain unconsummated; her aura is too mystical, too magical and too domineering for her to ever be coerced by a mere man.

The second challenge to the golden age formula appears in the set-piece dances between Mary and Bert. The consonance of their relationship is defined by the synergistic reciprocity of their routines: 'that they sing and dance so fluidly together is a metaphor for the perfection of their relationship' (Altman 1989: 83). These provide an excuse to challenge Mary's asexual persona through the musical's excuse for heterosexual affirmation and intimate cross-gender physical contact, but in neither instance is the expected male dominance and female acquiescence achieved. The two main dance routines, 'Jolly Holiday' and 'Step in Time', are both 'dream sequences' constructed by Mary's magic, yet choreographed and prescribed from Bert's perspective. Both dances are extensions of the musical narrative designed to advance the plot and develop the characterization, ensuring 'the song and dance becomes a self-conscious and explicit performative re-enactment of individual identity' (Taylor and Symonds 2014: 277). Thus in 'Jolly Holiday' the children are quickly dispatched to the fairground to heighten the potentiality of a romantic interlude, and it is clear that Bert and Mary are 'stepping out'. Yet the choreography excludes intimate contact: that has to be left to the semiotic symbolism of Bert's precocious cane, which whisks Mary's umbrella away in an amorous clinch. Bert's costume emphasizes his clown-like nature, whilst Mary's outfit of high-waisted, multi-layered white dress symbolizes her femininity, but also her purity and aloofness. This is not the eroticized virginal white shift of Maria in *West Side Story*, but a deliberate symbol of Mary's unavailability from her constrained, high-lace-collared and perfect hat down to her tightly buttoned white boots. The red silk cummerbund may symbolize her sexualized potential, but with Bert flipping and flopping about with animated penguins in a hip-hop-anticipating drop-crotch routine, this is not a dance designed to elevate his masculinity in her eyes. Thus, the childlike parameters of the chalk-drawing dream sequence, the interaction with the animation and the affirmation of Edwardian morals and ethics within their exchanges precludes further development in their relationship.

The function of 'Step in Time' is radically different, yet the outcome is the same. Coming towards the end of the film, the dance routine offers the perfect vehicle for Bert and Mary to metaphorically consummate their relationship, and yet once again it doesn't happen. Here, the dominant soot-besmirched Mary, dressed in the vernacular red of the fallen woman, repudiates the advances of her male suitors despite her cockney hoedown circumnavigation of the rooftops in the arms of Bert and other sweeps. Although the children are present, it is clear Mary is dancing for the male gaze, yet she reasserts her dominance by out-pirouetting the men whilst providing the merest glimpse of her provocative underskirt and bloomers in the process.

In both dance sequences, the brief, liminal transitions in Mary's character are explained by transformational expectations of the dream ballet. The audience is aware that this is where the female protagonist usually explores the framework for her subsequent acquiescence to the male protagonist, as 'characters in musicals who dance can find their identities expanded to include expressions of their innermost selves' (Symonds and Taylor 2013: 89). But not Mary. Her feminine dominance reasserts itself by beating dozens of animated male jockeys or by leading the male sweeps back down the chimney into the seat of her maternal congruity, then ejecting their hyperactive intrusions through the front door of 17 Cherry Tree Lane, reasserting her feminine efficacy, restoring domestic order and dampening all hopes of male valediction in the process.

The third challenge to golden-age certitude is in Mary's rendition of the 'outsider' role. Whilst her feminist stance and matriarchal facilitation may have been unusual for the time, the outsider role through which she projects these characteristics was not. Lovensheimer observes that 'nonconforming outsiders are indeed inherent in much dramatic literature' (2002: 5), but the outsider is usually male, moody, isolated, rebellious and culturally challenging. Mary is the opposite: she is female, well-balanced, loved by all, feisty, yet ultimately conformist, and seeking to re-establish the status quo. Despite this contradiction, she retains many of the characteristics of the outsider role: her intransigence, her absolute confidence in the fact that she is always right, her determination to force compliance with her ideals and her refusal to be absorbed into the society with which she is interacting (even if that means a painful departure and a return to isolation at the end).

The constraints of her role as a nanny can perhaps be explained by the fact that 'the domestic has more progressive possibilities, opening up oppor-tunities for women to gain power in patriarchy as well as helping to create a definitively female space' (Bilbao 2011: 22). Yet Grilli disagrees, noting that Mary is 'an outsider to the family [...] whose very presence and role as a governess displays its futility' (2007: 85). Nevertheless, Mary's outsider status allows her to provide us with a fresh perspective on the failing Banks family. Her magical abilities, reinforced by her unusual behaviour, ensure her illusory separation from the rest of society. Her motivation is selfless and extraneous, driven by Jane and Michael's literary plea dispatched up the chimney in shreds by their autocratic father, rather than the narrow-minded self-interests of the other characters. Outsiders are engrained within the mythology of children's literature – they expect rejection, and we empathize with their self-sacrifice as surely as they align themselves with the 'underdog', the victim or with powerless children.

Mary Poppins therefore both confirms and challenges the traditional outsider role. Mary's magical powers, external perspective, intransigence and transience all reinforce tradition, whilst her gender, unselfish motivation and societal interactions redefine the role. Mary is not the usual 'outsider who craves fame and attention' (Laird 2011: 195), being happy to slip quietly away at the end, content with a job well done.

Conclusions

In *Mary Poppins* Disney created a film musical that was 'a strong affirmation of the values of community and the vitality of human character and an idealized utopianism' (Bradley 2004: 91). Although contemporary readings reveal flaws in its political sensibilities, these arise from the narrative simplicity of its fairy-tale format, its context and our bipolar relationship with Disney. Thus, its ideology remains complex and contradictory. Mary is seen by some as the ultimate patriarchal sop, demonstrating that 'motherhood can be seen to intersect with ideas of feminine dependence' whilst requiring active intervention to address 'masculinity in crisis [leading to] the recon-figuration of domestic patriarchy' (McCleer 2002: 87). Others read her as a critical figure in the development of the female protagonist, a performance that 'possesses brilliant moments of feminist clarity' (Kearns 2012).

Disney Studios may have planned to reinforce formulaic patriarchal values, yet Travis's indomitable creation still shines through, threatening to 'neutralise the extra-diegetic tendencies represented by woman as spectacle' (Mulvey 1975: 11). The Hollywood affirmation of the male gaze is therefore both confirmed and denied by Mary's pretty, yet unattainable, feminist characterization in which 'representation and subjectivity are made to reveal themselves as gendered fictions rather than natural or inevitable realities' (Fortier 2000: 74).

Mary Poppins also tacitly usurps the genre throughout. On the surface, there are all the familiar trappings of the welcoming narrator, the diegesis of the various songs, right through to the illusion of the sweep's ballet and the concluding kite-flying family reunion. All appear very familiar. Yet there is also something disjointed and left deliberately unexplained: Mary's arrival and backstory, her attitude to Mr Banks, the complete lack of redeeming maternal characteristics in Mrs Banks, the absence of communication between Mary and Mrs Banks, the unresolved class and romantic aspira-tions of the doe-eyed Bert and the closing sterile cruelty of the severed relationship between Mary and the children. Indeed, the prerequisite happy ending is so shrouded by uncertainty that a cynic might suggest a fiscally astute Walt Disney already had his eye on a sequel, even if the difficulties of their working relationship precluded that happening whilst Travis was alive. More than fifty years after the original release, their reticence finally seems to have been overcome. Spurred on by the recent success of *Into the Woods*, Disney has re-contracted Rob Marshall to direct *Mary Poppins Returns*, starring Emily Blunt, as their 2018 Christmas film.

Contemporary analysis of *Mary Poppins* cannot fail to be informed by the radical changes in the past genre over half a century. The film has long since passed into cultural folklore and the form of the musical itself continues its role of societal social commentary with the gradual introduction of more feminist narratives and nuanced female leads, like Elle in *Legally Blonde*, Sophie in *Mamma Mia* and Elphaba in *Wicked*. Against these, the fledgling feminist indicators of *Mary Poppins* seem almost passé, despite recent attempts to redefine her character for the stage by producer and impresario Cameron Mackintosh. In 1994, he persuaded Travers to allow him to turn the stories into a stage musical, putting together an auspicious team including Richard Ayres, Bob Cowley, Matthew Bourne, Stephen Mear and Julian Fellowes to catapult Travers' Edwardian nanny into the twenty-first century and introduce her particular brand of feisty mysticism to a new generation. The reworked stage production opened in 2004, combining favourites from the film with new material drawn from other books, and has subsequently become a world-wide success. It is also clear that Mary's new, darker persona was created more in accordance with Travers' original creation.

Yet whilst the creative success of the stage musical may have done much to eradicate the insidious Disneyfication that so offended Travers in the film, '[Mackintosh] honours the material with a mixture of fastidiousness and indulgence that would put an approving smile on the face of its enigmatic super-nanny heroine' (Cavendish 2015). In the process, it has lost the radicalism of its feminist parvenu. And despite the newly attributed darkness of Mary's stage persona, it still struggles to escape the original Disneyfied incarnation and its reinforcement in the stage show.

> If this sanitizing of the exotic in 'Mary Poppins' makes it more digestible for young children, it also makes it less arresting for adults. As for the show's title character, the poor thing doesn't really have much of a personality other than that of an animated healing force. (Brantley 2006)

The passing of time has therefore only served to dilute the latent fecundity of Mary's feminist aspiration, whilst twenty-first-century realignments of gendered parental norms have weakened the inherent diadic maternal paradox of her original character.

We understand that Disney are the 'racketeers of illusion' (Wasco et al. 2001: 269) and that Mary was created to be 'practically perfect', yet beneath her apparent conformity she challenged the patriarchal affirmation of the Disney female stereotype, embodying 'many of the characteristics of the "liberated" woman according to the 1960s feminist rubric' (McCleer 2002: 98). Thus, *Mary Poppins* not only challenged the male gaze, but also started to move us away from Mulvey's patriarchally defined 'female gaze', perhaps even sowing the seeds for the subsequent development of an autonomous female gaze, where women no longer have to disguise their fetishistic scopophilia. This is far from the utopian scenario Disney thought he had created, yet aspects of his musical entertainment philosophy persist. Despite the attendant dystopian mythologies surrounding the contemporary flux of the genre, the musical continues to amuse, to entertain, to affirm and to challenge those who choose to engage with this wonderfully joyous anachronistic concoction.

References

Altman, Rick (1989). *The American Film Musical*. Bloomington: Indiana University Press.

Baudrillard, Jean (1988). *The Consumer Society: Myths and Structures*. London: Sage.

Begley, Sarah (2014). 'Mary Poppins was the Original Disney Feminist.' *Time Magazine*, 26 August. Available online: http://time.com/3178096/mary-poppins-feminist-anniversary/ (accessed 6 June 2015).

Bell, Elizabeth, Lynda Haas and Laura Sells (eds) (1995). *From Mouse to Mermaid: The Politics of Film, Gender and Culture*. Indianapolis: Indiana University Press.

Bilbao, Diana (2011). 'Female Subjectivity and Feminist Aesthetics in Revisions of the Maternal Melodrama.' PhD thesis, Mount Holyoke College, Massachusetts. Available online: https://ida.mtholyoke.edu/xmlui/handle/10166/726 (accessed 5 August 2013).

Bradley, Ian (2004). *You Got To Have a Dream: The Message of the Musical*. London: SCM Press.

Brantley, Ben (2006). 'Meddler on the Roof.' *New York Times*, 17 November. Available online: http://www.nytimes.com/2006/11/17/theater/reviews/17popp.html?pagewanted=all (accessed 19 January 2016).

Brody, Paul (2013). *The Real Life Mary Poppins: The Life and Times of P. L. Travers*. BookCaps Study Guides, Golgotha Press, Hustonville.

Brown, Craig (2013). 'The Rasputin Who Inspired Mary Poppins.' *Daily Mail*, 22 October. Available online: http://www.dailymail.co.uk/debate/article-2471112/CRAIG-BROWN-The-Rasputin-inspired-Mary-Poppins.html#ixzz3csNcJw00 (accessed 10 June 2015).

Brown, Noel (2012). *The Hollywood Family Film: A History, from Shirley Temple to Harry Potter*. London: Taurus.

Cavendish, Dominic (2015). *Mary Poppins*, Bristol Hippodrome, Review: 'A Razzmatazz Retort to the Age of Austerity.' *Telegraph*, 11 November. Available online: http://www.telegraph.co.uk/theatre/what-to-see/mary-poppins-bristol-hippodrome-review/ (accessed 19 January 2016).

Crowther, Bosley (1964). 'Mary Poppins (1964): Movie Review.' *New York Times*, 25 September. Available online: http://www.nytimes.com/pages/movies/index.html (accessed 5 June 2015).

Dholakia, Nikhilesh and Jonathan Schroeder (2001). 'Disney Delights and Doubts.' *Journal of Research for the Consumer* 1 (2). Available online: http://jrconsumers.com/ (accessed 12 June 2015).

Dyer, Richard (2002). *Only Entertainment*, 2nd edn. London: Routledge.

Encyclopædia Britannica (2015). *Mother Goddess*. Available online: http://www.britannica.com/topic/mother-goddess (accessed 13 June 2015).

Flanagan, Caitlan (2005). 'Becoming Mary Poppins: P. L. Travers, Walt Disney, and the Making of a Myth.' *New Yorker*, 19 December. Available online: http://www.newyorker.com/archive/2005/12/19/051219fa_fact1#ixzz27QmD4F5j (accessed 12 June 2015).

Fortier, Mark (2000). *Theory/Theatre: An Introduction*. New York: Routledge.

Giroux, Henry and Grace Pollock (2010). *The Mouse that Roared: Disney and the End of Innocence*. Plymouth: Rowan & Littlefield.

Grilli, Giorgia (2007). *Myth, Symbol and Meaning in* Mary Poppins. New York: Routledge.

Henderson, Amy (2013). 'How Did P. L. Travers, the Prickly Author of Mary Poppins, Really Fare Against Walt Disney?' *Smithsonian Magazine*, 20 December. Available online: www.smithsonianmag.com (accessed 22 June 2015).

Hiller, Jim and Douglas Pye (2011). *BFI Screen Guides: 100 Film Musicals*. London: Palgrave Macmillan.

Hughes, Kathryn (2005). 'A Spoonful of Bile.' *Guardian*, 3 December. Available online: www.theguardian.com/books/2005/dec/03/ (accessed 2 May 2015).

Johnson, Brett (2012). 'The American Musical Stage as a Site of Utopian Possibilities.' PhD Thesis, University of Missouri. Available online: http://hdl.handle.net/10355/35186 (accessed 4 April 2015).

Kearns, Megan (2012). *Accidental Feminism in Mary Poppins*. Women and Gender in Musicals Week, Bitch Flix, 25 September. Available online: http://www.btchflcks.com/?s=Women+and+Gender+in+ Musicals (accessed 12 March 2015).

Laird, Paul (2011). *Wicked: A Musical Biography*. Plymouth: Scarecrow Press.

Lovensheimer, Jim (2002). 'Stephen Sondheim and the Musical of the Outsider'. In William A. Everett and Paul R. Laird (eds), *The Cambridge Companion to the Musical*. Cambridge: Cambridge University Press.

McCleer, Anne (2002). 'Practical Perfection? The Nanny Negotiates Gender, Class, and Family Contradictions in 1960s Popular Culture.' *National Women's Studies Association Journal* 14 (2) (Summer). Available online: http://muse.jhu.edu/journals/ff/summary/v014/14.2mcleer.html (accessed 4 April 2015).

McDaniel, June (2011). 'Shaktism.' *Oxford Bibliographies*, 27 January. Available online: http://www.oxfordbibliographies.com/view/ document/ obo-9780195399318/obo-9780195399318-0085.xml (accessed 14 June 2015).

Muller, Jurgen (2003). *Movies of the 60s*. New York: Taschen.

Mulvey, Laura (1975). 'Visual Pleasure and Narrative Cinema.' *Screen* 16 (3) (Autumn): 6–18. Available online: http: imlportfolio.usc.edu/ctcs505/ mulveyVisualPleasureNarrativeCinema.pdf (accessed 4 December 2014).

Picardie, Justine (2008). 'Was P L Travers the Real Mary Poppins?' *Telegraph*, 28 October. Available online: http://www.telegraph.co.uk/culture/ donotmigrate/3562643/ Was-P-L-Travers-the-real-Mary-Poppins.html (accessed 7 June 2015).

Rainey, Sarah (2013). 'Saving Mr Banks: The True Story of PL Travers.' *Daily Telegraph*, 29 November. Available online: http://www.telegraph.co.uk/ culture/10483126/Saving-Mr-Banks-The-true-story-of-PL-Travers.html (accessed 13 June 2015).

Rojek, Chris (1993). 'Disney Culture.' *Leisure Studies* 12 (2): 121–35.

Scherb, Laura (2014). 'Feminism and Fandom: Wolf's Talk Examines Gender Roles in Broadway Musicals', 2 March. Available online: https://thetartan. org/2014/3/3/pillbox/divasdarlings (accessed 15 June 2015).

Sherman, Richard and Robert Sherman (1963). *Mary Poppins* Lyrics. Available online: http://www.allthelyrics.com/ (accessed 30 June 2015).

Shone, Tom (2013). 'Can Tom Hanks Rescue Walt Disney From Saving Mr Banks?' *Guardian* Review, 13 December. Available online: http://www. theguardian.com/film/2013/dec/13/saving-mr-banks-rescued-tom-hanks-review (accessed 23 June 2015).

Simons, Herbert and Michael Billig (eds) (1993). *After Postmodernism: Reconstructing Ideology Critique*. London: Sage.

Smulders, Sharon (2014). 'We Are All One: Money, Magic and Mysticism in Mary Poppins.' In Angela Hubler (ed.), *Little Red Readings: Historical Materialist Perspectives on Children's Literature*. Jackson: Mississippi University Press, 75–93.

Symonds, Dominic and Millie Taylor (eds) (2014). *Gestures of Music Theatre*. Oxford: Oxford University Press.

Taylor, Millie and Dominic Symonds (2014). *Studying Musical Theatre: Theory and Practice*. London and New York: Palgrave Macmillan.

Travers, Pamela Lyndon (2010). *Essential Modern Classics: Mary Poppins.* London: HarperCollins (first published 1934).

Walsh, Bill and Don DaGradi (1963). *Mary Poppins* Script, Transcript Dialogue. Available online: http://www.script-o-rama.com/movie_scripts/m/ mary-poppins-script-transcript-andrews.html (accessed 30 June 2015).

Wasco, Janet, Mark Phillips and Eileen Meehan (2001). *Dazzled by Disney? The Global Disney Audiences Project.* London; Leicester University Press.

Wolf, Stacy (2002). *A Problem Like Maria: Gender and Sexuality in the American Musical.* Ann Arbor: University of Michigan Press.

Wolf, Stacy (2011). *Changed for Good: A Feminist History of the Broadway Musical.* New York: Oxford University Press.

Zipes, Jack (1992). *Breaking the Magic Spell: Radical Theories of Folk and Fairy Tales.* New York: Routledge.

4

Musicals in the Mirror: *Enchanted*, Self-reflexivity and Disney's Sudden Boldness

Paul R. Laird

We have all seen young girls, perhaps between the ages of three and seven, who are obsessed with Disney princesses. As the father of a daughter whom we took to Disneyland in 2003 when she was eight years old, it was fascinating to note her reason for the visit: to be photographed next to her heroines while holding her own polyvinyl chloride model of that figure. Perhaps the highlight of our visit for our daughter was a visit to a souvenir shop where Belle from *Beauty and the Beast* told her stories, with appropriate paraphernalia for sale. We left the park that day separated from some money, but admiring how Disney has made its princesses such desirable icons.

The combined appeal of such figures as Snow White, Cinderella, Aurora, Belle, Ariel, Pocahontas and their beautiful sisters in commerce constitute a marketing juggernaut that has captured the imaginations of young girls for decades, allowing Disney to reap enormous profits from parents who remember the appeal of these figures from their own childhoods. Obviously, the characters of these princesses have changed as society and its expectations for women have modernized. For example, the relative helplessness of Snow White, Cinderella and Aurora, who appeared between 1937 and 1959, contrasts strongly with pluckier heroines for the 1980s and 1990s like Belle, Ariel and Pocahontas, but all of the princesses appear to have been conceived with an eye towards beauty and perfection.

Four years after our visit to the Magic Kingdom, Disney released *Enchanted* (2007), a multi-layered entrant into the tradition of Disney princess films that combines a postmodern earthiness and self-reflexive, satirical bent that plays off many previous Disney films. The self-reflexivity is not surprising because such a sense of homage towards beloved films delights audiences and can also function as a major advertisement for Disney's princess brand. The tone of *Enchanted*, however, is a telling combination between fawning admiration for the Disney princesses, certainly the case for the lovely Giselle, played by Amy Adams, and a modern grittiness caused by transporting the fairy tale spirit to New York City. Contrast between animated fairy tales and our world constitutes a major theme in the film, both in the way that the formerly animated beings from Andalasia interact with New York and in the family life of Robert and six-year-old Morgan, as the father tries to steer his daughter away from fairy tales. He wants her to know that real life is full of challenges, such as the wife and mother who deserted them. In *Enchanted*, Disney manipulates and lampoons the world that it had been creating since the release of *Snow White* in 1937. It is almost as if the gift shop where Belle tells her stories in Disneyland were next to a liquor store or seedy motel, reminding the visitor that there is a real world outside of the amusement park.

This chapter considers *Enchanted* as an unusual continuation of Disney princess films because it is both a tribute and a postmodern comment upon the genre. Its self-reflexive appropriation of its Disney antecedents will be addressed, both in terms of the use of homage and satire. The score by composer Alan Menken and lyricist Stephen Schwartz includes an intentional pastiche of past musical styles appearing in Disney animated features, approached in detail here in terms of the songs themselves and how they have been incorporated into the movie through the use of film-making techniques and parallel dramatic situations with earlier Disney features. Finally, *Enchanted* will be approached below through the various lenses of feminism, consumerism and postmodernism.

Enchanted and the Tradition of Disney Princesses

The initial idea for *Enchanted* and its postmodern take on a Disney princess started with screenwriter Bill Kelly, who sold his idea to Disney's Touchstone Pictures in September 1997 for a reported $450,000 (Daly and Soll 2007: 76–9). The film would represent Disney's first foray into the world of European fairy tales since *Beauty and the Beast* (1991) (Cecire 2012: 243). Kelly's first version of the story brought Giselle out of her animated home into Chicago, where she was mistaken for a stripper at a bachelor party. Disney took the script out of Kelly's hands and tried other writers, but after several false starts Kelly got his project back, in 2005, and began to work with director Kevin Lima, who was responsible for the animated *Tarzan* (1999) and the live-action *102 Dalmatians* (2000). Among Lima's contributions to *Enchanted* was deciding that Giselle would enter the real world in Times Square. Amy Adams earned the lead role in an audition in 2005, distinguishing herself from a pack of actresses with her sincerity and, as Lima remembered, 'She's filled with joy' (Daly and Soll 2007). Adams, who began her career in dinner theatre (Shnayerson 2008), studied voice to try to avoid having the songs dubbed by a professional singer. She succeeded brilliantly as both singer and actress, feted by critics and popular with audiences, and the film has grossed $340,487,652 worldwide (boxofficemojo. com). In a fascinating twist, Disney did not honour Giselle as an Official Disney Princess because of legal difficulties in securing the rights to Adams' image (Stevens 2007).

To be sure, the creators of *Enchanted* ultimately produced another Disney fairy tale. They access much of the modern world, but fairy tales win the day. Giselle changes and does not wish to return to her roots, but in New York, after helping to vanquish the evil queen/dragon, she finds a family to join and takes over Nancy's fashion design business where she performs Disney-like makeovers for little girls. By replacing Nancy, Susan Cahill has argued that Giselle represents the younger woman from a fairy-tale vanquishing the older woman who is perhaps more competent but also trapped in a less desirable, older woman's body, a theme that Cahill also notes in the films *Stardust* (2007) and *The Brothers Grimm* (2005) (Cahill 2010: 57–8). Robert, a dedicated cynic, finds his own fairy tale princess, and Morgan now has the same woman as her stepmother. Nancy loses Robert but enters the animated world with Edward as his new princess, even throwing her cell phone aside and breaking it on the cathedral floor. She assumes the masculine position in the kiss at the end of their wedding ceremony, ensuring that Edward's life and Andalasia may never be the same, but they are in the land of fairy tales. The final song, 'Ever Ever After', confirms the triumph of Disney and its fairy tales. As Maria Sachiko Cecire has noted: 'The film thus begins as an animated parody of Disney's formulaic fairy-tale narratives, but ends as an homage that rehabilitates the Disney brand and celebrates its apparent ability to turn reality into a fairy tale' (Cecire 2012: 244). One might suggest that part of Disney's interest in the film was inspired by the success of *Shrek* (DreamWorks 2001), which included references to many fairy tales with a decidedly postmodern twist. Henry A. Giroux and Grace Pollock compared *Enchanted* to *Shrek* and another famous product of popular culture: 'Despite a promising beginning, the film does not sustain the kind of postmodern self-reflexivity familiar to a generation raised on *The Simpsons* and brilliantly applied to fairy tales in *Shrek* (2001)' (Giroux and Pollock 2010: 120).

The self-reflexivity built into *Enchanted* reaches nearly the level of self-indulgence in relation to previous Disney features, but it also includes possible bows to films from other studios. The creators loaded the film with visual references, and most character and place names carry some resonance to an aspect of a previous Disney feature; director Kevin Lima once commented that he did not know how many references there are in the film, but they exist on several levels (www.indielondon.co.uk 2007). As Cecire has stated, these many evocations not only pay homage to the models, but add for the audience possible emotional connections to earlier scenes. Most of the budding relationship between Robert and Giselle develops in examples of self-reflexivity (Cecire 2012: 252). What follows is not a complete listing of references, but it demonstrates *Enchanted*'s habitual self-reflexiveness and that some references include a hint of mockery of the models. The story is closest to that of *Snow White* with an evil queen having it in for the heroine for some nefarious reason, but the ending borrows more from *Sleeping Beauty*. *Cinderella* references also abound. In all three of these previous Disney films, the villain is a woman, causing Kay Stone to observe that each film can be seen to be 'strongly reinforcing the already popular stereotype of the innocent beauty victimized by the wicked villainess' (Stone 1975: 44).

Enchanted and Other Influences: Narrative Inversions

Enchanted literally opens and closes with a storybook, as do *Snow White* (1937), *Cinderella* (1950) and *Sleeping Beauty* (1959), among other Disney films. As in *Snow White*, the evil queen wishes to put a beautiful young woman into a charmed sleep with a poisoned apple. A 'prince' rescues her with a kiss. *Enchanted* is more complicated, but there are many other minor references to *Snow White*. When Giselle wanders around New York in confusion, a disgruntled little person becomes entangled with her voluminous dress and she calls him 'Grumpy'. When looking for a place to sleep, she asks someone if there might be a place nearby where dwarfs live. As described in detail below, Giselle's 'Happy Working Song' is a parody of Snow White's 'Whistle While You Work'. Staying in a cheap hotel (called 'The Grand Duke', as in the comic character in *Cinderella*), Edward learns where to look for Giselle from a television newswoman on a device that he calls 'The Magic Mirror', the evil queen's informant in *Snow White*. Queen Narissa in *Enchanted* keeps appearing to her henchman Nathaniel in various fluids, also reminiscent of 'The Magic Mirror'. Narissa twice disguises herself as a hag, once in Andalasia when she pushes Giselle down the well, and at the ball in New York where she induces Giselle to take a bite of the apple. These scenes strongly resemble *Snow White* in some details, such as when the apple rolls out of Giselle's hand when she hits the floor. Narissa dies by falling while threatening Robert and Giselle, reminiscent of the evil queen in *Snow White* falling from the rocky crag while threatening the dwarfs.

The resonances that *Enchanted* shares with *Sleeping Beauty* are especially apparent at the end of the film, but a theme running through both stories is the power of a 'true love's kiss'. Also, Edward first learns of Giselle when he hears her singing in the woods, which is how Philip discovers Aurora in *Sleeping Beauty*. The creators of *Enchanted* invoked the tone and images of *Sleeping Beauty* when Narissa turns herself into a dragon and climbs to the top of the Woolworth Building. Giselle follows the dragon, which clutches Robert, a gender inversion of the usual rescue trope, on which the sassy dragon seemingly must comment lest the audience miss such obvious imagery. Giselle's efforts mark her as an aggressive Disney heroine, unlike the princesses in early features but common in later films such as *Pocahontas* (1995) and *Mulan* (1998). In the same way that Prince Philip throws his sword in *Sleeping Beauty* to injure Maleficent as a dragon, Giselle throws the one that she carries (pulled from the ballroom floor, redolent of *The Sword in the Stone* [1963]) to pin Robert to the antenna of the Woolworth Building and save him from a fatal fall. In the 1998 film, the title character Mulan uses a sword to pin the villain to the palace roof before killing him with a rocket prepared by her animal sidekick, another dragon. Reviewer Shannan Palma calls the dragon scene of *Enchanted* 'nonsensical' (Palma 2009: 194), but clearly the reference to *Sleeping Beauty* was too important to miss for the film's creators.

The story of *Cinderella* is not a major part of the plot of *Enchanted*, but several references and images from the 1950 animated feature appear in the later movie. Robert's prospective mate, Nancy, is a potential 'evil stepmother' for Morgan, who does not want her father to marry the woman. (In a perceptive casting twist, the actress who plays Nancy is Idina Menzel, famous as Elphaba, in *Wicked*, for which a poster appears over Edward's shoulder when he is on top of the bus in Times Square. It is also interesting to note that Menzel, highly regarded as a singer, only speaks in *Enchanted*, emphasizing that this 'evil stepmother' lacks the power of song.) Nancy's surname is Tremaine, the same as the evil stepmother in *Cinderella*. In the animated opening of *Enchanted*, Giselle dresses her dummy Prince Edward with the help of animals and later makes clothes in New York City with the help of rats and pigeons, like Cinderella, who works with mice and birds. Giselle takes a shower in Robert's apartment, assisted by pigeons with her towel, like the helpful birds in Cinderella's shower, and birds also help Giselle with her dress before 'Happy Working Song'. Giselle makes clothing out of drapes, not unlike Cinderella sprucing up her first dress for the ball with unused scraps from her sisters. Giselle arrives late for the ball at the end of

Enchanted, like Cinderella, but Giselle is already with one prince, Edward, before she leaves with Robert as her modern prince. As Giselle picks up Edward's sword to pursue Narissa as a dragon, she leaves one of her shoes, a glass slipper, that Edward then tries on Nancy, the perfect fit of which inspires the two to go to elope to Andalasia.

A few other moments in *Enchanted* demonstrate where references to other film musicals appear, both Disney projects and the occasional bow to film musicals from other studios. Vestiges of Disney's *Mary Poppins* (1964) appear with Julie Andrews serving as narrator at the opening, Edward flying out of the manhole in Times Square in a manner that resembles the famed nanny popping out of the chimney, and Giselle running into an old lady in Central Park who feeds the birds. Giselle shows interest in the fish tank at Robert's office and later spits one of the fish into a glass, surely a reference to *The Little Mermaid* (1989), and the song 'That's How You Know' is based on calypso tropes, redolent of 'Under the Sea' from that film. During that song, while Robert and Giselle share a picnic, a woman with a candelabra on her head approaches them, like Lumière in *Beauty and the Beast* (1991). The creators of *Enchanted* also make two brief references to *The Sound of Music* (20th Century Fox 1965) when Giselle makes clothes out of drapes in Robert's apartment (like Maria does for Captain von Trapp's children, although not so miraculously) and during 'That's How You Know' when Giselle comes running across a green expanse in Central Park with the New York buildings behind her like mountains, an urban substitute for Maria's meadow at the opening of *The Sound of Music*.

Self-reflexivity in *Enchanted* goes well beyond what might be included to tickle fans of Disney's other films. Director Kevin Lima and his collaborators crafted an elaborate homage to the Disney animated films while also bringing the genre to the present by juxtaposing the cartoon world with modern New York, surely intended in part as a commercial gesture to benefit other Disney products. Reviewer Shannan Palma believes that the many references add to the film's appeal because they 'rescue the film from straightforward feature-length commercial status and instead reposition the film's allusive qualities within the long-standing Hollywood tradition of homage' (Palma 2009: 195). The modern world's intrusion into the naïve love between Edward and Giselle (portrayed as completely innocent of sexual matters, a condition of Disney princesses on which Stone has commented [Stone 1975: 46]) at times carries adult sensibility, perhaps also part of updating Disney's brand in its princess films. Queen Narissa's henchman Nathaniel, as portrayed in both the animated and real worlds, clearly lusts after the queen, and before Giselle addresses the urban vermin that have come to help her clean Robert's apartment, one of the rats appears to be licking its anus. At the end of the song a pigeon eats a cockroach as they both sit on the back of a piece of furniture. It is hard to imagine a hawk eating one of the rabbits in *Snow White*! In another scene, a small dog urinates on Edward's boot. Writing for the *New York Times*, Manohla Dargis called *Enchanted* a 'gently heretical redo' aimed at 'some of the very stereotypes that have been this company's profitable stock in trade' (Dargis 2007). Evocations of an earthier spirit are not absent from Disney's animated features – one recalls Claude Frollo's seething lust for Esmeralda in *The Hunchback of Notre Dame* (1996), portrayed in the song 'Hellfire' – but Disney intentionally approached a new audience in *Enchanted*. Combined with the film's rampant self-reflexivity, the project smacks of a commercial savvy that goes beyond the appealing performances and memorable combination of animation, computer graphics and live action. Cecire offers another take on Disney's mixture of self-reflexivity and the modern world, calling it 'neomedievalism', with many of the images from earlier animated features, based on stories from the Middle Ages and replete with tropes of a romanticized version of the era, mixed with later ideas and all of it removed from any kind of historical continuum (Cecire 2012: 244). French sociologist Jean Baudrillard has commented that part of the Disney brand is that the corporation 'seeks to erase time by synchronizing all the periods, all the cultures, in a single traveling motion, by juxtaposing them in a single scenario' (Baudrillard 1996: n.p.).

Music, Commercial Viability and 'Pastiche' as Parody

Like most Disney animated features, *Enchanted* has several songs to help tell the story, and perhaps have a commercial life outside of the film. Alan Menken wrote all of the music, both songs and underscoring, continuing his role as Disney's primary animated film composer since the 1980s. Stephen Schwartz penned the lyrics, having previously worked with Menken on *Pocahontas* and *The Hunchback of Notre Dame* in the 1990s. Schwartz had been exiled from the Disney camp when he agreed to write *The Prince of Egypt* (1998) for DreamWorks shortly thereafter, even though he had already started the songs for *Mulan*, for which he was writing both music and lyrics. Apparently a decade later Disney could again consider working with Schwartz (Laird 2014: 231–56). He reported that the screenplay for *Enchanted* was substantially finished before they started the songs (De Giere 2008: 491–5). Director Kevin Lima and scriptwriter Bill Kelly had already decided where some songs would be placed, but they also accepted suggestions from the musical team. The five songs include 'True Love's Kiss', 'Happy Working Song', 'That's How You Know', 'So Close' and 'Ever Ever After'.

Lima and Kelly decided to begin the film with a song in Andalasia, for which Menken and Schwartz wrote the intentionally saccharine 'True Love's Kiss'. The screenplay already included a scene where Giselle would call forth the kinds of animals available in New York City – flies, rats, pigeons and cockroaches – to help clean Robert's apartment, but Schwartz was not sure whether Lima and Kelly had decided that a song like 'Happy Working Song' belonged there (De Giere 2008: 491). Schwartz reported that the musical team suggested composing 'That's How You Know' for a Central Park scene that already existed (ibid.). The placement for 'So Close' at the ball was not only in the script, but the number's title had already been chosen before Menken and Schwartz came on the scene (ibid.). Among other possibilities, the ball allowed a self-reflexive moment related to several previous animated features, perhaps the most famous of which is the dance between the main characters in *Beauty and the Beast*. Schwartz stated that the final number 'Ever Ever After', sung as a voiceover by Carrie Underwood, was something for which he advocated, believing that *Enchanted* needed to end as a musical and underscore each character's newfound happiness (De Giere 2008: 492).

Schwartz noted that the score's 'pastiche' nature emanated from an overall scheme where the songs progress from typical Disney fare of the early animated features to the modern world, but the process 'wasn't conscious from the very beginning' (De Giere 2008: 492) This progression from parodying older Disney songs to newer styles, a sort of journey from fantasy to reality, provides the film with a satisfying musical arc. The five songs are a surprisingly small part of the movie, sounding for only about a total of 18 minutes (and even those excerpts are interrupted by dialog and action), but the tunes often recur in the orchestral underscoring, especially 'True Love's Kiss'.

Schwartz said that 'True Love's Kiss' was inspired by the music of classic Disney animated features such as *Snow White*, but that he and Menken also 'made fun of it a bit' (De Giere 2008: 492). Cecire has suggested that the opening sequence with this song functions somewhat like an entire princess animated feature in about eight minutes of screen time with Giselle desiring her prince and ending up in his arms after she escapes the ogre, a parody that 'pokes fun at the formulaic nature of the genre' and sets up the satire of *Enchanted* (Cecire 2012: 249). The song 'True Love's Kiss' operates on two levels. Children respond to the sweetness and innocence, but those with more sophisticated ears will catch the overplayed sentiment and Giselle's naïve assertion that it is only the lips of lovers that touch. Menken wrote a simple melody in C major and quadruple metre based upon wide, ascending leaps and conjunct descents, changing to triple metre when

Giselle invites forest animals to help her complete the statue she is making of the man who recently appeared in her dreams. The forest animals come running and sing part of the song as a waltz before the return of the opening key, and later the original time signature, as Giselle and her friends finish the number's first section. Elements of the song return over the next few minutes as the scene plays out with Giselle escaping a troll and falling into Edward's arms.

Schwartz's lyrics, in tandem with Disney's animated action, play a major role in developing the song's two levels of understanding. The innocent opening recitative includes cutesy, spoken lines from two rabbits and two birds. The distasteful troll with his runny nose (perhaps reminiscent of Harry's encounter with troll mucous in *Harry Potter and the Sorcerer's Stone*) provides one of the earthier elements that the *Enchanted* animators included. After Giselle falls into Edward's arms he sings the song again, this time with lyrics referring to finding the one who completes the lover's duet, reminiscent for musical theatre fans of the song 'Ah! Sweet Mystery of Life' from Victor Herbert's *Naughty Marietta* (1910), where a woman will only find love when she meets a man that literally finishes her song.

'Happy Working Song' is self-consciously modelled after 'Whistle While You Work' from *Snow White* (1937). The heroine finds herself in the sloppy cabin occupied by seven dwarfs and enters the familiar role of feminine domesticity as she decides it must be cleaned. Assisted by a small army of deer, squirrels, chipmunks, rabbits, turtles, mice and other animals, Snow White cleans the cabin while admonishing animals that attempt unacceptable shortcuts. The animators offered moments for more mature members of the audience that might find the whole thing cloyingly cute, such as a mouse upset that two squirrels have swept a great deal of dirt into his hole, or a chipmunk winding a spider web into a ball and confronting the web's angry spinner. A young buck used as a moving clothes rack seems less than pleased with his chore, but for the most part the animals are more than glad to lighten Snow White's load. Musically it is a simple, conventional number with Snow White's voice adding ornamentation as she enters scenes previously dominated by animals and vocalizes mindlessly at the end while applying the last strokes with a broom. The song never reaches a final cadence, perhaps commenting that a woman's work never ends.

David Whitley offers a telling interpretation of 'Whistle While You Work' in the film's context and what children might see in it. He comments on the importance placed on cleaning by the title character in the cabin and that the dwarfs themselves later must wash up before dinner, making dirt and grime a major theme in *Snow White*. Perhaps this is just adults impressing on the young that they must help clean, but, as Whitley notes:

Within the housecleaning sequence alone, we are invited to experience
the dirt repeatedly through direct contact with the animals' bodies, as
they swish cobwebs and accumulated dust up with their tails, lick plates
clean with their tongues, and rub clothes along the ridges of upturned
turtles' carapaces as simulacra for washboards. (Whitley 2013: 82)

Some children love dirt, so perhaps the film's creators were simply engaging
with their young audience.

Computer Graphics and Confronting the Cinematic Past in the Musical Numbers of *Enchanted*

If the animators of *Snow White* meant to give the young members of their
audience a thrill with their graphic depiction of grime, the creators of
Enchanted revelled in the disgusting, making their parody of 'Whistle While
You Work' an over-the-top display of domestic messes. Giselle finds herself in
the apartment that Robert shares with his daughter Morgan, awakening the
next morning to a mess that she cannot abide. Singing into the Manhattan
morning, her voice retains its fairy-tale quality in live action and calls forth
hundreds of rats, mice, pigeons, flies and roaches. Surrounded by them in
the apartment, Giselle is slightly disturbed by the identity of her assistants,
but she puts them to work. In the bathroom we are confronted with more
graphic cleaning situations than animators of another generation would have
dared to place in *Snow White*: dozens of roaches coming through the drain
to clean the ring around the bathtub, a mouse pulling a large hairball out of
the drain with its tail and three rats scrubbing the toilet with toothbrushes.
When the vacuum comes out, some roaches are accidentally scooped up,
but Giselle rescues them, showing surprising knowledge of the modern
convenience. She takes a break out on the balcony to pine after her Edward,
whom she knows will come for her, then returns to help in the kitchen.

The computer graphics include some images similar to those seen in *Snow
White*, such as animals rolling clean dishes towards the cupboard and birds
putting them away. A bird drops and shatters a plate, causing Morgan to come
running. Giselle throws flowers into a vase, a final touch seen a bit earlier
in the *Snow White* sequence where birds prepare the flowers. The dramatic
situation of 'Happy Working Song' also recalls other Disney working songs,
including 'Spoonful of Sugar' from *Mary Poppins* and 'A Dream Is a Wish
Your Heart Makes' from *Cinderella*. Menken's melody is in quadruple meter
and primarily diatonic, but with enough melodic leaps to help provide the
requisite perkiness. Schwartz's lyrics are carefully chosen, veering between

Giselle's innocence and the gross messes being cleaned. Dargis, in her review for *the Times*, found the number 'so flat-out bizarre and grotesquely funny ... that it threatens to send the story off the rails' (Dargis 2007).

'That's How You Know', a production number in Central Park, presents a multi-layered commentary on the role of music in movie musicals. Trying to show Robert how Nancy might know that he loves her, Giselle earnestly starts to sing, just as she might in Andalasia. This embarrasses Robert, who asks her to stop, but he cannot thwart the power of song. A calypso group immediately takes up the tune, surprising Robert, who apparently does not know what should happen in a film musical. The calypso group follows Giselle as her back-up musicians, and the circle expands to include many performers. Giselle goes through a wide array of situations and pieces of advice for Robert in the four-minute running time for 'That's How You Know' with the help of many New Yorkers of all ages and diverse races. Robert seems nonplussed through most of the song, but he is most perplexed when Giselle tells two doves to take a heart-shaped wreath of flowers to Nancy, who telephones her appreciation just after the song ends. Robert appears charmed and grateful and Giselle beams at him. She has started to win him over to the possibility of fairy tales, and unintentionally they begin to fall in love. The song's presentation is directly comparable to large production numbers from old-time Hollywood musicals (*Enchanted* 2008, documentary on 'That's How You Know'). Disney has approached large production numbers in their animated features in such segments as 'Under the Sea' from *The Little Mermaid* and 'Topsy-Turvy' from *The Hunchback of Notre Dame*, but this live-action extravaganza in *Enchanted* projects another effect entirely with extensive dancing and acrobatics. There is nothing here from the earthier side of life. Giselle and her many new friends extol the virtues of love with such events as elderly men and women meeting and dancing together, a dancing chorus of wedding couples and other tender images.

Schwartz noted that the song's musical models came from later Disney animation features, specifically referencing the calypso feeling of 'Under the Sea' from *The Little Mermaid* (De Giere 2008: 492), but the tune also recalls ethnic numbers in *The Lion King* and other films. The diversity of characters celebrating with Giselle somewhat flies in the face of the whiteness of most Disney films. In 'That's How You Know' Menken combined rhythms and a counter-melody that sound like calypso, brought alive in the film by players of steel drum, cabasa and conga. Although artless simplicity in lyrics can be difficult to produce, Schwartz provided just that, mixing questions of how a woman wonders if a man loves her with suggestions of actions that could confirm that fact. The unalloyed joy of 'That's How You Know' is a break from the consistent conflict between the real world of New York and Giselle's fairy-tale existence, beginning the inversion that takes place in *Enchanted*, where the imaginary world wins the day. As Cecire has commented, Giselle's encounter with New York has shown her ability to accomplish the 'translation of reality into a hybrid fairy-tale space' (Cecire 2012: 247).

It seems inevitable that there would be a ball in New York where Giselle and Robert can finish falling in love. Giselle has grown and now seems almost as much a New Yorker as an Andalasian. The song, 'So Close', occurs diegetically as Jon McLaughlin sings it with the orchestra at the ball. The conductor calls it 'The King and Queen's Waltz' and asks that everyone dance it with someone they did not accompany to the ball, allowing Edward to dance with Nancy and Robert with Giselle. The song is in 4/4 with prevailing triplet motion, not a waltz, and the couples clearly dance in quadruple meter. Schwartz noted that the conception of 'So Close' was based upon the title tune of *Beauty and the Beast*, partly because director Kevin Lima wanted to reproduce in live action the spinning camera angles seen when the Beast and Belle dance (De Giere 2008: 492–3). Giselle and Robert dance beautifully while the other dancers vacate the middle of the floor for them. Nancy then breaks in and Giselle goes to leave with Edward. While he retrieves her wrap, Giselle looks wistfully at Robert and Nancy dancing before Narissa, as a hag, interrupts with the poisoned apple.

The lyricist further reported that the director asked that the last line of the song refer to the couple's physical proximity but different fates (suggesting the actual line that Schwartz used), because this appears to be the final moment together for Robert and Giselle (De Giere 2008: 493). Menken wrote a flowing tune with a wide range that takes the tenor to a *d-flat*, sung in falsetto. Robert, played by Patrick Dempsey, sings some of the lines quietly to Giselle, a moment that Schwartz fought for because the actor did not wish to sing (De Giere 2008: 493–4). Schwartz's lyrics convey the song's dual message while relying less on rhyme than in other tunes in the film.

'Ever Ever After' completes the chronological journey that Menken and Schwartz followed in this score, bringing them to the present with a country/rock song written for pop diva Carrie Underwood singing a voiceover. Edward and Nancy decide that they can be a couple after he tries on her the glass slipper that Giselle left and it fits; they rush off to Andalasia to be married. Other minor story points also resolve. Robert and Giselle find happiness in Manhattan, Nathaniel signs the book that he wrote after staying in Manhattan and the chipmunk Pip returns to Andalasia, where he hosts his own book signing. The music that Menken wrote is a typical pop ballad with rich melodic syncopation and some large, effective ascending intervals, obviously working carefully with Schwartz in terms of the many times that they repeat the title text. The accompaniment includes a *rumba* rhythm (3+3+2) and throbbing quaver notes in the bass line, imparting great energy. Schwartz's lyrics include references to the triumph of fantasy, appropriate when the fairy-tale world has carried the day, but then the message moves into the real world. As the A section repeats he calls for a new trend of truthfully living one's emotions, Giselle's usual posture. We see her new business of providing Disney princess-like fantasies for little girls and then at home with Robert and Morgan, dancing around as they have fun with their little girl.

Robert has accepted Giselle's world and become a participant in it with Morgan, the daughter that he had hoped to raise without fairy tales. Despite his earlier intentions and the fun that the movie's creators have had with the Disney canon, *Enchanted* ends with two couples living 'happily ever after'. Dargis was hardly surprised that the fairy-tale ethos emerged victorious, stating that 'It would be too much to expect Disney to wholly dismantle its own mythologies', and she believes that the film 'trips up' from the time that Queen Narissa arrives in Manhattan, the moment when *Enchanted* begins to find its fairy-tale ending (Dargis 2007). Cecire adds that the final song assists the film's marketing potential because 'the montage recalls the breadth of Disney's transmedia empire as it evokes the pop-up book, animated and live-action cinema, the music video, the American country music genre, and fan-made online videos' (Cecire 2012: 256).

Conclusions

Palma strongly criticized what she sees as the film's 'ham-fisted postfeminism', much of it caused by the fairy-tale ending (Palma 2009: 195). Morgan disdained her father's gift of a book about successful women, rejecting the possibility of female empowerment, and instead Morgan wins the fairy-tale mother that she wanted, while Giselle, who towards the end of the film seems so confident, still must bite into a poisoned apple and become the helpless 'sleeping beauty' that can only be re-awakened by a kiss from her latest prince. Palma takes the creators of *Enchanted* to task for the film's inherent consumerism, especially in the shopping scene between Giselle and Morgan where the thrilled child, who barely knows her own mother, wonders aloud if this is what it is like to shop with one's mother, an attitude that Palma suggests will 'reinforce the understanding that shopping is central to the mother–daughter bonding experience' (ibid.).

Giroux and Pollock have compared Giselle's shopping spree as a declaration of her self-actualization to that of *Pretty Woman*, another Disney movie with a strong consumerist message (Giroux and Pollock 2010: 121). Cecire takes this critique a few steps further by noting that Giselle and Morgan use Robert's credit card on their shopping trip, meaning that the female must be saved by a male's economic power, although later Giselle asserts her own economic power during the closing montage when we see her new business of outfitting young consumers in princess makeovers (2012: 254). As Giroux and Pollock have noted (2010: 121), Disney even has shops that offer the same service that Giselle provides in the film in the real-life Bibbidi Bobbidi Boutiques. Cecire states that Giselle's special ability is that of a seamstress, part of her princess identity and one that keeps her safely within the female realm, not threatening Robert's male prerogative (2012: 254). At its core, *Enchanted* remains similar to Disney's animated features of the 1980s and 1990s, surveyed so convincingly by Giroux and Pollock in *The Mouse That Roared*, where they conclude:

> Disney's view of women's agency and empowerment is more than simply limited: it reproduces the idea that a child born female can only realize a gendered incarnation of adulthood and is destined to fulfill her selfhood by becoming the appendage, if not the property, of a man. (Giroux and Pollock 2010: 108)

Cecire concludes that the consumerist stance in *Enchanted* is perhaps the most important message from the film for Disney – the seller of princess goods – demonstrating that '... magical transformation can be bought. This is a powerful assertion for Disney to make; as part of the film's model for how to transform reality in the image of a Disney fairy tale, it encourages not only recalling and celebrating Disney films but also purchasing products' (2012: 253). The acquisition of that 'magical transformation' through economic transaction is, finally, what all of this is about. The consumer can buy the film on DVD, the products tied to that film and come experience the full Disney transformative experience at one of their amusement parks, allowing one to overcome the doldrums of ordinary existence for a few moments and become like Giselle as she escapes the cartoon world of Andalasia and realizes her own dreams in the 'real' world of modern Manhattan. Strangely, Disney eschews its usual fantasy world here, a major inversion from its past princess films. Finally, according to Cecire, *Enchanted* perhaps ends the traditional Disney princess narrative (2012: 257), but the company is now free to play with the legacy with more doses of postmodern irony, while remaining the primary purveyor of princess dreams to consumers of all ages, especially those cute young ones for whom parents have so much trouble refusing the gown that is their heart's desire.

References

Baudrillard, J. (1996). 'Disneyworld Company,' trans. François Debrix. *Liberation*, 4 March. Available online: https://journals.uvic.ca/index.php/ctheory/article/view/14846/5716 (accessed 30 October 2016).

boxofficemojo.com (accessed 14 June 2015).

Cahill, S. (2010). 'Through the Looking Glass: Fairy-Tale Cinema and the Spectacle of Femininity in "Stardust" and "The Brothers Grimm".' *Marvels & Tales* 24 (1): 57–8.

Cecire, M. S. (2012). 'Reality Remixed: Neomedieval Princess Culture in Disney's *Enchanted*.' In T. Pugh and S. Aronstein (eds), *The Disney Middle Ages: A Fairy-Tale and Fantasy Past*. New York: Palgrave MacMillan, 243–59.

Daly, S. and L. Soll (2007). 'Fall Movie Premiere November: *Enchanted*.' *Entertainment Weekly* 949/950, 24 August: 76–9. Available online: http://web.b.ebscohost.com.www2.lib.ku.edu/ehost/detail/detail?vid=4&sid=b49c0560-f99b-4ccc-8093-c4b6896c77ef%40sessionmgr101&bdata=JnNpdGU9ZWhvc3QtbGl2ZQ%3d%3d#AN=26299737&db=a9h (accessed 14 June 2015).

Dargis, M. (2007), 'Someday My Prince Will … Uh, Make That a Manhattan Lawyer.' *New York Times*, 21 November.

De Giere, C. (2008). *Defying Gravity: The Creative Career of Stephen Schwartz from 'Godspell' to 'Wicked'*. New York: Applause Theatre & Cinema.

Enchanted (2008). DVD. Burbank, CA: Walt Disney Video. Extra features/short documentaries: 'Fantasy Comes to Life', 'Happy Working Song', 'That's How You Know' and 'A Blast at the Ball'.

IndieLondon (2007). 'Enchanted – Kevin Lima Interview.' Available online: http://www.indielondon.co.uk/Film-Review/enchanted-kevin-lima-interviewk (accessed 20 June 2015).

Giroux, H. A. and G. Pollock (2010). *The Mouse That Roared: Disney and the End of Innocence*, updated and exp. edn. Lanham, MD: Rowman & Littlefield.

Laird, P. R. (2014). *The Musical Theater of Stephen Schwartz: From* Godspell *to* Wicked *and Beyond*. Lanham, MD: Rowman & Littlefield.

Palma, S. (2009). 'Review: *Enchanted*.' *Marvels & Tales* 23 (1): 194.

Shnayerson, M. (2008). 'Some Enchanted Amy.' *Vanity Fair*, November. Available online: www.vanityfair.com (accessed 22 June 2015).

Stevens, D. (2007). 'Princess Mastercard: There's Something Rotten About *Enchanted*.' Available online: http://www.slate.com/articles/arts/movies/2007/11/princess_mastercard.html (accessed 14 June 2015).

Stone, K. (1975). 'Things Walt Disney Never Told Us.' *The Journal of American Folklore* 88 (347) (January–March): 44.

Whitley, D. (2013). 'Learning with Disney: Children's Animation and the Politics of Innocence.' *Journal of Educational Memory, Media, and Society* 5 (2) (Autumn): 75–91.

Part Two

Disney Adaptations: On Stage and Beyond

Disney as Broadway *Auteur*: The Disney Versions of Broadway Musicals for Television in the Late 1990s and Early 2000s

Geoffrey Block

It is common to denote Disney as the author it is not rather than the brand it is. Nevertheless, several years before our story begins, the Disney company brought adaptations of two of its most successful animated film musicals to Broadway stages. The first was the 1991 film musical *Beauty and the Beast*, which was adapted for Broadway in 1994 and eventually ran on for 5,461 performances. The second film was the rip-roaring box office hit *The Lion King*, also in 1994, which roared even more loudly than the *Beast* when it moved to Broadway in July 1997. As of this writing, *The Lion King* is still roaring and currently reigns as the fourth longest-running and highest-grossing show of all time.

The *Beast* and the *Lion* were stage adaptations of film musicals, a genre with a rich legacy going back to the 1930s. In the same year as it brought *The Lion King* to Broadway, Disney launched a new enterprise when it began to move Broadway to television along with direct-to-DVD releases. This chapter is about a quartet of Disney-branded television adaptations that debuted between 1997 and 2005: *Cinderella* (1997), *Annie* (1999), *The Music Man* (2003) and *Once Upon a Mattress* (2005), three popular stage musicals and one classic television musical.

Attributing the work done by the creative teams behind these new versions to an abstraction like the Disney corporation would certainly be as naïve as attributing Apple corporation's design innovations to their CEO. Nevertheless, rather than attempt to unravel the many contributions and negotiations, in this chapter the efforts of the many are, regrettably but necessarily, subsumed under the Disney brand. Not to do so would be as naïve as to attribute all the work discussed here to one or more creative *auteurs*. Hence my ironic title, 'Disney as *auteur*'.

Although these musicals were made for television, the television showings were primarily promotional events intended to generate a market for the DVDs, which could be watched over and over by parents with small children. The broadcasts/DVDs, each packed with familiar stars, stories and songs, diverged from their predecessors as popular and artistically successful modern entertainments designed to appeal to younger audiences and evolving sensibilities. The broadcasts also captured a modern multicultural vision of America. This chapter will explore Disney's four made-for-television musicals and the ways in which they responded to their sources and target markets to reflect a revised vision of America.

Problematic Early Disney Films

The history of Disney films as far back as the 1930s is fraught with characters whose presence has been interpreted as racist, sexist or offensive to a particular group. On at least three occasions, Disney went to the expense of removing offending characterizations, and in one recent case removed problematic song lyrics from future prints. For example, fifteen years after *The Three Little Pigs* (1933) appeared with its classic song 'Who's Afraid of the Big Bad Wolf', Disney replaced the Wolf's costume and accent – a stereotyping of a Jewish peddler not unlike the putatively Persian but implicitly Jewish peddler Ali Hakim in *Oklahoma!* – with an ethnically neutral Fuller Brush salesman who spoke with a falsetto (Grant 1993). In 1963, Disney removed from future prints and showings the young black centaurette named Sunflower, a shoeshine girl who buffed the centaurs' hooves in the pastoral scene set to the music of Beethoven's Sixth symphony of *Fantasia* (1940) (Korkis 2012: 115–23). More recently, the Merchant's opening song from *Aladdin* (1992) originally included the lines 'Where they cut off your ear if they don't like your face, it's barbaric, but hey, it's home.' In response to complaints from the American-Arab Anti-Discrimination Committee, the offending lines were replaced with innocuous ones prior to the film's video release.

Other Disney characters have created controversies. With the exception of their leader, aptly named Jim Crow, sung by the future Jiminy Cricket in *Pinocchio* Cliff Edwards, the crows in *Dumbo* (1941) are voiced by African-American actors. The crows who express their disbelief at seeing that Dumbo can fly in the jazzy song 'When I See an Elephant Fly' have troubled many, for example Richard Schickel in his ambivalent 1968 treatment of the Disney legend: 'There was one distasteful moment in the film. The crows who teach Dumbo to fly are too obviously Negro caricatures' (Schickel 1968: 265). Still, Disney's crows have their defenders, including film critic Leonard Maltin:

There has been considerable controversy over the Black Crow sequence in recent years, most of it unjustified. The crows are undeniably black, but they are black *characters*, not black *stereotypes*. There is no denigrating dialogue, or Uncle Tomism in the scene, and if offense is to be taken in hearing blacks call each other 'brother', then the view is merely being sensitive to accuracy. (Maltin 1973: 52)

Another film, *The Song of the South* (1946), cinematically significant as the first film that combines animation and human actors (i.e. live action), based on the stories of the white writer and folklorist Joel Chandler Harris, became so controversial that Disney has refused to publish or screen the film commercially since 1986. Indeed, the film has been accused of idealizing the racial situation in the South during Reconstruction. Interestingly, *Song of the South* has been singled out for blame, when other arguably more problematic films have been spared, for example *Gone with the Wind* (1939), in which a major character, Ashley Wilkes, waxes nostalgic for the Southern way of life. Far more than Disney's depiction of Harris's world, Wilkes's viewpoint contributed to the 'glorification of the old rotten system of slavery' (Leff 1999). Another unfortunate moment in *Wind* occurs when the central male character, Rhett Butler, dresses up in Ku Klux Klan garb to raid a black shanty town to avenge the harassment of Scarlet O'Hara. If we argue we should make allowances for and continue to market *Gone with the Wind* or the overtly racist *Birth of a Nation* (1916), another film that clearly possesses artistic merit and historical significance, we might also consider reinstating *The Song of the South* for public consumption. Disney's African-American animator Floyd Norman also speaks for the defence:

> The film remains a sweet and gentle tale of a kindly old gentleman helping a young child get through a troubled time. The motion picture is also flavored with some of the most inspired cartoon animation ever put on the screen. If you're a fan of classic Disney storytelling, I guarantee you'll not find a better film. (Norman 2012: ix–xii; see also Brode 2005: 53–62; Korkis 2012: 67–74; Maltin 1973: 78)

The Disney Broadcasts and their Stage Sources

On 2 November 1997 the Disney organization showcased its first television adaptation of a stage musical on its ABC network flagship programme *The Wonderful World of Disney*. The work chosen for this historic new Disney enterprise, *Cinderella*, was based on Richard Rodgers and Oscar Hammerstein II's heralded and historic made-for-television version of the classic fairy tale *Cinderella*, starring the bright young Broadway star of the then-running mega-hit *My Fair Lady*, Julie Andrews, in the title role.

That first television *Cinderella* with Julie Andrews was broadcast live on 31 March 1957. According to legend, this CBS production, fortunately preserved in black and white on kinescope, was seen by more than 100 million viewers and temporarily curtailed traffic worries in major cities all over America. To celebrate the arrival of colour videotape, which offered a far superior picture and could easily be rebroadcast, CBS created a new version of *Cinderella* in 1965 with the eighteen-year-old newcomer Lesley Ann Warren. This version was re-shown annually until 1974. Thirty years after the second *Cinderella*, Disney decided the time was ripe to rethink and recast the popular fable for a new generation of television viewers.

Over the next eight years Disney adapted three more shows for the little (but getting bigger by the year) television screen: two classic Broadway musicals first staged in the late 1950s, *The Music Man* (Broadway 1957; Disney 2003) and *Once Upon a Mattress* (Broadway 1959; Disney 2005), and the mega-hit *Annie* (Broadway 1977; Disney 1999). In contrast with the earlier non-Disney made-for-television adaptations of *Gypsy* (1993) and *Bye Bye Birdie* (1995), which included occasional adult-themed components, the musicals chosen for the Disney quartet were probably chosen in part because of their suitability for young audiences. While this chapter focuses on the artistic aspects and multicultural casting and does not attempt to place these works within larger social contexts, it is clear that these versions were intended to reach massive audiences, and no doubt massive research went into their planning.

Unlike *Cinderella*, *The Music Man* and *Annie* not only began their life on the Broadway stage, but also inspired film adaptations shortly after or during their initial Broadway runs. *The Music Man*, which had charmed Broadway audiences in 1957 (the same year as the first televised *Cinderella*), received the Tony Award (winning by one vote over *West Side Story*), ran 1,375 performances and was filmed in 1962. Prior to its Disney version, *Once Upon a Mattress* had been filmed twice for television, in 1964 and 1972, on both occasions starring the creator of the role, Carol Burnett, as Princess Winnifred. In the Disney version, Burnett returned, this time as the Queen. Unusually, the first feature film of *Annie* appeared in 1982, *before* the end of its enormously successful run, which began in 1977 and ended when the show closed in 1983 after 2,377 performances.

Cinderella: Meaning and Social Significance through Song

One of the central creative decisions confronting the prospect of a film or television adaptation is the extent to which one wishes to remain faithful to the stage original. In the case of *Cinderella*, there was no stage musical to which to be faithful. Instead, the precedents were two television broadcasts, only the first of which was created by both Rodgers *and* Hammerstein. The second *Cinderella* appeared in 1965, after Hammerstein's death in 1960, although Rodgers was alive to approve a new book with a new approach as well as to make decisions about several song additions from other Rodgers and Hammerstein stage musicals. Rodgers died in 1979 and the producers and creators of the 1997 Disney version tinkered with the work, but in the end, although the new version removed traces of sexism to create a prince for a new era, the new adaptation preserved the fundamental storyline and most of the songs from the original 1957 broadcast. Since the new broadcast was allotted an additional eleven minutes, several songs were added.

These new songs derived from vastly differing dramatic contexts. The first newly interpolated song, 'Falling in Love with Love', originally from *The Boys from Syracuse* (1938), enjoyed a perennial place in the Rodgers and Hart songbook. Its presence gave the previously songless Stepmother (now played by a major Broadway star, Bernadette Peters) something to sing. Although the melody was borrowed from an old show, the new musical production staff converted Rodgers' gentle waltz in *The Boys from Syracuse* into a somewhat frenetic Latin-tinged number in duple meter, a modernization not unlike Peggy Lee's 1950s popular jazzy duple-metered rendition of 'Lover', another Rodgers and Hart waltz from the 1930s.

A second song, Rodgers and Hammerstein's 'There's Music in You', was hidden in a little-known film, *Main Street to Broadway* (1954). 'There's Music in You' was given to the Fairy Godmother in an expanded musical role designed for the show's producer, Whitney Houston, to close the show (the Prologue also featured the Godmother/Houston singing a slow version of 'Impossible'). The narrative began with Cinderella and the Prince singing 'The Sweetest Sounds' in two separate spaces before they first meet. This song was recycled from the title song introduced in the 1962 musical *No Strings*, the only musical for which Rodgers wrote lyrics as well as the music.

The words to the Stepmother's 'Falling in Love with Love' and the Fairy Godmother's 'There's Music in You' do not add to the dramatic meaning of the new conception, although the words 'Make a wish come true' in the latter song fit in well with the Cinderella concept. The addition of 'The Sweetest

Sounds', however, adds dramatic meaning and offers deeper social significance. In the 1965 *Cinderella* the Prince and Cinderella meet outside the
latter's cottage and the future princess, who does not realize the identity of
the thirsty stranger, responds to his distress and offers him water. Although
she identifies herself to the stranger, it is only when he is addressed by his
aide as High Highness that she grasps who she has been talking to. The
Prince then sings 'The Loneliness of Evening', which had been discarded
from the stage version of *South Pacific* (but salvaged as underscoring in the
film version). In contrast to 'Loneliness of Evening', 'The Sweetest Sounds'
gives the Prince and Cinderella a chance to reveal their fundamental similarities and compatibilities before they meet at the ball.

The royal carriage brushes the Disney Cinderella back, causing her
to drop the armful of packages she is forced to carry for her shopaholic
stepmother and stepsisters. Disney's gentlemanly prince helps Cinderella
pick up the packages and they converse about the etymological meaning
of her name. We also learn that this new-age prince is prepared to treat a
woman 'like a *person*', 'with kindness and respect'. The future partners then
sing a partial reprise of 'The Sweetest Sounds', their sweet sounds of conversation and song of their promising first meeting. Soon the Prince tells his
mother, as she plans a ball, that he wants to marry for love. In short, 'The
Sweetest Sounds' has, as the Queen quips, gotten the ball rolling and their
incognito meeting effectively sets up the inevitable pairing of the Prince and
his future Princess (Block 2003: 171–201).

The Music Man: Restoring Broadway

The 1962 film adaptation of *The Music Man* tried to create a faithful snapshot
of its Broadway predecessor. To achieve this goal, it took a chance on casting
the untested film potential of Robert Preston, who played the charismatic
and charming but exploitative charlatan band salesman Harold Hill on
Broadway. The film also retained the original choreography of Onna White
and made only one significant departure from the stage score. With proven
musical female film star Shirley Jones from the *Oklahoma!* and *Carousel* film
adaptations as Marian the librarian and a strong supporting cast, the faithful
1962 film is still regarded as one of the great film adaptations, although
unlike *West Side Story*, *My Fair Lady*, *The Sound of Music* and *Oliver* it failed
to become the fifth film adaptation of the 1960s to be rewarded with an
Academy Award for Best Picture.

The Disney remake in 2003 offered a new generation a new star, Matthew
Broderick, who demonstrated his acumen as a capable singing actor in the

successful 1995 revival of *How to Succeed in Business* and when he co-starred with Nathan Lane in the Broadway phenomenon *The Producers* (2001). Parents of the new viewers were likely to remember the youthful Broderick from *Ferris Bueller's Day Off* (1986). Kristin Chenoweth, who played Marian, had been featured as Lily St Regis in the Disney *Annie* and was on the verge of major Broadway stardom as the originator of the good witch Glinda in *Wicked*, which appeared the same year as the Disney *Music Man*.

In perhaps the most notable creative decision, the Disney *Music Man* restored two crucial songs from the stage version – 'My White Night' and 'It's You', both of which had been discarded in the 1962 film. It remains unclear why composer Meredith Willson or the producers of the 1962 adaptation wanted to replace 'My White Night' in the first place. Unsubstantiated rumours report that this song was actually composed by Willson's mentor, Frank Loesser, who was allegedly unwilling to release his ownership of the rights, and a similarity has been noted between 'My White Night' and a song cut from Loesser's *The Most Happy Fella* (Miller n.d.). It is clear, however, from Willson's 1959 memoir *But He Doesn't Know the Territory* on the genesis of *The Music Man* that 'My White Night' was fully realized long before the show first opened on Broadway. Not only does Willson describe in his memoir how he resolved the challenges of creating this song, but he quotes the lyrics to the entire original verse of the song followed by 'this new part [that] then went right into "The White Night" refrain, i.e. the refrain that begins with "My White Knight / Not a Lancelot / Nor an angel with wings / Just someone to love me"' (Willson 1957: 114–17).

Even if Loesser helped Willson with 'The White Knight' refrain (the song was published by Loesser's Frank Music Corp.), Willson would not need to ask Loesser for permission to use this or any other song. Moreover, since the verse of the new song 'Being in Love' retains the *identical* refrain to 'My White Night', it is perhaps more likely that the decision to write a new refrain for the 1962 film adaptation was guided by the reality that only songs written expressly for the screen were eligible in the Best Song category of the Academy Awards. Although it was not nominated, 'Being in Love' was eligible for this honour. 'My White Night' was not.

Annie: A Respectful Revival for a New Generation

In comparison with the film adaptation of *The Music Man*, the *Annie* film adaptation, directed by the famous John Huston, who admitted to his inexperience and distaste for both musicals and children, took considerable liberties with the original stage score, adding several new songs created by the original composer (Charles Strouse) and lyricist (Martin Charnin) and deleting *six* of the original fourteen songs. Since it first appeared, the 1982 *Annie* has enjoyed few defenders, and remains one of several maligned adaptions of popular musicals of the era, such as *A Chorus Line* in 1985 and *Evita* in 1996. The cycle was finally broken with the arrival of the Academy Award-winning *Chicago* in 2002, one year prior to Disney's *The Music Man*. Along with Disney's decision to produce a new *Music Man* for television that respected its stage and film predecessors, a respectful new *Annie* for a new generation also seemed like a great idea. The Disney *Annie* not only featured a fine and tested cast – Kathy Bates (Miss Hannigan), Victor Garber ('Daddy' Warbucks), Allan Cumming ('Rooster' Hannigan), Audra McDonald (Grace Farrell), Kristin Chenoweth (Lily St Regis), and talented newcomer Alicia Morton (Annie) – it even brought back the original stage Annie, Andrea McArdle, in a cameo role, 'Star-To-Be'.

Once Upon a Mattress: Long Live Queen Burnett

The 90-minute Disney version of *Once Upon a Mattress* (music by Mary Rodgers, daughter of Richard, and lyrics by Marshall Barer) dropped several songs. Three of these, 'An Opening for a Princess', 'The Minstrel, the Jester, and I' and 'Yesterday I Loved You', had also been discarded for the 1964 and 1972 broadcasts. The Disney version also considerably abbreviated the Prologue number 'Many Moons Ago', 'Quiet', which opened Act II, the instrumental numbers 'Fight-Fight', 'Tents' and 'Three O'clock in the Morning', and the reprises of 'In a Little While' and 'Spanish Panic'. The character of the Minstrel and his songs were either cut all together ('The Minstrel, the Jester, and I') or abbreviated ('Many Moons Ago'). In 'Normandy', the Minstrel's duet with Lady Larken was changed into a duet for Sir Harry and Lady Larken and moved to a later part of the story. The Disney version also eliminated the Jester's only song, 'Very Soft Shoes'. With the time saved, there was room to add another song for Burnett (written not by Rodgers and Barer but by long-time associates Ken and Mitzie Welch), and to provide the Queen, now played by a major star, a second song. The new song, 'That Baby of Mine', also incorporated a short reprise of Winnifred's 'Happily Ever After' at its close (Mandelbaum 2006).

The desire to give new generations of young viewers their own *Cinderella* was sufficient justification to produce yet another. In the case of the 1997 televised *Cinderella*, the new production offered high production values, a bevy of new and established stars, new opportunities for new songs, and a modern sensibility. In addition to offering a new Harold Hill (Broderick) for a new generation, a new *Music Man* could take advantage of the opportunity to reinstate 'My White Night', which had been discarded in the 1962 film in favour of a new song, 'Being in Love', as well as 'It's You', also excluded from the earlier film. A new made-for-television *Annie* presented an opportunity to rectify numerous distortions of a film that no one seemed to work. Similarly, a new *Once upon a Mattress* could combine the old (Burnett and Tom Smothers) with the new (Denis O'Hare, Tracey Ullman, Zooey Deschanel and Matthew Morrison). As we will soon observe, perhaps most importantly, the four Disney television adaptations of musicals created fresh opportunities to present a vision that accords revered classics the opportunity to symbolically join the multicultural modern world.

It's an Integrated World After All: Non-traditional and Colourblind Casting in Disney's Stage Adaptations for Television

Bias and stereotyping have received considerable critical attention in the evaluation of films, including Disney's, but usually the problem is the exclusion of ethnic and racial groups and their resulting invisibility. This chapter addresses the ways this perpetual racial imbalance has been addressed, especially by Disney's made-for-television adaptations.

The most common way to address (and redress) this imbalance is through the practice known as 'non-traditional' or 'colourblind' casting. Over the past few decades 'non-traditional' and 'colourblind' casting has become a familiar presence in live theatre, although it is less common in film and television. The commonplace aspect of this practice, however, does not mean that people don't notice and don't comment, especially when white is entirely replaced by black. For example, people noticed when Orson Welles produced the first all-black *Macbeth* in 1936. The same was true in 2008 when a production with an all-African-American cast of Tennessee Williams's play *Cat on a Hot Tin Roof* inspired a National Public Radio (NPR) broadcast called 'Casting beyond Colour Lines'. One year later the Yale Repertory Theatre in New Haven staged an all-black *Death of a Salesman*. When Phylicia Rashad, Bill Cosby's wife on *The Cosby Show*, was cast as the despicable white matriarch of *August: Osage County*, one offended critic argued that 'it doesn't make sense that she would have white siblings and children' (Heilpern 2009). Perhaps we are not supposed to notice, but we do.

Actors' Equity has defined non-traditional casting 'as the casting of ethnic [male] and female performers in roles where race, ethnicity, or gender are not germane to the characters or play's development' (Sun 2000: 87). When the character is playing an African-American (Joe in *Show Boat*, Jim in *Big River*, nearly the entire cast of *Porgy and Bess*) or a person of a less precise origin but generally portrayed as black (e.g. nearly all stage and film productions of *Othello* after the age of Laurence Olivier), most directors would no longer cast a Caucasian in these roles, even if they were permitted to do so (in the case of *Porgy and Bess*, legal restrictions require casting actors with African heritage for all the African-American roles). In theory it should not be an issue whether to cast an Asian or non-Asian in the role of the Asian Engineer in *Miss Saigon*, but after producers won the battle with Actors' Equity over the casting of the non-Asian actor Jonathan Pryce in this role, the war was over. Actors with Asian heritage playing Asian characters are now the rule.[1]

One outspoken critic of non-traditional or colourblind casting has been the African-American playwright August Wilson, who argued publically and forcefully against the practice.[2] For Wilson, 'Colourblind casting is an aberrant idea that has never had any validity other than as a tool of the Cultural Imperialist' and 'to cast us in the role of mimic is to deny us our own competence' (Wilson 1998: 498).[3] Wilson is the exception. Most practitioners and writers on theatre, including theatre critics, make a note of the colourblind casting and leave it at that, for example when the secondary couple in Rodgers and Hammerstein's *Carousel*, Carrie and Enoch, were played by two different mixed-race couples, one in London (1992) and one in New York (1994), in a widely acclaimed production directed by Nicholas Hytner. Some critics also noted in connection with this production that in New York the role of Nettie ('You'll Never Walk Alone') was sung by the great African-American mezzo-soprano Shirley Verrett, a major opera star in the late 1960s and early 1970s. On the other hand, no one seemed to notice the casting of the great soprano Jessye Norman when she played Sieglinde, the twin sister to Gary Lake's Siegmund, or the racial relevance of any of her other roles for that matter.

Sometimes colourblind casting can uncomfortably resemble old-fashioned stereotyping. In 2012, in addition to a handful of non-Caucasian cowboys and ranchers in Seattle's Fifth Avenue Theatre's *Oklahoma!*, the director cast an African-American actor to play the surly, lascivious, threatening and eventually murderous Jud Fry. This was a problem for some, exacerbated by a prop choice, a rope noose. *Seattle Times* theatre critic Misha Berson addressed these decisions in her review:

> The production's easy social mingling of white settlers and their African-American neighbors as they dance, drink, bathe and mete out frontier justice together may be a historical stretch. (Oklahoma's black pioneers tended to reside in all-black towns.) But we buy it: theater is fantasy, not literal reality. And multiracial casting in classics is now common – and,

when used to reflect and explore our own social dynamic, enriching. But depicting Jud as a homicidal black brute, prone to quivering rages, who forces himself on a virginal white girl? What point is intended? In the 'Poor Jude is Dead [Daid]' sequence, Curly's urging the farmhand to hang by a rope inevitably brings to mind racist lynchings – not the mock suicide the satirical lyrics allude to. (Berson 2012)

In an introductory note to the libretto of Richard Rodgers' *No Strings* (1962), a show about a prize-winning author's relationship with a top African-American model in France (the musical that begins with 'The Sweetest Sounds'), the librettist Samuel Taylor, at Rodgers's insistence, inserted this 'Author's Note': 'The part of Barbara Woodruff in *No Strings* is designed to be played by an American coloured girl in her early twenties. It is proposed that she also be beautiful, have style, and wear clothes well; be intelligent, witty, warmly human, and wise. The play itself never refers to her colour' (Taylor 1962: 1). Casting a white actor as Barbara Woodruff, originally played by Diahann Carroll, would directly subvert the author's intention, but what if a director chose to cast David Jordan (originally played by Richard Kiley) with an African-American actor?

In addressing the ramifications of non-traditional and colourblind casting on the NPR broadcast referred to earlier, one of the guests, Ayanna Thompson, the editor of *Colourblind Shakespeare: New Perspectives on Race and Performance*, states in the case of the Broadway production of *Cat on a Hot Tin Roof* with an all-black cast 'you're not supposed to notice the race in the play' ('Casting Beyond Colour Lines'). In response to this comment, Lynn Neary, the host of the programme, asked whether this is 'really possible' and 'doesn't it [non-traditional casting] frequently, at least, really change the way you would look at a play or think about a play when you see somebody of a different race or not?' (NPR 2008).

Thompson acknowledged we may not be blind to racial casting, but expressed the view 'there are productions that want the cast and want the audience to be blind to race' before moving on to a reminder that the treatment of race and gender alike have changed on the stage over time. As a Shakespearean, she naturally reminds us that when casting his plays 'all the female parts were played by young boy actors and any black characters that were in the Renaissance were played by white actors in black face'.

One of the most remarkable features of the four Disney television adaptations of three mainstream musicals and a historic television broadcast is that they incorporate non-traditional and colourblind casting in ways that bring these shows into the modern multicultural world. The most pervasive example of non-traditional colourblind casting is the 1997 *Cinderella*. The 1957 and

1965 *Cinderella*s cast no actors or actresses of colour, but in the 1997 Disney version four central characters were played by African-American actresses: Cinderella (Brandy Norwood), her Fairy Godmother (Whitney Houston), her future mother-in-law, the Queen (Whoopi Goldberg), and one of her stepsisters, Minerva (Natalie Desselle). Norwood, Houston, and Goldberg in particular were major stars at the time, with considerable cross-cultural appeal. The Prince, played by Paolo Montalban, was a Filipino-American actor (no relation to the Mexican actor Ricardo Montalban), and the ball was a thoroughly integrated and multicultural event.

In an earlier essay on the three *Cinderella*s I asked questions about whether the racial casting, which seems to expand the notion of 'blind' casting, might be interpreted as significant to a new back story (Block 2003: 171–201). Do the Disney casting choices allow us to consider the possibility that Cinderella's father was African-American? Can we attribute her ill treatment in any way to racial prejudice? Other than its casting, the new screenplay offers no clues to a revisionist interpretation of the show, but the casting alone seems to bear its own intrinsic meaning. Five years earlier, in Disney's *Aladdin*, Jasmine had a Middle Eastern physical appearance and two years earlier the title character in *Pocahontas* was an American Indian princess. Despite these cultural breakthroughs, it was not until 2009, Barack Obama's first year as President, that Disney cast an African-American as the princess in *The Princess and the Frog*, opposite a white male counterpart, as in the pioneering Disney *Cinderella* twelve years previously.

Conclusions

Since the prolific and influential George Abbott, who directed the original Broadway and first television broadcast, 'insisted that that not one word of publicity on this matter was ever to be released', to this day few know that these early productions of *Once Upon a Mattress* made the historical choice to cast the light-skinned African-American actress Jane White as the Queen (Barer 1984: 48), probably the first time on Broadway a black character played a putatively European–American role. White even played the Queen in the 1972 version, the third time she was cast opposite Carol Burnett's Winnifred. Although none of the major characters in Disney's *Once Upon a Mattress* were African-American, the production included two in important roles. The first, Ayanna Sealey, was one member of a trio of singing and dancing Ladies in Waiting, a role that includes several lines of dialogue and included a crucial component of an Andrew sisters-type ensemble with Winnifred in 'The Swamps of Home'. The African-American actor Michael Boatman, in the larger role of the Court Jester, has his fair share of lines, launches the finale singing a reprise of 'Man to Man Talk' and appears in the cast publicity shots.

The worlds depicted in *Cinderella* and *Once Upon a Mattress* are timeless kingdoms. On the other hand, *Annie* and *The Music Man* were originally conceived for two specific American locales and eras – New York City, 11–19 December 1933 in the former and River City, Iowa (a *nom de plume* for Mason City) on 4 July 1912. For this reason, the casting of an African-American in a pivotal role in the Disney *Annie*, Audra McDonald as Grace Farrell, Oliver Warbucks's personal secretary (and, less consequentially, the casting of the African–American actress Nanea Miyata as July, one of the six orphans), offer rich social meanings not present in the all-white original cast.

Interestingly, for the 1982 film, the role of the magical Punjab, a character derived from the comic strip rather than the stage show and played by the noted African-American actor Geoffrey Holder, was removed from the Disney *Annie*. Again, we are not supposed to notice, but if we did, Disney is clearly suggesting that in 1933 it would not be so unusual to contemplate a bi-racial marriage. Ironically, when in the 2014 musical film adaptation of *Annie* a marriage proposal between the modern-day Warbucks, William 'Will' Stacks, played by the African–American actor Jamie Foxx and his white secretary played by Rose Byrne, would not be viewed as unusual, Stacks only asks Grace out to dinner (although the invitation is followed by a passionate kiss).

Considering its time and setting, the conspicuous African-American presence in the Disney *Music Man* is perhaps the most remarkable racial transformation in Disney's made-for-television musicals. According to published census figures, the population of the state of Iowa in 1910 was 2,225,000, of whom 2,209,000 were white (93.8 per cent) and 15,000 black (0.3 per cent). In the white America of 1957 and 1962, blacks were as invisible on stage and screen as they were in Mason City (or River City) in 1912. Within seconds of the Disney 2003 version, we see a close-up of an African-American, Salesman #1, chanting 'Cash for the merchandise' in the opening number, 'Rock Island'. When the show moves to River City in the second number, 'Iowa Stubborn', we quickly are presented with a totally integrated community and prominent inter-racial groupings, close-ups of black citizens of every age in shot after shot. Individual blacks sing lines like 'But we'll give you our shirt' in 'Iowa Stubborn'. In the scene that includes the song 'Seventy-Six Trombones' we see five African-Americans, another three in the song 'Marian' and more than one African-American in 'Shipoopi' (along with perhaps the only Asian in the town).

Viewers can observe a cheerful African-American woman buying musical instruments at one end of the show and an angry African-American woman demanding her money at the other end when Harold Hill has been shown to be a fraud. We also can notice a bi-racial couple in the ice cream partner (who sing 'Aren't We Sincerely in Love?') and a bi-racial marriage between Jacey Squires, one of the four school board and barbershop quartet members, and his African-American wife Mrs Squires, a leading townswoman who picks on Marian in 'Pick-A-Little'. And with naturalness and seeming plausibility we also hear an African-American pianist play a cross between ragtime and novelty piano in the ragtimy song 'The Sadder but Wiser Girl' and also sing a short duet with Matthew Broderick (Harold Hill). Thus even in the absence of central African-American characters (as of 2012 still only 1.2 per cent of the Mason City population), what we see in the 2003 Disney *Music Man* is a classless, thoroughly integrated and racially harmonious rural American town. We're not in *Song of the South* anymore. Welcome to Disney's twenty-first-century vision of America, an America not unlike our own.

Table 5.1 Principal Songs Comparison: Broadway vs Disney Versions of *Cinderella*

Book and lyrics – Oscar Hammerstein
Music – Richard Rodgers
Bold – added songs
Underlined – additional reprise or altered song position

Broadway *Cinderella* (31 March 1957)	Disney *Cinderella* (2 November 1997, 88 mins)
	The Sweetest Sounds
The Prince is Giving a Ball	The Prince is Giving a Ball
In My Own Little Corner	In My Own Little Corner
	Falling In Love With Love
	In My Own Little Corner (reprise)
Impossible	Impossible
It's Possible	It's Possible
Gavotte	Gavotte
Ten Minutes Ago	Waltz for a Ball
Stepsisters' Lament	Ten Minutes Ago
Waltz for a Ball	Stepsisters' Lament
Do I Love You Because You're Beautiful?	Do I Love You Because You're Beautiful?
When You're Driving through the Moonlight	A Lovely Night (with abbreviated When You're Driving though the Moonlight)
A Lovely Night	**Do I Love You Because You're Beautiful?** (reprise)
The Search	[The Search]
Finale	
In My Own Little Corner	**There's Music in You**
Impossible	

Table 5.2 Principal Songs Comparison: Broadway vs Disney Versions of *Annie*

Book: Thomas Meehan
Lyrics – Martin Charnin
Music – Charles Strouse
Bold – added songs
Underlined – additional reprise or altered song position

Broadway *Annie* (21 April 1977)	Disney *Annie* (7 November 1999, 90 mins)
Act I	
Maybe	Maybe
It's the Hard Knock Life	It's the Hard Knock Life
	Hard Knock Life (reprise)
Tomorrow	Tomorrow
We'd Like to Thank You, Herbert Hoover	
Little Girls	Little Girls
Little Girls (reprise)	
I Think I'm Gonna Like it Here	I Think I'm Gonna Like it Here
N.Y.C.	N.Y.C.
N.Y.C. (reprise)	N.Y.C. (reprise)
Lullaby	Lullaby
Easy Street	Easy Street
You Won't Be an Orphan for Long	
Maybe (first reprise)	Maybe (first reprise)
Act II	
Maybe (second reprise)	
You're Never Fully Dressed Without a Smile	You're Never Fully Dressed Without a Smile
You're Never Fully Dressed Without a Smile (reprise)	You're Never Fully Dressed Without a Smile (reprise)
Easy Street (reprise)	
Tomorrow (first reprise)	
Tomorrow (second reprise)	
Something Was Missing	Something Was Missing
Annie	
I Don't Need Anything But You	I Don't Need Anything But You
Maybe (third reprise)	Maybe (second reprise)
A New Deal for Christmas	Tomorrow (reprise)
	Little Girls (reprise)
Finale	
	I Don't Need Anything but You (reprise)

Table 5.3 Principal Songs Comparison: Broadway vs Disney Versions of
Music Man

Book, lyrics and music – Meredith Willson
Bold – added songs
Underlined – additional reprise or altered song position

Broadway *Music Man* (19 December 1957)	Disney *Music Man* (16 February 2003, 133 mins)
Act I	
Rock Island	Rock Island
Iowa Stubborn	Iowa Stubborn
Ya Got Trouble	Ya Got Trouble
Piano Lesson	Piano Lesson
Goodnight, My Someone	Goodnight, My Someone
Ya Got Trouble (reprise)	Ya Got Trouble (reprise)
Seventy-Six Trombones	Seventy-Six Trombones
Sincere	Sincere
The Sadder But Wiser Girl	The Sadder But Wiser Girl
Pick-A-Little, Talk-A-Little/	Pick-A-Little, Talk-A-Little/
Goodnight, Ladies	Goodnight, Ladies
Marian the Librarian	Marian the Librarian
	Gary, Indiana
My White Knight [replaced by Being in Love in 1962 film]	My White Knight
The Wells Fargo Wagon	The Wells Fargo Wagon
Act II	
It's You [cut in 1962 film]	It's You
Shipoopi	
Pick-A-Little, Talk-a-Little (reprise)	Pick-A-Little, Talk-A-Little (reprise)
Lida Rose/Will I Ever Tell You	Lida Rose/Will I Ever Tell You
Gary, Indiana	Gary, Indiana (reprise)
It's You (reprise)	Shipoopi
Till There Was You	Till There Was You
Seventy-Six Trombones/Goodnight My Someone (reprise)	Seventy-Six Trombones/Goodnight My Someone (reprise)
Till There Was You (reprise)	

Table 5.4 Principal Songs Comparison: Broadway vs Disney Versions of *Once Upon a Mattress*

Book – Jay Thompson, Marshall Barer and Dean Fuller
Lyrics – Marshall Barer
Music – Mary Rodgers

Broadway *Once Upon a Mattress* (5 November 1959)	Disney *Once Upon a Mattress* (18 December 2005, 90 mins)
Act 1	
Prologue: Many Moons Ago	Prologue: Many Moons Ago (abbreviated)
An Opening for a Princess [also absent from the first two TV versions]	
In a Little While	In a Little While
In a Little While (reprise)	
Shy	Shy
The Minstrel, the Jester, and I [also absent from the first two TV versions and unrecorded on the 1959 Cast Album]	
Sensitivity	Sensitivity
The Swamps of Home	The Swamps of Home
Fight-Fight, Spanish Panic, Tents (instrumental)	Spanish Panic (Instrumental) [introduced and concluded with Sensitivity]
Normandy	
Spanish Panic No. 2 (instrumental)	
Song of Love	Song of Love
Act II	
Opening – Act II (Quiet)	
Happily Ever After	Happily Ever After
Man to Man Talk	Man to Man Talk
	Normandy [duet for Harry and Lady Larken; originally for the Jester and Lady Larken] [chorus only]
	That Baby Of Mine/Happily Ever After (abbreviated) [new song composed by Ken and Mitzie Welch for Carol Burnett, who played the Queen]
	Very Soft Shoes
Three O'clock in the Morning (instrumental)	
Yesterday I Loved You [also absent from the first two TV versions]	
Nightingale Lullaby [variant of Many Moons Ago]	Nightingale Lullaby [sung by the Wizard] [variant of Many Moons Ago]
Finale	
Man to Man Talk and Happily Ever After	Man to Man Talk and Happily Ever After

References

Barer, M. (1984). '300,000 Mattresses.' *Dramatics* 56 (2) (14–21 October): 47–8.

Berson, M. (2012). 'Provocative "Oklahoma!" Hits 5th Avenue Stage.' *Seattle Times*, 10 February.

Block, G. (2003). 'Broadway Comes to Television: The Three *Cinderellas*.' In G. Block, *Richard Rodgers*. New Haven: Yale University Press, 171–201.

Brode, D. (2005). *Multiculturalism and the Mouse: Race and Sex in Disney Entertainment*. Austin: University of Texas Press.

Daboo, J. (2005). 'One Under the Sun: Globalization, Culture and Utopia in *Bombay Dreams*'. *Contemporary Theatre Review* 15 (3): 330–7.

Grant, J. (1993). *Encyclopedia of Walt Disney's Animated Characters*. Los Angeles: Disney Editions.

Heilpern, J. (2009). 'Should a Fuss Be Made over Colourblind Casting?' *New York Observer*, 9 June.

Korkis, J. (2012). *Who's Afraid of the Song of the South?* Orlando: Theme Park Press.

Leff, L. J. (1999). '*Gone with the Wind* and Hollywood's Racial Politics.' *Atlantic Online*, December.

Maltin, L. (1973), *The Disney Films*. New York: Crown.

Mandelbaum, K. (2006). 'Many Moons Ago'. *Broadway Buzz*. Available online: Broadway.com (accessed 6 November 2014).

Miller, F. (n.d.). 'The Music Man.' Turner Classic Movies Film Article. Available online: www.tcm.com/this-month/article/12694%7CO/The-Music-Man.html (accessed 23 August 2014).

Norman, F. (2012). 'Foreword'. In J. Korkis, *Who's Afraid of the Song of the South?* Orlando: Theme Park Press, ix–xii.

NPR (2008). 'Casting Beyond Colour Lines'. National Public Radio, 5 February.

Schickel, R. (1968). *The Disney Version: The Life, Times, Art and Commerce of Walt Disney*. New York: Simon & Schuster.

Sun, W. H. (2000). 'Power and Problems of Performance across Ethnic Lines: An Alternative Approach to Nontraditional Casting.' *The Drama Review* 44 (4): 86–95.

Taylor, S. (1962). 'Author's Note'. In *No Strings*. New York: Random House.

Willson, M. (1957). *But He Doesn't Know the Territory*. New York: G. P. Putnam's Sons.

Wilson A. (1998). 'The Ground on Which I Stand.' *Callaloo* 20 (3): 493–503.

The Hunchback of Notre Dame (1996): Too Far 'Out There'?

Olaf Jubin

The following chapter discusses the struggles Disney faced when adapting *The Hunchback of Notre Dame*, as Victor Hugo's 1831 romantic masterpiece could not easily be bent to fit the template the film company had developed with its previous cartoon musicals. It will also chart the public and critical reception of the 1996 animated feature and its subsequent stage incarnations both in Germany (1999) and the US (2014/15).

After the hugely successful *The Little Mermaid* (1989), *Beauty and the Beast* (1991) and *Aladdin* (1992), with each new cartoon musical out-grossing the previous one, the Disney animation unit not only felt secure in its artistic approach, but was also ready to face new challenges. As director Kirk Wise pointed out in the mid-1990s, 'One of the criteria for each new Disney animated film is to do something we've never done before' (cited in Rebello 1996: 44). *Pocahontas* (1995) had gone further than any other cartoon feature to show how far the artists at Disney were willing to go in their quest to explore what is possible in the field of animation when it comes to story-telling and expressing even the subtlest of emotions: for the first time, there is no happy ending for the heroine and her lover, the whole movie gears up for a major battle that never comes, and the final close-up of the American Indian princess attempts to show realistically her feelings in a manner comparable with a human actor (Biskind 1995: 85).

Yet it was the subsequent feature with its baffling choice of source material that illustrated just how ambitious Disney had become: Hugo's *Notre Dame de Paris* with its strongly drawn characters and melodramatic incidents had already inspired several musical versions,[1] but its adaptation into a cartoon musical was particularly exacting, as Disney animated features are characterized by their economic story-telling and fairly short running times of no more than 90 minutes; thus they are not ideally suited to do justice to a novel of somewhere in the region of 200,000 words.

The movie industry had been very quick to recognize the novel's potential as screen material – it proffered colourful characters, melodramatic plot developments and major set pieces all centred around one of the most famous buildings in the world. Several adaptations, made in 1923, 1939, 1956 as well as 1982 (the last one for television), had already explored the opportunities provided by the book for heart-wrenching drama and rousing spectacle before the Disney animators went to work. Although all of these previous film adaptations had cut and reshaped the source material depending on their intended target audience as well as the censorship demands and production possibilities of their time, it was an enormous task to align the novel's preoccupation with carnal desire and human cruelty with Disney's reputation of creating entertainment that the whole family can enjoy.

Hugo's novel features a carefully woven love quadrangle, with not one but four men lusting after sixteen-year-old dancer Esmeralda: the repressed priest Claude Frollo, the deaf hunchback Quasimodo, the vainglorious Captain of the Guard Phoebus as well as the hapless poet Gringoire. At the end of the story, most of the main protagonists perish: Esmeralda is hanged, Frollo is thrown off the cathedral by Quasimodo, who dies of grief next to the corpse of his beloved dancer. There is also the demise of several supporting characters (Esmeralda's mother, Sister Gudule, Frollo's younger brother Jean as well as Clopin, the leader of the beggars), meaning that Hugo's tome could be summed up as dealing predominantly with death and sex, the latter markedly an absolute 'no-no in the Disney universe' (Biskind 1995: 85). One thing was evident to the artists working on *Hunchback* right from the start. In the words of Kirk Wise, who co-directed the movie together with Gary Trousdale, 'We were not going to end it the way the book ended, with everybody dead' (cited in Thompson 1996). Add to that the fact that Hugo intentionally did not include a male romantic lead (Burr 1997: 72), and it becomes clear that there are huge obstacles to overcome when turning the novel into a typical Disney offering full of uplift and humour and suitable for both adults and children.

Hugo's sociopolitical melodrama was suggested as a potential project for the Disney animation unit by Creative Affairs Vice President David Stainton during a story conference in 1993; when he was younger, Stainton had come across the *Classics Illustrated* comic book version of the novel (Sundel et al. 1944)[2] and later read the work itself in high school (Rebello 1996: 44; Thompson 1996). He considered it a great choice of source material, precisely 'because of the challenge it so clearly presented for a streamlined, restructured treatment in animation' (cited in Rebello 1996: 44).

The Disney staff were also intrigued by those elements of the story with which even people who have not read the book are familiar and which would allow them to use the full (colour) palette of their artistry when rendering them in hand-drawn animation. These features include:

- Quasimodo's 'adoration'[3] for Esmeralda (basically a variation of the *Beauty and the Beast* fairy tale, itself so memorably tackled by Disney in 1991);
- The bell ringer being crowned the King of Fools at the Festival of the Flight into Egypt and then being mercilessly taunted and tortured by the crowd;
- Quasimodo's acrobatic scaling of the bells and the architecture of the cathedral;
- The attack on Notre Dame by the mob with the bell ringer defending the church by throwing down wooden beams, rocks and pouring down molten lead. (Rebello 1996: 17)

Of course, these plot elements and visual images have entered the public consciousness mainly because of previous film adaptations; with this in mind, one can assume that Disney also wanted to showcase the fact that animation could compete with live-action films when it came to adapting the classics. Yet, while they were aware that they needed to tread carefully when portraying the church and Quasimodo, clearly the least traditional of Disney's customary 'outsider' protagonists, they could not have anticipated what would affect the later stage adaptations in Berlin and the US, all of which will be explored in the following discussion.

At the Centre of Attention: The Church

One major obstacle to overcome was Hugo's decidedly anti-clerical stance, his harsh criticism of organized religion and its practitioners. It is interesting how author Stephen Rebello in his book *The Art of The Hunchback of Notre Dame*, written in close collaboration with Disney Feature Animation and published by Hyperion, one of Disney's own companies, tackles the subject. Rebello justifies this particular feature of the novel by pointing out to his readers that Hugo conceived and wrote the novel 'during a personal crisis of faith' (Rebello 1996: 72), strongly implying that only somebody shaken in his belief may question organized religion, as if being a devout Christian automatically precludes criticism of the church.

He then goes on to assert tersely that the 'Disney moviemakers chose to make Frollo a feared and powerful judge rather than a cleric as Hugo did' (Rebello 1996: 73) without offering any explanation as to the reasoning behind this drastic alteration. Other writers were less coy: Anne Thompson and Ty Burr reveal that the company wanted to avoid another public outcry from American conservatives like the one that was triggered by the British film *Priest* (which depicted a secretly gay cleric) when it was released stateside by Disney subsidiary Miramax (Thompson 1996; Burr 1997).

In the end, Disney not only gave Frollo a secular profession, but also provided a clerical foil, in the form of the archdeacon who interferes at regular intervals and makes his dissatisfaction with some of Frollo's more devious schemes known: it is the archdeacon who prevents the judge from murdering the misshapen baby, an intervention that symbolically takes a stand against both euthanasia and abortion – key issues with conservative groups specifically in the US – and he also protests against Frollo's verdict to have Esmeralda burnt as a witch. The studio also decided to leave most of the more incendiary comic elements improvised by its voice actors out of the film. Jason Alexander, who played gargoyle Hugo, later admitted: 'We were on thin ice with a lot of the religious overtones. Most of our nun and priest jokes are not in [the finished film]' (Thompson 1996).

Disneyfication of a Character: From Quasimodo to Quasi

The studio may have been able to avoid a backlash from conservative Christians, but they had a hard time in coming to terms with the violent undercurrent of the original novel. In spite of their attempts to render the darker elements of the story less frightening to younger audience members, to balance the 'often adult subject matter with humor' (Rebello 1996: 44), the film still features themes of genocide, infanticide, torture[4] and execution, not to mention sexual desire and perversion.

The Hugo adaptation with its two directors (Gary Trousdale and Kirk Wise) and five credited screenwriters (Tab Murphy, Irene Mecchi, Bob Tzudiker, Noni White and Jonathan Roberts) turned out to be 'the darkest, most adult animated film Disney has ever made' (Thompson 1996). Even the company was surprised when the ratings board of the Motion Picture Association of America/MPAA decided to give the movie a 'G' rating (for general audiences), as Disney had secretly prepared itself for a higher category, namely 'PG' (parental guidance suggested) (ibid.). But since the film ends in a mood of cheerfulness and uplift and because the studio agreed to make minor adjustments to the scene of Esmeralda dancing in the flames,[5] the MPAA agreed to give the movie its lowest rating.

Perhaps inspired by the English title of the classic book, the Disney animators decided to put Quasimodo front and centre in their version of the story – a first, as they proudly underlined (Rebello 1996: 47). It was also novel to depict the bell ringer as close to the age he is given in the source material – the actors who essayed the role before and after the animated movie musical came out were usually in their forties. The task of turning the grotesque-looking, bitter, vicious and deaf Quasimodo into a likable, kid-friendly protagonist proved a formidable challenge that at times seemed insurmountable: at least ten of the studios most gifted animators tried their hands at coming up with the right look (Rebello 1996: 53–5), and to find the character's voice took two years, a process which was initially so frustrating for actor Tom Hulce that he considered leaving the production (Thompson 1996).

Finally, as evidenced by the character's nickname, 'Quasi', the studio settled for a face and form that may be unusual, but are far from gruesome or ugly; instead, his 'unconventional outward appearance' cannot really hide his 'transcendent spirit' (Rebello 1996: 53). The bell ringer is shown to the audience right from the beginning of the film, after the prologue, and is introduced as kindhearted when he helps a little bird literally to fly the nest, a scene that is overtly symbolic of Quasimodo's own predicament and his emotional journey throughout the movie (Norden 2013: 170).

Every Disney hero/heroine needs at least one sidekick, mainly so that the character does not have to speak to him/herself;[6] as Quasi spends most of his time cooped up in the bell tower of Notre Dame, the studio decided to partner him with three talking gargoyles, one of the more controversial features of the film. In a typical example of the self-referential and meta-filmic humour found throughout the movie, they are called Victor, Hugo and – rather perplexingly, as it is not a French name – Laverne.

Although Disney attempted to justify the addition of these stone-figures-brought-miraculously-to-life as 'creatures of Quasimodo's imagination' (Rebello 1996: 134), their depiction in the film itself does not bear this out: while the gargoyles turn back into stone immediately when other characters are around or look at them, they freeze right where they are, meaning that they do not return to their regular position on the façade of the cathedral, but objectively constantly change places, a fact that all other people in the movie conveniently fail to notice.

The Bell Ringer as 'the Other'

Quasimodo may find public admiration at the end of the movie with the Parisians parading him around on their shoulders, but what he hasn't found is love with another human; although the movie sets him up as the main hero, this is the rare Disney film where the boy doesn't get the girl. Instead, it is the beautiful people who become a couple: seductive Esmeralda and strapping Phoebus.

Why is it that the misshapen bell ringer cannot wind up with the woman he so indubitably adores? First of all, the filmmakers in public statements consistently stressed the character's innocence and child-like demeanour,[7] but the movie additionally introduces several plot devices to validate its ending: Phoebus saves Quasimodo's life by catching him when he falls off the roof of Notre Dame, so when the bell ringer puts Esmeralda's hand into the captain's (thereby blessing their union) this can also be interpreted as simple gratitude. Moreover, it could be argued that Quasi at least now has the love of the people, but as the movie has already shown us when he was crowned King of Fools, this admiration isn't necessarily long-lasting and can quickly turn into cruel rejection. Therefore, how much consolation can the audience take in Quasi being carried off like a hero when crowds 'are notoriously fickle' (Rebello 1996: 168–70)?

Although at the age of twenty clearly no longer a teenager, Quasimodo's infatuation with Esmeralda, who is much more overtly sexual than previous Disney heroines (Lacroix 2004: 221), even doing a medieval version of a pole dance, is categorized as 'puppy love' (Rebello 1996: 65) by the film's co-director Gary Trousdale, and not as adult sexual passion and thus was not to be seen as the main thrust of the narrative: 'Our story is more about "Will Quasimodo get out from under Frollo and become part of the outside world?" than "Does he get the girl?"' (cited in Rebello 1996: 65).

Disney asserted that it was mostly attracted to the story because of what was seen to be its underlying message. In this context, the rationale given by Thomas Schumacher, at the time of filming Executive Vice President of Feature Animation and now Head of Disney Theatrical Productions, is worth quoting:

> Our earlier movies say things like 'It's okay to be you …' but that usually meant 'it's okay to be you *if* you're a really handsome, winning, young street urchin or you're a frightening, ill-tempered beast who in the end becomes handsome.' This movie says, 'It's okay to be you if you're not necessarily "normal" or "beautiful" to the rest of the world,' which I call a big step forward. (Rebello 1996: 48)

Unfortunately, this seems to have been a case of 'one step forward, two steps back', as Martin F. Norden emphasizes in his analysis of the film as a portrayal of Quasimodo as disabled. The studio had refused to work with disability consultants during the film's pre-production phase (Norden 2013: 171), and after its release the finished movie was heavily criticized by groups representing people with disabilities (PWDs).[8] Norden agrees with their evaluation: 'The movie appears to critique the view that "different" people should be kept separate and isolated, yet it simultaneously perpetuates it and, worse, wallows in it' (2013: 164). Norden continues: 'In many respects, [Quasi] is a multi-faceted character, but each facet reflects some aspect of a longstanding disability stereotype' (2013: 169).

The filmmakers resort to the old cliché of PWDs compensating for their imperfect bodies with inner beauty (Norden 2013: 166) and represent the bell ringer as 'emotionally stunted' (Norden 2013: 168–9); his 'sweet innocence' (Norden 2013: 169) betrays a person who, despite being an adult in years, remains a child at heart (Norden 2013: 171), a young man who consequently is both infantilized as well as desexualized. For Kathi Wolfe, a blind freelance writer, the movie portrays PWDs in a most unfortunate light: 'It says that our only friends are stone gargoyles, that we are never ordinary people but monsters or superheroes; that no matter how heroic we are, we will never have a loving, romantic relationship' (cited in ibid.).

Like several other Disney cartoons – *The Little Mermaid* and *Beauty and the Beast* being the most obvious examples – *Hunchback* also invites a queer reading, and not just because 'Out There' is also the name of a high-profile gay advocacy group (Thompson 1996). The studio denied that 'there was any intentional homosexual identification in Quasi's quest for tolerance' (ibid.),[9] but with a hero who is seen as the unattractive 'other' by the majority of the Parisians and in the end finally 'comes out (in)to society', the film aims to send a powerful message of acceptance that alas finally is undermined by the ending, whether one reads Quasimodo as gay or disabled.

Reactions of the Critics and the General Public

At the time of the cartoon's release, then-President of Walt Disney Feature Animation Peter Schneider was quoted as insisting: 'Our movies can go anywhere to tell a story' (cited in Thompson 1996). It seems that, despite some bravura elements, its musical retelling of *The Hunchback of Notre Dame* proved him wrong; in this case, the divide between the dark, violent source material and the Disney brand of wholesome family entertainment was too wide to straddle, neither pleasing those who expected fidelity to the novel nor satisfying those who wanted a child-friendly musical.

Reviews for the cartoon were decidedly mixed;[10] while there was a lot of praise for the Menken/Schwartz score,[11] critics emphasized that the film was not suited to very young children, warning their readers that 'some scenes may be much too intense or violent' (Sterritt 1996: 12), partly because – like the song 'Hellfire' – they dealt with Frollo's unhealthy, lewd obsession with Esmeralda.[12] That the film distributor had decided to advertise its latest release with the slogan 'Come join the party' also came in for criticism as inappropriate and therefore misleading (ibid.). The way the studio tailored the original narrative to fit its purpose similarly caused concern, not least since this resulted in sharp shifts of tone (Ansen 1996: 83), and David Sterritt predicted: 'Literary purists will shudder at change after change' (Sterritt 1996: 12).

In the US, the film barely managed to bring in $100 million at the domestic box office, a sum still regarded as a benchmark for any movie that wants to be considered a hit, but since the cartoon had cost around $100 million to produce, this was in no way satisfying. The box office receipts also represented a steep decline not just from the phenomenal success of *The Lion King*, with its $313 million haul, but also from *Hunchback*'s predecessor, *Pocahontas*, which had earned $142 million in North America and was already regarded as something of an under-achiever. *Hunchback* did better internationally, as it accumulated $225 million abroad, which put the global earnings at $325 million (www.boxofficemojo.com).

Disney had high hopes for *The Hunchback of Notre Dame* and its merchandise, expecting the soundtrack to outsell the one for *Pocahontas*, which had moved 2.2 million units in the US alone, yet those hopes were quickly dashed: neither Bette Midler's pop version of 'God Help the Outcasts' nor the rousing 'Someday', performed by All-4-One, were very successful.[13] There was also another important area in which the *Hunchback* soundtrack failed to impress: at the Academy Awards. After securing multiple Oscar-nominations and at least one win with each of their previous cartoon musicals, the Victor Hugo adaptation and its score were completely ignored by the Academy of Motion Picture Arts and Sciences.

The studio had also struck lucrative tie-in deals with several major global corporations like American Express, Nestlé, Mattel, Payless ShoeSource, General Mills and Burger King to the tune of $150 million (Benezra 1994: 4). But Disney and its business partners were in for a rude awakening. As the movie 'produced unspectacular box-office results', its merchandise failed to sell as well (Fitzgerald and Pollack 1996: 1), resulting in an unexpected financial shortfall.

The Move to the Stage: The 1999 German Production

When the cartoon feature opened in American cinemas in June 1996, the press had already speculated that Disney saw *Hunchback* as a potential screen-to-stage transfer (Thompson 1996). Despite the film's less-than-stellar box office receipts, the journalists were proven right, but it still came as a surprise how and where the stage version was produced: it opened in Berlin, making it the first (and thus far only) adaptation of a Disney movie to premiere abroad and in a language other than English. Disney had negotiated a co-venture with German company Stella Entertainment, at that time the biggest private producer of musical theatre in Continental Europe, which would give the American corporation full artistic control while leaving Stella with all the financial risk.

The 1999 stage version of *Hunchback* – German title *Der Glöckner von Notre Dame*[14] – opened the newly built Musical Theater am Potsdamer Platz. For this third stage adaptation of one of their cartoon musicals, Disney chose Tony Award-winner James Lapine, best known for his collaborations with Stephen Sondheim, as book author and director, who rewrote most of the dialogue (Schuermann 2003: 57) while staying close to the plot of the 1996 cartoon, with one major exception – he insisted on having Esmeralda die at the end, as she did in the novel. This lent additional urgency to her eleven o'clock anthem 'Someday', which is repeated as a rousing finale at the very end of the show. Lapine's book is more sombre than the cartoon musical; it re-introduces (melo)dramatic components from the novel and restricts those elements that could be deemed 'pure entertainment', for example by having only two major dance numbers throughout the evening (Schuermann 2003: 60) (in 'Topsy Turvy' and 'Balancing Act').

Like all Disney screen-to-stage transfers, the 1999 Berlin *Hunchback* uses three major devices to expand the ninety-one-minute film into a more-than-two-hour theatrical experience: songs that were originally written for the movie, but then were cut, are restored (such as 'Someday'), dialogue is musicalized (for instance in 'The Top of the World' and 'Esmeralda') and new songs are introduced to give more depth to certain characters. Phoebus now has an entrance song called 'Rest and Recreation' that marks him as a hedonist and the difficult position of the gypsies in medieval Parisian society is explained in the elaborate production number 'Balancing Act', which replaces 'The Court of Miracles'. All in all, there were ten new songs.

It is difficult to gauge who Disney assumed to be the target audience for the stage adaptation of *Hunchback*; co-producer Stella could have told the corporation that it certainly wouldn't be families, as in contrast to Broadway and the West End the idea of parents accompanying their children to a commercially produced musical as a joint outing has never taken hold in the German and Austrian market. There are multiple reasons for this: on the one hand, the steep ticket prices for commercial open-end productions put a visit to a musical outside the price range of many families, especially as in these two countries, where most theatre and all opera is subsidized and therefore can offer cheap tickets to pupils and students, there are many alternatives for a family excursion.[15]

On the other hand, many of the classic family musicals – like *The Sound of Music* (1959), *Oliver!* (1960), *Annie* (1977) or the more recent *Billy Elliot* (2005) and *Matilda* (2011) – have never entered the repertory of German-language theatres, because strict local child labour laws complicate casting the juvenile roles to such a degree that long runs are more or less impossible. In addition, one could argue that the stage version of *Hunchback* includes elements that make it unsuitable for children, partly by harking back to the source material: Esmeralda is burnt at the stake and dies (presumably of smoke inhalation), while Quasimodo kills Frollo by throwing him off the roof of the cathedral. During the fight for Notre Dame, Clopin's leg is chopped off (Lapine et al. 1999: 74).

The Berlin stage production also revealed that Disney (and Stella) had competition from an unexpected quarter, and that competition coloured audience expectations to a substantial degree: the 1956 film version starring Anthony Quinn and Gina Lollobrigida, a French–Italian co-production that, although it turned a profit in its North American release,[16] is mostly forgotten in the United States[17] and not held in very high esteem by those Americans who do remember it.[18] But this film was a major success in Europe and is most likely the film adaptation that most Germans are familiar with.[19] That Gina Lollobrigida was invited to attend the premiere of the Berlin stage production as the guest of honour merely reinforced the impression of the general public of the 1956 film as a classic and thus as the standard against which to measure the stage *Hunchback*.

Therefore, it turned out that for most critics and audience members the point of comparison was not necessarily the Disney cartoon, but the Franco-Italian *Hunchback*,[20] which was adapted by Jacques Prévert and directed by Jean Dellanoy. Of all the live-action versions of Hugo's book, it follows the original story the most closely (only deleting the subplot of Sister Gudule), and thus is by far the darkest adaptation, without any form of comic relief, that ends like the novel with the deaths of the main protagonists, Frollo, Esmeralda and Quasimodo. It is not surprising that compared to this the 1999 Berlin production with its singing gargoyles and hopeful ending was seen as insufficiently serious and was denounced for its 'Disneyfication' of a great literary masterpiece, an uneasy compromise between the novel's European mentality and American showbusiness. For instance, reviewer Manuel Brug panned the screen-to-stage transfer as being 'stranded somewhere in the shallow waters of half-heartedness' (Brug 1999). The stage musical *Hunchback* had its premiere on 5 June 1999 in the Musical Theater Berlin; a few months later, in November 1999, the Stella corporation declared insolvency (Jansen 2008: 239). In the next two-and-a-half years, several attempts at rescuing what had once been one of the world's biggest private investors in musical theatre failed, so its assets were sold off to the highest bidder in the summer of 2002. *The Hunchback of Notre Dame* closed after three years on 20 June 2002, without having turned a profit; there were claims that the theatrical adaptation with its production costs of 45 million Deutschmarks (Brug 1999)[21] had been far too expensive (Gerlach and Sieler 2002: 27) and that the licensing fees Stella had to pay Disney had been so huge that it was impossible for the production to get out of the red (Anon. 2002: 40).

The 2014/15 US Stage Version: Caught between Opposing Audience Expectations

The Berlin stage adaptation of *Hunchback* left as its only trace a German-language cast recording.[22] One reason why it disappeared more or less completely may have been that is was scaled specifically to the facilities of the theatre in the German capital and there was no Broadway or West End venue of sufficient size and technological sophistication to house it (Schuermann 2003: 60). In 2003, there was talk of adapting it to television, for *ABC's Wonderful World of Disney* (Anon. 2003), but nothing ever came of this. It was only fifteen years after the German production that the material was once again presented to a theatre audience: in a co-production, it first played at the La Jolla Playhouse in California, before moving east in spring 2015 to the Papermill Playhouse in New Jersey. This version had a new book by Peter Parnell and was directed by the lyricist's son, Scott Schwartz.[23] Although it had a different libretto and in some ways adheres more closely to Hugo's novel,[24] certain aspects of the 2014/15 productions build on the Berlin version. As James Lapine did before him, Scott Schwartz also included several meta-theatrical elements, for instance having Michael Arden as Quasimodo turning into the misshapen bell ringer in front of the audience by strapping on his hump and changing his posture and demeanour in full view, a device that proved more popular with critics than with regular audiences, if the comments left on message boards are any indication.[25] As before, the character of Frollo, who had been a tradi-tional Disney villain in the cartoon,[26] was reworked to make him more like the multi-faceted, conflicted priest of the novel, and the comic relief was reduced to the point where people who had seen the production warned others: 'There is absolutely no humor in this musical until the second act ...'[27]

Even more controversial was the decision of the artistic team to maintain the conceit of having large sections of the story described to the audience instead of dramatizing it. The function of the narrator no longer fell to Clopin (as it did in Berlin); instead it now was various members of the ensemble, referred to as 'congregants', who narrated parts of the story. This time it was not only the regular theatregoers but the professional ones as well who objected, with comments ranging from '[t]he narrators really kill any sense of action'[28] to 'much of it feels like shorthand storytelling that dampens the production's theatricality' (Isherwood 2015).

Once again the attempt to reconcile two contrasting artistic sensibilities seemed doomed to fail. Charles Isherwood underlined right at the beginning of his review: 'Bridging the gap between those two aesthetics – Hugo's darkly thundering melodramatics and the smiley-faced warmth of a Disney cartoon – proves tricky' (Isherwood 2015). But these two warring aesthetics also bring with them two incompatible kinds of audience expectations: on the one hand, there are those who go to the show hoping for a musical retelling of the novel they have read or heard about, and, on the other hand, there are people who grew up with the Disney cartoon and want to see it live on stage, leaving not just the creative but also the marketing team behind any stage version in a very difficult position. Both the cast and the director of the La Jolla/Paper Mill Playhouse *Hunchback* cautioned audiences that their version would be dark and not really suited for children, with Scott Schwartz specifying: 'There's nothing that parents would find objectionable, but that's the core of the story, and we're not shying away from it' (cited in Henerson 2014).[29] Clearly, Disney Theatrical Productions was aware of this conundrum; in an attempt to free the artistic team from having to operate within the constraints of the Disney brand (including what now constitutes the brand of Disney Theatrical Productions), the company's name was nowhere to be found on posters or the cover of the programme. But this protective move proved futile, as many people still attended the production on the assumption that the stage version would closely follow the cartoon and then were upset when it didn't.

Several reviewers expressed concern that this latest incarnation of *Hunchback* would have problems attracting an audience (Scheck 2015), and shortly after the end of the New Jersey run it was announced by members of the cast that *Hunchback* would not go to Broadway (Robbins 2015). Later there was news that this incarnation of the *Hunchback* would receive a cast recording (Anon. 2015b, 'Exclusive') and in mid-July 2015 Alan Menken and Stephen Schwartz made it known that the show would soon be licensed for regional and amateur theatres (Henry 2015). Some people had suspected that this exploitation of subsidiary rights and not the hope for a major New York production was the main motive behind the 2014/15 rewrite all along.[30]

Conclusion: The Shackles of Brand Awareness

In his 1996 book *The Art of The Hunchback of Notre Dame* Stephen Rebello makes the controversial claim that, were Walt Disney still alive today, he would by now resort to adapting material from the great classic authors such as Charles Dickens,[31] Mark Twain, Nathaniel Hawthorne or Ernest Hemingway (Rebello 1996: 42). Trying to justify this rather daring statement, Rebello points towards those Disney films based on other literary classics, like *Alice in Wonderland* (1951; Lewis B. Carroll), *Peter Pan* (1953; James M. Barrie) or *20,000 Leagues under the Sea* (1954; Jules Verne) as proof of Walt Disney's attraction to celebrated literary works. What Rebello fails to see is that all of his examples are based on novels or plays that are regarded as children's classics and do not include stories that are intended predominantly for adult readers.

If the complicated production history and ambivalent reception of *The Hunchback of Notre Dame* illustrates one thing, it is that it is more or less impossible to reconcile Disney and what it stands for with themes of violence, sexuality and politics or with a critical stance against traditional authorities, such as organized religion. No matter how ambitious and talented the Disney artists are – both those working for its animation unit and its theatrical branch – there remain some subjects that are too far 'out there' for them to grapple with satisfactorily. Just like Quasimodo, they are prevented from moving around freely and exploring all possibilities; instead, they are reigned in by a stern father figure, ordered to stay within the place he has designed for them, and are expected not to question his belief system, including his faith in the church and his definition of what constitutes an acceptable outer appearance and a suitable love interest.

References

Anon. (1958). 'Top Grosses of 1957.' *Variety*, 8 January, p. 30.

Anon. (2002). 'Stella-Insolvenz.' *Musicals. Das Musicalmagazin* 95: 39–40.

Anon. (2003). '*The Hunchback of Notre Dame* – On Stage and Live Action TV.' Available online: http://www.musicalschwartz.com.the-hunchback-stage. htm (accessed 21 February 2003).

Anon. (2014). '*Hunchback* La Jolla Previews.' Available online: http://www. broadwayworld.com/board/printthread.php?thread=1077691&boardid=1 (accessed 2 December 2014).

Anon. (2015a). '*The Hunchback of Notre Dame* at Paper Mill.' Available online: http://www.broadwayworld.com/board/printthread.php?thread= 1081000&boardid=1 (accessed 17 March 2015).

Anon. (2015b). 'Exclusive: *The Hunchback of Notre Dame* Cast Album in the Works.' www.broadwayworld.com, 15 May. Available online: https://www. broadwayworld.com/article/Exclusive-THE-HUNCHBACK-OF-NOTRE-DAME-Cast-Album-in-the-Works-20150515 (accessed 25 July 2015).

Ansen, D. (1996). 'A Broadway Quasimodo.' *Newsweek*, 24 June, p. 83.

Baumann, H. (1999). 'Gina, wo bist du, wenn wir dich brauchen?' *Ballett International/Tanz Aktuell* 7: 28–9.

Benezra, K. (1996). '*Hunchback* Rings up $150M Support.' *Brandweek*, 5 February, p. 4.

Billboard (n.d.). 'All-4-One Chart History'. Available online: http://www. billboard.com/artist/278662/All-4-One/chart?f=379 (accessed 25 July 2015).

Biskind, P. (1995). 'American Beauty: With *Pocahontas*, Disney Has Created a Real Love-among-the-Toons Story.' *Premiere* 7: 84–5.

Brug, M. (1999). 'Zigeunerbaron im High-Tech-Fahrstuhl.' *Die Welt*, 7 June. Available online: http://www.welt.de/print-welt/article573090/ Zigeunerbaron-im-High-Tech-Fahrstuhl.html (accessed 25 July 2015).

Burr, T. (1997). 'Saved by the Bell.' *Entertainment Weekly*, 7 March, p. 72.

Corliss, R. (1996). 'A Grand Cartoon Cathedral.' *Time*, 24 June, p. 75.

Fitzgerald, K. and J. Pollack (1996). '*Hunchback* Does a Bellyflop.' *Advertising Age*, 22 July, p. 1.

Gerlach, G. and M. Sieler (2002). 'Abgeschrieben: Zum verzweifelten Kampf der Stella-Academy-Schüler, die eigene Zukunft zu retten.' *Musicals. Das Musicalmagazin* 95: 27.

Gleiberman, O. (1996). 'Towering Achievement.' *Entertainment Weekly*, 21 June, p. 43.

Der Glöckner von Notre Dame (1999). *Die Höhepunkte der Weltpremiere im Musical Theater Berlin*. Original Cast Recording, Stella Music 547 836-2.

Harnick, L. E. (2001). 'Lost and Found in Translation: The Changing Face of Disability in the Film Adaptations of Hugo's *Notre Dame de Paris: 1482*'. In

A. Enns and C. R. Smit (eds), *Screening Disability. Essays on Cinema and Disability*. Lanham and Oxford: University Press of America, 87–95.

Henerson, E (2014). 'A Devil of a Role: Stage Veteran Patrick Page Gets Dark and Twisted in *The Hunchback of Notre Dame*.' Available online: http://www. playbill.com/news/article/a-devil-of-a-role-stage-veteran-patrick-page-gets-dark-and-twisted-in-the-hunchback-of-notre-dame-334003 (accessed 11 November 2014).

Henry, S. (2015). 'Schwartz and Menken Reveal What's Next for Disney's *The Hunchback of Notre Dame*.' Available online: http://www. broadwayworld.com/article/Schwartz-and-Menken-Reveal-Whats-Next-for-Disneys-THE-HUNCHBACK-OF-NOTRE-DAME-20150718 (accessed 18 July 2015).

IMDb (1996). 'Box Office/Business for *The Hunchback of Notre Dame* (1996).' Available online: http://www.imdb.com/title/tt0116583/business?ref_=tt_dt_ bus (accessed 19 July 2015).

Isherwood, C. (2015), 'Review: *The Hunchback of Notre Dame* at Paper Mill Playhouse.' *New York Times*, 18 March. Available online: http://www. nytimes.com/2015/03/19/theater/review-hunchback-of-notre-dame-at-paper-mill-playhouse.html?_r=0 (accessed 19 March 2015).

Jansen, W. (2008). *Cats & Co. Geschichte des Musicals im deutschsprachigen Raum*. Berlin: Henschel.

Lacroix, C. (2004). 'Images of Animated Others: The Orientalization of Disney's Cartoon Heroines from *The Little Mermaid* to *The Hunchback of Notre Dame*.' *Popular Communication* 2 (4): 213–29.

Lapine, J., A. Menken and S. Schwartz (1999). *The Hunchback of Notre Dame: Full Libretto*. Unpublished manuscript.

MusicalWorld (n.d.). 'Musical *Die Schöne und das Biest* in Stuttgart.' Available online: http://www.musical-world.de/theater/musicals-alphabetisch/s/ schoene-und-das-biest/stuttgart/ (accessed 25 July 2015).

Norden, M. F. (2013). '"You're a Surprise from Every Angle": Disability, Identity, and Otherness in *The Hunchback of Notre Dame*.' In J. Cheu (ed.), *Diversity in Disney Films: Critical Essays on Race, Ethnicity, Gender, Sexuality and Disability*. Jefferson and London: McFarland, 163–78.

Rebello, S. (1996). *The Art of The Hunchback of Notre Dame*. New York: Hyperion.

Robbins, C. (2015). 'Paper Mill's *Hunchback of Notre Dame* Will Not Transfer to Broadway. Fans Start Petition,' 6 April. Available online: http://www. broadwayworld.com/article/Paper-Mills-HUNCHBACK-OF-NOTRE-DAME-Will-Not-Transfer-to-Broadway-Fans-Start-Petition-20150406 (accessed 7 April 2015).

Rotten Tomatoes (n.d.). 'Reviews: *The Hunchback of Notre Dame* (1996).' Available online: http://www.rottentomatoes.com/m/1073037-hunchback_ of_notre_dame/ (accessed 25 July 2015).

Scheck, F. (2015). '*The Hunchback of Notre Dame*: Theatre Review.' *Hollywood*

Reporter, 16 March. Available online: http://www.hollywoodreporter.com/
print/781731 (accessed 17 March 2015).

Schuermann, K. (2003). *The German-Language Musical at the Turn of the 21st
Century*. Ann Arbor: University of Missouri Press.

Sterritt, D. (1996a). 'Disney Stands Tall with *Hunchback*.' *Christian Science
Monitor*, 21 June, p. 12.

Sterritt, D. (1996b). 'Other Adaptations of Hugo's Classic.' *Christian
Science Monitor*, 21 June. Available online: http://www.csmonitor.
com/1996/0621/062196.feat.film.2.html (accessed 4 July 2014).

Sundel, A., R. Crandall and G. Evans (1944). *The Hunchback of Notre Dame by
Victor Hugo: Classics Illustrated No. 36*. Newbury: Classic Comic Store Ltd.
(reprint 2011).

Thompson, A. (1996). 'Playing a Hunch.' *Entertainment Weekly*, 21 June.
Available online: https://groups.google.com/forum/#!topic/alt.disney.
secrets/9j97YwK4V3A (accessed 4 July 2014).

Tonkin, B. (1996). '*The Hunchback of Notre Dame*.' *New Statesman*, 12 July,
p. 40.

The Lion King: A 'Blockbuster Feline'[1] on Broadway and Beyond

Barbara Wallace Grossman

From its spectacular success as an animated film to its brilliant reimagining as a stage musical, *The Lion King* remains one of Disney's most celebrated and enduring ventures, an example of creative synergy at its best. As the highest-grossing hand-drawn animated film in history and the highest-grossing Broadway production to date, its record-shattering trajectory is impressive indeed. A January 2017 press release from Disney Theatrical Productions trumpeted the enviable accomplishments of *The Lion King*, now in its twentieth year as a stage production. Winner of more than seventy global theatrical awards, it 'continues ascendant as one of the most popular stage musicals in the world':

> Since its Broadway premiere on November 13, 1997, 24 global productions have been seen by more than 90 million people. Produced by Disney Theatrical Productions (under the direction of Thomas Schumacher), *The Lion King* is only the second show in history to generate five productions worldwide running 10 or more years. Translated into eight different languages (Japanese, German, Korean, French, Dutch, Spanish, Mandarin and Portuguese), productions of *The Lion King* can currently be seen on Broadway; London's West End; Hamburg; Tokyo; Madrid; Mexico City; Shanghai; Scheveningen and on tour across North America, for a total of nine productions running concurrently across the globe. Having played over 100 cities in 19 countries on every continent except Antarctica, *The Lion King*'s worldwide gross exceeds that of any film, Broadway show or other entertainment title in box office history.[2]

More than the award-winning film it reinterpreted, it was the exhilarating stage production envisioned and directed by Julie Taymor that made *The Lion King* an extraordinary artistic achievement as well as a commercial phenomenon. It established Disney as a formidable presence on Broadway and global stages, and demonstrated the power theatre still has to delight, awe and engage audiences of all ages. This chapter will discuss the development and unexpected success of the animated film, Disney's bold decision not only to adapt *The Lion King* as a musical for the stage, but also to entrust the project to an innovative team of artists headed by Taymor, and its stunning realization as a daring theatrical event in which risk-taking at all levels yielded boundless rewards.

Genesis of the Animated Film: From 'Bamblet' to Simba

The fourth animated feature produced by a resurgent Disney in the late 1980s and 1990s, *The Lion King* (1994) was the first not based on an existing story and reflected the studio's interest in exploring material of multicultural significance. In development at roughly the same time as *Pocahontas* (1995), it was considered the less prestigious project, and thus gave many talented young animators the opportunity to work on a major film. Originally conceived as a kind of animated *National Geographic Special* about lions in the savanna called *King of the Jungle*, it was a film without music.[3] As the creative team struggled to find a storyline, however, the project changed. 'We were intentionally trying to work in the realm of archetypes,' co-director Roger Allers recalled, explaining how the trope of a prodigal son's spiritual journey, 'coming of age' and 'taking of responsibility' emerged as the best way to depict Simba the lion cub's birth, childhood and eventual manhood.[4] With the addition of lyricist Tim Rice to the Disney fold, it became a musical.

Redolent with mythological and biblical resonance as well as echoes of Disney's *Bambi* (1942), many critics saw striking parallels to Shakespeare's *Hamlet*. As screenwriter Irene Mecchi – later co-author of the stage script – quipped, 'It was described to me as "Bambi in Africa" with *Hamlet* thrown in, so "Bamblet."'[5] The villainous Scar was first imagined as a rogue lion not associated with the pride, but when he became the king's brother the similarities to *Hamlet* were obvious. Although lines from the play were jettisoned, the evil uncle and the troubled prince, the juxtaposition of tragic and comic scenes, and the son urged by his father's spirit to 'remember' remain.

That the animals and the African landscape in the film are realistically drawn resulted from a research trip several members of the production team took to Kenya. The vibrant colours observed in the natural world inspired bold design choices, including the decision to make Pumbaa the flatulent Warthog bright red. It also reinforced major thematic elements: the idea of the 'circle of life' with its emphasis on the interconnectedness of all living things, the power of generational continuity and the importance of individual initiative.[6]

As in the three 'neo-Disney' classics preceding it – *The Little Mermaid* (1989), *Beauty and the Beast* (1991) and *Aladdin* (1992) – music plays an important role in *The Lion King*. From the first, the film is aurally and visually stunning. The opening chant as the sun rises immediately takes audiences to the African savanna. 'Nants' ngonyama bakithi baba / Here comes the lion, my people, the father of our nation,' a male voice calls in Zulu.[7] 'Sithi hu ngonyama / We hail this coming of the lion,' others respond. A rhinoceros lifts its head silhouetted against the orange sky, antelopes leap, meerkats rise up on their haunches, a leopard trots to the top of a hillock as pelicans soar over a waterfall, wildebeests file past a mist-covered mountain, and flamingos and leaping gazelles make their way to Pride Rock. As a female voice sings 'From the day we arrive on this planet,' rhythmic Zulu chanting grounds 'Circle of Life' unmistakably in Africa.

Music: A Varied 'Sonic Landscape'

Of the five Elton John/Tim Rice songs in the film, only 'Circle of Life' sounds African. Three others are more standard 'pop' fare: young Simba's jaunty 'I Just Can't Wait to Be King', irrepressible Timon and Pumbaa's joyful 'Hakuna Matata' and the romantic ballad 'Can You Feel the Love Tonight?' performed by the adult Simba and Nala, its wry comic ending courtesy of Timon, who tells Pumbaa their 'pal is doomed'. An exception to the 'pop' rule is 'Be Prepared', which the black-maned Scar delivers with chilling malevolence in the hyenas' lair. As he enlists them in his plot to kill Mufasa and Simba, vocal and visual pyrotechnics combine to create a Hellish scene, with goose-stepping hyenas marching in formation before their diabolical leader amid volcanic eruptions of green and red smoke.

As entertaining as these compositions are, it is Hans Zimmer's rich and varied score – with additional music by South African Lebo M and his chorus singing in Zulu – that renders the landscape, sets the tone and conveys emotion as brilliantly as the animators do. Interestingly, while the animators did not anthropomorphize the animals, they made them human in expression and character. For Zimmer, who said he had 'never written for talking, fuzzy animals', the key was to 'treat them as human characters with emotions'. He saw his score as creating a 'sonic landscape that these drawings can sit on and these characters can live within'.[8] 'This Land' pays lush orchestral homage to the savanna before breaking into energetic drumming and chanting. The tumultuous 'To Die For' captures the terror of the stampede in which Mufasa is trampled by a herd of computer-generated wildebeests. The music segues into Mozart's haunting 'Ave Verum' as a tearful Simba tries to revive his dead father.

In 'Under the Stars', luminous voices and instruments underscore the pivotal scene in which Nala challenges Simba to return to Pride Rock and he confronts his demons. Pacing under the night sky, he worries he is powerless to change the past as a fragment of 'Ave Verum' – a musical theme meant to evoke Mufasa – plays again. Rafiki appears and, as background chanting builds, leads Simba to a pond in which he sees his father's reflection, then his image in the night sky. Choral voices soar as Mufasa admonishes his son, 'Remember who you are.' After the vision dissipates in the gathering clouds, Rafiki urges Simba to learn from the past rather than running from it. As Simba charges toward the Pridelands, drumming and choral chanting ('Busa Simba / Rule Simba') intensify.

After evoking the devastation of the land Scar has blighted, 'King of Pride Rock' underscores the confrontations that bring the film to its suspenseful end. In the climactic clash between villain and hero, Scar tries to leap on Simba, but misjudges the distance and falls to the burning ground below. Flames engulf him as the hyenas, who know he has betrayed them, move in for the kill. Vocal and instrumental music soar as Simba ascends Pride Rock to claim his rightful place as king. With 'Busa Simba' building in volume, the land becomes green once more. Animal subjects gather in celebration of the birth of Simba and Nala's cub as the last lines of 'Circle of Life' are reprised.

The Film's Critical Reception

Following the film's release in June 1994, critical response was mixed. The *New York Times*' Janet Maslin, for example, found it 'contrived', 'derivative' and 'predictable'.[9] Chicago's Roger Ebert thought it was 'surprisingly solemn in its subject matter' and possibly 'too intense for very young children'.[10] His television partner Gene Siskel disliked the story's 'flimsiness' and called Simba 'a bore'.[11] Subsequent charges included sexism (insufficient number and development of female characters), racism (portrayal of hyenas Shenzi and Banzai as African–American and Latino because voices were provided by Whoopi Goldberg and Cheech Marin), conservatism, heterosexism, cultural appropriation, literary vandalism, aberrant sexuality, promotion of undemocratic social relations and governments, even plagiarism (of a 1960s Japanese television show called *Jungle Emperor*, known as *Kimba the White Lion* in the United States). Among the more bizarre reactions were objections from religious conservatives who claimed they saw the word 'SEX' in the night sky, and a lawsuit reputedly brought against Disney for alleged

defamation of hyena character. 'Amoral', 'dystopian', 'ahistorical' and 'inces-
tuous' are also words that have ludicrously been applied.

Most reviews of the film, however, were laudatory. More important,
the popular response was overwhelmingly positive, with ticket sales far
surpassing expectations. *The Lion King* became the highest-grossing film of
1994, making over $310 million in domestic box office sales. By the end of
December it had been screened in twenty-five countries, earning hundreds
of millions more internationally. In 1994 alone it exceeded $1 billion in total
merchandise sales and had become what Michael Eisner, then Chairman
and CEO of The Walt Disney Company, called a 'cultural phenomenon' with
a significantly greater 'end result' than anyone had anticipated.[12] At the 1995
Academy Awards ceremony the film earned Oscars for best original song
('Can You Feel the Love Tonight?') and Hans Zimmer's score. It triumphed
in the same categories at the Golden Globes, where it also won Best Motion
Picture – Comedy/Musical.

The Stage Adaptation: Not 'a Cartoon Brought to Life'

Given the film's worldwide appeal, it is not surprising that Eisner saw the
potential for a stage adaptation[13] and promising material for the company's
newest venture, Walt Disney Theatrical Productions. Formed in 1994, it
already had its first musical on Broadway, *Beauty and the Beast*, which had
opened at the Palace Theatre in April. A faithful recreation of the animated
film, the stage version had an energetic cast costumed to look as much
like their cartoon counterparts as possible, lavish production numbers and
spectacular special effects.[14] In addition, Disney Development Company
had acquired a theatre in December 1993, the dilapidated and abandoned
New Amsterdam on 42nd Street, once considered the most beautiful
playhouse in New York. Empty since 1982, it was purchased in 1992 by the
42nd Street Development Project, a group committed to restoring historic
theatres.

Eisner had been asked to play an active role in the revitalization of
the seedy area by acquiring the New Amsterdam for Disney theatrical
productions. Initially disinterested, he changed his mind after touring it
in March 1993. Once plans were finalized in July 1995 for the renovation
and long-term lease of the building, Disney hired architect Hugh Hardy, a
specialist in theatre design and restoration, to oversee what turned out to
be an eighteen-month, $36 million project (Henderson 1997: 127–32).[15] A
magnificently restored New Amsterdam Theatre made the idea of a stage
production of *The Lion King* even more attractive.

At a theatrical development meeting with colleagues from Walt Disney Feature Animation, Eisner expressed his strong interest in *The Lion King* and received a uniformly negative response. As producer Donald Hahn recalled, 'Everybody said, "You've got to be kidding. *The Lion King?* What are they gonna do, wear rubber heads and dance around?"'[16] Undeterred, Eisner made Thomas Schumacher, currently President of Disney Theatrical Group, responsible for the adaptation, telling him he just needed a brilliant idea. Schumacher's was to contact Julie Taymor, a Manhattan-based director, designer, puppeteer and 'conceptualist' he knew by reputation and whose innovative work in theatre and opera intrigued him. He understood that a literal adaptation like *Beauty and the Beast*'s would be wrong for *The Lion King*. How right he was to turn to Taymor to reimagine the story theatrically. When he asked her in 1995 to direct the stage production, he urged her to create something wholly original. Excited by the project's scope, she 'set off to devise a concept that would transform the film into a full-fledged musical' (Taymor 1997: 21).

While Broadway buzzed about the unlikely alliance between 'the corporate giant and the bohemian artist',[17] Taymor focused on developing two key elements: a script and a design concept that would serve the story without compromising her distinctive style. Shaped by several years in Indonesia and Japan, her aesthetic reflected the strong influence of Asian theatrical forms, particularly the use of masks and puppets. From Indonesian shadow and wooden rod puppetry to Japanese Bunraku, Taymor had an extensive theatrical vocabulary and moved easily between theatrical worlds. The result was an eclectic fusion that could be exhilarating. In *The Lion King* she and her creative collaborators would draw on wide-ranging theatrical styles and traditions with astonishing results.

'This isn't to be a cartoon brought to life,' Taymor insisted. 'This is an actual theatricalization of *The Lion King* as a script.'[18] For her, theatricalization involved a process of 'expansion' that began with making Simba a more complex character. She saw him as a troubled adolescent and puzzled over the best way to portray what she called his 'lost years'. Soon joined by Roger Allers and Irene Mecchi as co-authors, they devised a scene intended to give the audience insight into his confusion and guilt. It became the second act's 'Simba's Nightmare', in which he almost causes Timon's death by daring him to jump across a river teeming with crocodiles. Paralyzed by a terrifying flashback to the stampede when his friend falls into the water, Simba finally manages to rescue the drowning meerkat (Taymor 1997: 22–4).

More than this scene, which provides less insight into Simba's character than dramatic stage action, it is the one that follows that reveals his struggle to understand his destiny. Looking up at the stars, Timon and Pumbaa ask

Simba what he thinks the 'sparkly dots' are. He hesitantly replies, 'Somebody once told me the great kings of the past are up there – watching over us.'[19] When his companions find that hilarious, he leaves them to sing 'Endless Night', a moving number that was not in the film but whose melody appeared in *Rhythm of the Pridelands* (1995).

A concept album in which the film's Hans Zimmer, Lebo M, Mark Mancina and Jay Rifkin explored musical ideas they wanted to develop further, *Rhythm of the Pridelands* became an essential source of material for the stage production. It contributed five songs, all with a strong South African chorus and lyrics in African languages including Xhosa, Zulu and Tswana.[20] 'He Lives in You' became act one's 'They Live in You' in which Mufasa shares his belief in past kings who watch over Simba. Reprised as 'He Lives in You' in Act II, it is a song for Rafiki, Simba and the chorus affirming their deep faith in 'his' protective presence. 'One by One' provides spirited entr'acte expression of African pride and resilience performed by the ensemble scattered throughout the theatre. 'Busa', fragments of which appeared in the film, was incorporated into the 'Grasslands Chant' sung near the top of the show by the ensemble inventively costumed as savanna grass.[21]

What became 'Endless Night' was originally called 'Lala', a song about familial loss. Taymor wrote new lyrics, which allowed Simba to address Mufasa: 'You promised you'd be there / Whenever I needed you / Whenever I call your name / You're not anywhere / I'm trying to hold on / Just waiting to hear your voice / One word, just a word will do / To end this nightmare.' The epiphany he seeks comes from the chorus, representing voices of hope in the night. They help him understand that just as 'the night must end', 'the clouds must clear' and 'the sun will rise', his father will always be there to guide him.[22]

Taymor approached Nala similarly, convinced she had to be a more three-dimensional character. No doubt sensitive to charges that the film lacked a strong female presence, she knew she could develop Nala with greater complexity (Taymor 1997: 24). An additional scene in the second act and the moving song after it – the fifth adapted from *Rhythm of the Pridelands* – were critical to the expansion of Nala's role in the musical. First, an ugly confrontation in Scar's cave follows a new John/Rice composition, 'The Madness of King Scar', in which Scar complains he is unloved and decides he needs a queen. As soon as Nala enters, he lecherously advances. She resists, but he presses his face and body against hers until she lashes out at him. Stifling his rage, he declares she will be his 'one way or another'. With a defiant 'Never, Scar, never!' she flees as he bellows, 'You belong to me / You all belong to me.'[23]

There was an almost identical scene in an earlier version of the film. Considered too suggestive of rape, however, it was cut. Thus when the movie Nala leaves the Pridelands, she is foraging for food, not escaping from a dangerous sexual predator. Restored to the musical, it not only shows Nala's courage – along with enhancing Scar's odiousness as a character – but motivates her flight. Just before her departure, she expresses her emotions in 'Shadowland', developed from Lebo M and Hans Zimmer's 'Lea Halalela / Holy Land', itself an elaboration of a musical theme in the film. As she sets out on her journey, Nala bids farewell to the lionesses and her home. They exhort her to 'always remember [her] pride' – a word that resonates on the animal and human level – and she promises to return.

Another significant revision involved Rafiki, whom Taymor saw as a 'marvellous shaman baboon' and whose gender she changed. Male in the film, on stage Rafiki is female, a 'strong essential feminine presence' and 'force of nature' (Taymor 1997: 25–6). In addition to creating another major woman's role, this eliminated confusion about the singer of 'Circle of Life'. In the film, after Lebo M's opening call, a woman carries the song, but exactly who she is remains unclear. Now the singer is Rafiki, immediately establishing her as the story's spiritual guide.

The new numbers greatly enhanced the African content of the stage production, as did three additional compositions: Lebo M's 'The Lioness Hunt' and 'Grasslands Chants' in Act I, and Act II's 'Rafiki Mourns' by Tsidii Le Loka, the musical's original Rafiki. The film's John/Rice songs remained basically unchanged, although Timon's comic coda was dropped from 'Can You Feel the Love Tonight?' allowing the romantic focus to remain on Simba and Nala, who now had an elaborate aerial ballet. Along with 'The Madness of King Scar', Elton John and Rice contributed Zazu's patter song 'The Morning Report' and 'Chow Down', a hard rock number for hyenas Shenzi, Banzai and Ed. (Perhaps in response to criticism of the film for alleged racial stereotyping, the musical's gritty trio may sound like streetwise punks on the original Broadway cast album, but their voices have no discernible racial or ethnic identity.) The result is a powerful melding of Western and African styles, rhythms and sounds.

Taymor's fiercely non-literal approach to the stage production originated in a concept she called the 'double event', which shaped her remarkable costume, mask and puppet design. Because she considered *The Lion King* 'a human drama in animal guise', she wanted 'the human being to be an essential part of the stylization' (Taymor 1997: 30). Rather than hiding actors inside animal body suits or behind masks that obscured their faces, she insisted that human and animal – live actors and the characters they played – be visible simultaneously. The masks she sculpted captured the expression she thought represented each character's dominant trait, but audiences would also see the actor's changing face underneath. This mixture of human performer with fixed animal mask constituted a 'double event', as did the yoking of puppeteer and puppet.

Engaging the Audience: Making 'Stage Mechanics' Visible

Taymor believed this approach was the best way to engage audiences emotionally and intellectually in a participatory experience. 'Audiences relish the artifice behind theater,' she explained. 'When we see a person actually manipulating an inanimate object like a puppet and making it come alive, the duality moves us.' Convinced, moreover, that audiences were 'ready to fill in the lines' if 'given a hint or suggestion of an idea', she knew that activating their imagination was paramount. Ultimately, that was what would make her production a live, 'visceral', theatrical event, rather than simply a replication of the 'two-dimensional' film on stage (Taymor 1997: 29, 79).

In January 1996 Taymor travelled to Florida to share her ideas with Michael Eisner. When she explained the rationale for having 'stage mechanics' visible throughout the show, he understood the concept and approved its development. The next check-in with Disney would be an August workshop consisting of 'a presentation of costume sketches, prototypes of masks and puppets, and models of scene designs; a sit-down reading of the new script and music; and the staging of a few key scenes' (Taymor 1997: 45, 49). The intervening months would see a period of intense collaboration with the stellar team she had assembled, notably co-designer of puppets and masks Michael Curry, scenic designer Richard Hudson and lighting designer Donald Holder, who would use nearly 700 instruments in the show's lighting plot.[24]

For Hudson and Holder, the biggest challenge was 'to create a sense of vast panorama, an infinite landscape under a wide open sky' (Taymor 1997: 74). For Curry and Taymor, it was mask design. Originally intended to be carried in backpacks and then thrust forward like shields, masks for Mufasa and Scar depended on mechanization. When backpacks proved unwieldy, Taymor and Curry attached the mask to a harness worn as a headdress above the actor's head. Using a cable control hidden in the sleeve of his costume, the actor could move the mask forward and backward or side to side. In a vertical position, it gave the actor a more human stance. Thrust forward horizontally, it suggested a lunging animal. The surprisingly light carbon graphite masks also helped to convey character: 'majestic' for Mufasa, 'abstract angularity' for Scar (Taymor 1997: 52–3).[25] Ever eclectic, Taymor said she took her inspiration for the elaborately patterned and textured costumes both actors wore from many sources. Mufasa's collar, for example, 'is really Balinese. His bodice is very Masai. The bottom is Indonesian.'[26]

Masks for the lionesses were simpler, designed to sit on the actors' heads like 'large urns'. Young Simba and Nala wore stylized makeup, but had stationary masks resembling Roman helmets when they matured. Each hyena's carved mask was attached to a harness on the actor's chest and connected by bungee cord to the back of the costume. Part mask, part puppet, the mask could be controlled with strings attached to the actor's head. The actor could also move its jaws by removing his hand from one of the hoof-tipped 'crutches' that extended from his lower arms and placing it directly into the mask (Taymor 1997: 56, 70).

Puppets rather than masks defined the designs for Timon, Pumbaa and Zazu. For the wisecracking meerkat, it was a grinning Bunraku-inspired puppet worn and manipulated by the actor in jungle green makeup and body suit. Pumbaa was a puppet the actor wore, built to allow the audience to see the actor's body between its ribs and struts. His large head rested on the actor's front, his ears attached to the actor's shoulders, his hind legs on lines attached to the actor's legs. The actor used his arms to move the warthog's mouth and operate a long red tongue. Complete with stripes of face makeup and a spiky wig, the actor's head became Pumbaa's hair. Finally Zazu, whom Taymor envisioned as 'part British butler, part majordomo,' wore Western formal dress – tails, cravat and bowler hat – fashioned from African indigo tie-dyed fabric. The actor, whose face was painted blue and white, controlled the Zazu hornbill puppet, which perched on his head and arm, and whose mouth, eyes and wings he manipulated. Because Taymor felt strongly about 'maintaining the absolute humanity' of Rafiki, however, she chose not to give her a mask or any kind of puppet. Instead, colourful makeup suggested a baboon's face, and the actor's physical expressiveness conveyed the animal character (Taymor 1997: 64–9).

There are 200 puppets in the production, including rod puppets, shadow puppets and life-sized puppets. The largest, at thirteen feet long and nine feet wide, is the elephant, which lumbers down the orchestra aisle at the top of the show powered by four actors; the smallest is a five-inch shadow-puppet mouse at the tip of Scar's cane.[27] There also are ingenious examples of 'corporate puppetry' in which one person conveys the movement of a group like a herd of gazelles by wearing or manipulating a device carrying multiple figures. Along with exquisite costumes designed in painstaking detail, they enable the cast to portray twenty-five types of animals, birds, fish and insects, as well as savanna grass, jungle foliage and exotic flowers. As British costume and puppet supervisor Jack Galloway observed, 'It's so rare to have costumes that transcend just being costumes, that become scenery and … architectural elements on stage.'[28] The brilliance of this production is that every design element is integrated into its aesthetic, with all combining to create the unique world of the show from its opening moments. Taymor translates 'Circle of Life' into a wondrous pageant, as Hudson's giant saffron sun rises, Holder lights a glorious day, Rafiki begins to chant and animals – whose human actors are always visible – move onstage from the wings and down the aisles from the back of the auditorium.

The story may be familiar, but how Taymor and her colleagues tell it is strikingly original, using a variety of theatrical techniques, some dating back hundreds – if not thousands – of years. To show drought on the African plain, a circle of blue silk is pulled through a hole in the stage, gradually vanishing. When lionesses weep, white ribbons fall from their eyes. A sheet of billowing silk represents a waterfall. For the stampede, Hudson turned to baroque stagecraft: 'The use of rollers to simulate the oncoming wildebeest harks back to 18th-century European theater … Placing side portals one behind the other to create false perspective goes back to the scenic designs of the Italian Renaissance, but it's a very simple method of making a canyon' (Taymor 1997: 99).

The combination of human ingenuity, modern technological wizardry and presentational theatre techniques defined *The Lion King*. So did the element of risk-taking for everyone involved. Disney referred to the project as the 'big experiment', trusting Taymor's talent, but unsure of the end result. Like every other member of the creative team, except Tim Rice, she had no Broadway experience. Using puppets and masks was unconventional and possibly misguided. Taymor had no guarantee that Disney would ultimately accept her bold vision, audiences would respond to the 'double event' as she intended, or that people would recognize the work's artistic merit and not simply its commercial value. For the design and technical team, translating Taymor's daring ideas into practical terms was an ongoing challenge. For actors who had to manipulate puppets and masks, make complicated costume changes and navigate moving scenery, the expectations were daunting.

At the August 1996 workshop in a New York rehearsal studio, Taymor presented much of the new material, including Rafiki's change of gender, 'The Madness of King Scar', 'Endless Night' and 'Shadowland'. Disney executives were pleased with the script and music, but still expressed doubts about the use of puppets and masks for the principal characters. Taymor would have to prove the soundness of her concept at a 'prototype demonstration' on 10 February 1997, which she insisted take place at the New Amsterdam Theatre. In the interim, she and her colleagues had to refine the designs.

After months of work and two weeks of rehearsal, in which technical difficulties with puppets and masks persisted and actors' anxieties increased, she
staged parts of two scenes for her Disney producers. Each was done twice:
once with puppets and masks, once with actors in costumes and makeup
only. Fortunately, the demonstration allayed Disney's concerns and allowed
Taymor to forge ahead with the more 'extreme and unique' approach. Using
puppets and masks was 'the bigger risk', Eisner noted, 'but the artistic reward
promises to be bigger as well' (Taymor 1997: 126).

After the February workshop, there was 'an intensive drive toward
opening night'. Choreographer Garth Fagan worked closely with Taymor to
determine how and where dance would be most effective. He had to develop
a movement language appropriate to the show's special world so that dance
would 'look like an integral part of this community, of this *Lion King* land'. It
would include 'strong elements from Africa' and would also have 'fantastic,
unusual patterns and shapes', some of them African and others 'just magical'
(Taymor 1997: 148). Essential to the musical's expansion from screen to
stage, memorable Fagan creations include the lioness hunt, the trickster
dance in 'I Can't Wait to Be King', the ballet interlude in 'Can You Feel the
Love Tonight?' and the fight choreography for the finale.

Of the thirteen principal roles, seven were filled with actors from the
August or February workshops, with others cast subsequently. Beyond
acting, singing and dancing, Taymor wanted performers who embraced the
challenge of working with puppets. 'Rather than expressly hiring puppeteers',
she sought 'inventive actors who move well'. The twenty-seven-member
chorus had twelve dancers and fifteen singers, some of whom had been in
the February workshop. Selecting the rest was fraught because Lebo M's
demand that at least half be South African clashed with the rules of Actor's
Equity, which eventually permitted six, in addition to Lebo himself and his
wife, Nandi. Fagan's rigorous auditions soon winnowed hundreds of dancers
to the requisite number for the ensemble (Taymor 1997: 136, 138).[29]

Five weeks of rehearsal culminated in a run-through for a small audience
including Eisner, Schumacher and co-producer Peter Schneider. Then it was
on to the Orpheum Theatre in Minneapolis, Minnesota, for the show's world
premiere. Chosen perhaps because the theatre had just been refurbished for
Phantom of the Opera and was technically sophisticated enough to handle
the demands of *The Lion King*, Minneapolis was also thought to be a bit 'off
the radar' in terms of public scrutiny. It may also have been seen as a good
city in which to draw more middle-American, Disney-friendly, audiences.

The company arrived in mid-June, beginning with technical rehearsals and
preview performances. There were daily crises, from Taymor's unexpected
gallbladder surgery on the first day of tech to the elephant not fitting through

the auditorium door at the start of the show to the risks involved in staging the climactic battle between Scar and Simba at the show's close. Even the chaotic backstage area, whose 'danger' Taymor found strangely exciting, posed challenges. Unaware of the offstage drama, audiences responded enthusiastically. At the first preview on 8 July they cheered the opening animal parade so loudly that Taymor was 'stunned'. By 31 July, she felt ready to open. She called that performance, which Eisner attended and the audience punctuated with applause, 'glorious' (Taymor 1997: 167–73, 177).

The Lion King closed its Minneapolis engagement at the end of August, with the company returning to New York to prepare for Broadway. In September, after recording the cast album and finalizing additional changes, there were more demanding technical rehearsals with a new backstage crew. The production had its first New York preview on 15 October, opening at the New Amsterdam Theatre on 13 November 1997. Critical response was generally positive, with all acknowledging the production's visual splendour. Some, though, carped at other aspects, from the 'well-worn, simplistic story', banal dialogue and 'second-rate' John/Rice songs[30] to mediocre acting, 'clumsy' choreography, and tension between Taymor's vision and Disney's sensibility.[31] Extending the concept of the double event in a way she had perhaps not anticipated, Taymor noted in interviews that it was really two shows seen by two audiences. White theatregoers saw it as a primal fable; black audience members as a story about race.[32] Reductive generalizations notwithstanding, no one denied that The Lion King was an impressive artistic achievement. 'With this production', Variety observed, 'the Walt Disney Co. stages itself as a serious and ambitious contender on the legit scene.'[33]

The Lion King triumphed at awards ceremonies the following spring, notably at the 1998 'Tonys', where it won six, including choreography (Fagan), costume design (Taymor), lighting design (Holder) and scenic design (Hudson). Taymor became the first woman recognized as Best Director of a Musical, while the production itself unexpectedly won Best Musical, eclipsing Ragtime. The Lion King, moreover, was enjoying spectacular commercial success. The production, which had been budgeted at $18 million and reportedly cost almost twice as much, unleashed a stampede for tickets as unrelenting as the wildebeests on stage.

'There is Simply Nothing Else Like It'[34]

The 'big risk' continues to yield astronomical rewards for Disney and keeping its 'crown jewel' fresh is paramount. In June 2010, with Taymor's approval, ten minutes were cut from the show: its running time is now

2:30 including intermission.[35] Along with twenty-two other 'creatives', she supervises new productions around the world, often incorporating culturally specific changes and localized references to make the show more appealing to theatregoers in a particular country. Globally, nearly 1,100 people are directly employed by *The Lion King*.[36]

In the United States, where *The Lion King*'s Broadway home has been the Minskoff Theatre since 2006, there have been innovative advertising campaigns and marketing strategies as well as commendable education and outreach efforts. These include 'autism-friendly' performances with quieter music, less intense lighting, 'calming areas' and relaxed rules for audience behaviour. There are condensed versions of the show for young performers: *The Lion King JR.*, which runs for an hour, and *The Lion King KIDS*, which uses five Rafikis to tell the story in thirty minutes. Both were launched in 2015, along with *The Lion King Experience*, a multimedia curriculum for students and teachers designed to introduce a wide range of theatrical – and life – skills through the lens of the show.[37] These will make *The Lion King* accessible to people who have not yet seen the professional stage production, some of them deterred no doubt by perennially high ticket prices.

In her book's afterword, Taymor expresses gratitude to Disney for having given her 'an opportunity to experiment, take risks, and develop a piece of theatrical art ... intended to be commercial as well', noting that 'The merging of these two worlds is a rare phenomenon' (1997: 190). Rare indeed, it is emblematic of the duality that permeates the production and remains its greatest strength. *The Lion King* itself was a daring 'double event' in which radical theatre and corporate enterprise met in happy symbiosis, where trust, cooperation and seemingly limitless financial support from Disney were fundamental, and an inspired creative team drew on diverse traditions and a brilliant shared vision to make stage magic.

References

Ayres, Brenda (ed.) (2003). *The Emperor's Old Groove: Decolonizing Disney's Magic Kingdom*. New York: Peter Lang.

Bell, Elizabeth, Lynda Haas and Laura Sells (eds) (1995). *From Mouse to Mermaid: The Politics of Film, Gender, and Culture*. Bloomington and Indianapolis: Indiana University Press.

Brantley, Ben (1997). 'Cub Comes of Age: A Twice-Told Cosmic Tale.' *New York Times*, 14 November. Available online: http:www.nytimes.com/mem/theater/treview.html?pagewanted=print&res=9a01efd81738f937a257 52c1a96158260&_r=0> (accessed 30 March 2014).

Budd, Mike and Max H. Kirsch (eds) (2005). *Rethinking Disney: Private Control, Public Dimensions*. Middletown, CT: Wesleyan University Press.

Cerniglia, Ken and Aubrey Lynch II (2011). 'Embodying Animal, Racial, Theatrical, and Commercial Power in *The Lion King.' Dance Research Journal* 43: 3–9.

Disney on Broadway (2014). *The Lion King* 10-part Education Series (2009–2010). Available online: https://www.youtube.com/playlist?list=PL749105D5 0D29325E (accessed 22 July 2015).

Disney Theatrical Group (2010). *The Lion King,* New Broadway Script. Updated 12 July 2010, unpublished, courtesy of Disney Theatrical Group. Music and Lyrics by Elton John and Tim Rice. Additional Music and Lyrics by Lebo M, Mark Mancina, Jay Rifkin, Julie Taymor, Hans Zimmer. Book by Roger Allers and Irene Mecchi. Adapted from the screenplay by Irene Mecchi, Jonathan Roberts and Linda Woolverton.

Disney Theatrical Productions (2016). '*The Lion King* – Fun Facts.'

Disney Theatrical Productions Education Department (c. 2008). *The Lion King* Study Guide. Available online: www.telecharge.com/showimages/ TheLionKingStudyGuidepdf (accessed 22 July 2015).

Ebert, Roger (1994). 'The Lion King.' *Chicago Sun-Times,* 24 June. Available online: http://www.rogerebert.com/reviews/the-lion-king-1994 (accessed 15 June 2015).

Evans, Greg (1997). 'The Lion King.' *Variety,* 14 November. Available online: http://www.broadwayworld.com/reviews/The-Lion-King (accessed 31 July 2015).

Giroux, Henry A. and Grace Pollock (2010). *The Mouse That Roared: Disney and the End of Innocence.* Lanham, MD: Rowman & Littlefield.

Henderson, Mary C. (1997). *The New Amsterdam: The Biography of a Broadway Theatre.* New York: Hyperion.

The Lion King (2003). DVD 2-Disc Special Edition: Disc 1 Feature; Disc 2 Supplemental Features. Burbank, CA: Walt Disney Video.

Maslin, Janet (1994). 'The Hero Within the Child Within.' *New York Times,* 15 June. Available online: http://www.nytimes.com/movie/review?res (accessed 15 June 2015).

Miller, Scott (2007). 'Songs for a New World' in Scott Miller, *Strike Up the Band: A New History of Musical Theatre.* Portsmouth, NH: Heinemann.

Simon, John (1997). 'The Lion King.' *New York Magazine,* 15 November. Available online: http://www.broadwayworld.com/reviews/The-Lion-King (accessed 31 July 2015).

Siskel, Gene (1994). 'Entertaining "Lion King" Lacks the Flair of Disney's Best.' *Chicago Tribune,* 24 June. Available online: http://www.chicagotribune.com (accessed 15 June 2015).

Taymor, Julie with Alexis Greene (1997). *The Lion King: Pride Rock on Broadway.* New York: Hyperion.

Walt Disney Records (1994). *The Lion King Original Motion Picture Soundtrack,* 60858-2.

Walt Disney Records (1995). *Rhythm of the Pridelands,* M5V 3L4.

Walt Disney Records (1997). *The Lion King Original Broadway Cast Recording.*

Not Only on Broadway: Disney JR. and Disney KIDS Across the USA[1]

Stacy E. Wolf

The Little Mermaid on Broadway was a bust. Though the 1989 animated movie musical grossed $84 million domestically at its initial release, has since earned $211 million worldwide and spawned an entire industry of kid-sized green rubber monoflippers, glittery corsets and long red flowy Ariel wigs, the 2008 Broadway musical was panned – 'an unfocused spectacle', the *New York Times*' Ben Brantley called it – and closed after fifty previews and 685 performances (Hill 2014; Box Office Mojo 2015). After the jaw-dropping success of *Beauty and the Beast* (1994–9) and *The Lion King* (1997, and still running strong as of 2017), which not only transformed the Broadway musical but also reshaped the entire Times Square neighbourhood and the global economy of musical theatre, Disney thought the beloved *Mermaid* could not fail. And yet it did. And like everything that happens at Disney, it failed big: $20 million worth (Schumacher 2015).[2]

As soon as it was clear that *Mermaid* was going down the tubes, executives at Disney Theatrical Group (DTG) put their heads together to figure out how to salvage the product. They might have tossed the whole musical; they might have gone back to the drawing board and tried to make it into a bigger, brighter and better Broadway show; or they might have thought about a new audience for the product.

Fast forward to January 2013, the Junior Theater Festival at the Cobb Galleria Centre in Atlanta, Georgia. This annual weekend event gathers 4,200 middle school-aged kids from twenty-three states across the country who perform 15-minute excerpts from musicals they have performed at home – either in school or at a community theatre or afterschool programme. They participate in singing, dancing and acting workshops, and attend all-conference sessions with guests from Broadway shows, including cast members from *Newsies* (then on Broadway) and Alan Menken sharing stories. That year, twenty-one (of eighty-two different groups) chose to perform a number from *The Little Mermaid*, or rather, from *The Little*

Mermaid JR., a 60-minute revision and adaptation of the Broadway script.[3]
More than 400 tweens sang and danced to 'Under the Sea' that weekend in
nondescript conference hotel meeting rooms *sans* lights and set, and wearing
the requisite festival 'costume' of jeans and matching JTF logoed t-shirts.
Backed by a fully orchestrated taped accompaniment to the calypso melody,
the kids exhibited commitment and passion to rival that of Broadway's stars.[4]
These performances were just the tip of the iceberg of *The Little Mermaid*'s
reincarnation as a Disney JR. show.

Across the US, in 2013, hundreds of schools, afterschool programmes and
community theatres produced the almost new show. More than 2,000 productions were scheduled between September 2014 and December 2016, with
more to be added (Music Theatre International Shows 2016). In addition, the
licences they purchased were accompanied by a Director's Guide, containing
suggestions and production advice. Within a few short years of amateur
licensing for a reworked, kid-friendly, hour-long *Little Mermaid JR.*, Disney
had gone a distance to offset the Broadway production's loss.

The Little Mermaid's journey from Broadway to Atlanta – now performed
by sixth and seventh graders – and then across America in a new, full-
length professional production (about which more later), while the starkest
example of Disney Theatrical Group's creative savvy and economic acumen,
is only one example of a Disney show that raked in the bucks through kids'
performances. Following the example of the fast-growing catalogue of
pared-down versions of classic musicals that were developed and licensed by
Music Theatre International starting in 1994, Disney Theatricals recognized
that children would be eager to play the characters they knew from the
Disney movies they grew up with. As DTG President Thomas Schumacher
asked rhetorically, 'Who wouldn't rather play Gaston [in *Beauty in the Beast*]
than Sky Masterson [in *Guys and Dolls*]?' (Schumacher 2015).

But that's not all. Fast forward again to May 2014 to I. T. Creswell Arts
Magnet Middle School in Nashville, Tennessee. Another *Little Mermaid JR.*,
this one a lavish affair, with a gorgeously painted backdrop of 'under the
sea', brightly coloured costumes, wigs and a long, semi-transparent, glittery
piece of cloth stretched across a wide proscenium stage, representing the
watery underworld. Ariel, played by an effervescent African-American girl
in a blazingly bright red wig and sparkling mermaid costume, listened half-
heartedly to Sebastian, played an expressive white boy all in red (he's a crab),
who belted the irresistible tune. After the first verse, a troop of kids playing
sea creatures danced on to the stage, led by ten girl dancers of all races
who wore black or red halter tops and layered fabric Latin dance pants and
executed a jazz routine across the upstage and sides of the stage. Other kids
leapt on to the stage, too, and a few carried see-through umbrellas as 'jellyfish'.

Everyone sang and moved on stage at once, bringing the song to life in an explosion of colour and energy (though through the first verse, their singing was almost drowned out by children in the audience screaming about the bubbles released from the catwalk, caught by the light) (*The Little Mermaid* 2014). This delightful school performance was only one of two complete casts of *The Little Mermaid JR.* who rehearsed for four months, while many of their classmates built sets and costumes. Creswell was among the six Nashville elementary and middle schools selected that year to participate in Disney Musicals in Schools, an ambitious initiative designed to seed musical theatre programmes in underserved public schools across the US. Creswell's student population is 86 per cent black, 10 per cent white, 3 per cent Hispanic/Latino and 1 per cent Asian, and 75 per cent of the children receive free and reduced lunch (Nashville School Finder 2015). Administered locally by the Tennessee Performing Arts Center, Disney Musicals in Schools (DMIS) was created because underprivileged children lack access to 'in-school arts programs', according to Ken Cerniglia, DTG's Dramaturg and Literary Manager, and Lisa Mitchell, Senior Manager of Education and Outreach (Cerniglia and Mitchell 2014: 140); that is, it aims to benefit kids who might not have been exposed to musical theatre previously and who likely wouldn't make it to the Junior Theatre Festival extravaganza.

Disney's twenty-first-century tripartite of projects for children – licensable, kid-friendly musical theatre adaptations of Disney movies and shows, supplementary production materials and teachers'/directors' guides, and public school outreach programmes across the US – transform child consumers into producers. By participating in – that is, by *doing* musical theatre – children become active agents and effective meanings makers of musicals. They become Disney artists.

These activities bridge what might seem an impossible incongruity in Disney's philosophy and its artistic and educational practices: that this global conglomerate worth $179.5 billion, according to Forbes, and ranked eleventh of the world's Most Valuable Brands in wealth and corporate power, is also a leader in philanthropic support of the arts by way of musical theatre education across the US (*Forbes* 2015). Disney's stringent product quality control, which is only possible because of their vast resources for Research and Development (R&D) and sustained oversight, virtually guarantees success for any production anywhere in the country. Their power – both economic and cultural – also explains how they, ironically, might diversify musical theatre socioeconomically and even, perhaps, challenge Broadway's hegemonic whiteness. And Disney isn't alone. As Frank Bruni writes in the *New York Times,* by 2015 corporations surpassed lawmakers and politicians in making real social change on issues such as same sex marriage and immigration. Companies like AT&T, Marriott and Microsoft, for example, 'have produced compelling recent examples of showing greater sensitivity to diversity, social justice and the changing tide of public sentiment than lawmakers often manage to'. According to *Newsweek*, 'Inclusiveness "may not be good politics in this day of polarization and micro-targeting, but it seems to be good business"', and Bruni concludes: 'Corporations aren't always the bad guys. Sometimes the bottom line matches the common good, and they the agents of what's practical, wise and even right' (Bruni 2015). When public schools' arts funding is decimated, a corporation like Disney can step in. What might seem like contradiction between Disney's dual agendas – its capitalist commercial practices and its outreach aspirations – seem to cohabitate surprisingly comfortably in DTG's rhetoric and practices.[5]

Critiques of Disney's insatiable desire to possess the souls of children and the pocketbooks of their parents abound, as do scathing attacks on their sexist, racist and heternormative representations, on their imperialist exoticization of African (*The Lion King; The Jungle Book; Tarzan*) and Middle Eastern (*Aladdin*) cultures. In this chapter, I acknowledge these and other criticisms of the Disney Corporation, but want to look at their musical theatre ventures for and with children through a different lens. Embracing the contradictions in Disney's rhetoric and practices as well as my own ambivalence about their systematic, occasionally alarming reach and influence, I nonetheless want to explore Disney's unique musical theatre projects and their uniquely progressive – artistically, pedagogically and socioeconomically – potential.

Developing the Repertoire of the Disney JR. and Disney KIDS Catalogue

In 2004, Disney began licensing their titles, which included *High School Musical* and *Beauty and the Beast*, for amateur productions through Music Theatre International, the largest global distributor of musical theatre titles. Concurrently, they started adapting musicals for children, both 60-minute JR. versions designed for middle school-aged youth and 30-minute KIDS' scripts for elementary school-age children (Cerniglia and Mitchell 2012). By 2013, they had licensed more than 40,000 productions that featured 1.5 million student performers of Disney JR. titles *Aladdin JR., Aladdin JR. Dual Language Edition* (in English and Spanish), *Alice in Wonderland JR., Beauty and the Beast JR., High School Musical JR., High School Musical 2 JR., The Little Mermaid JR., Mulan JR., My Son Pinocchio JR.,* and *Peter Pan JR.,* and

Disney KIDS'*101 Dalmatians KIDS, Aladdin KIDS, Cinderella KIDS, The Aristocats KIDS, The Jungle Book KIDS, Sleeping Beauty KIDS* and *Winnie the Pooh KIDS* (Cerniglia and Mitchell 2014: 139; Disney Theatrical Licensing Middle and Elementary 2015).[6]

Disney Theatrical Group developed a method for creating JR. and KIDS' versions as meticulously as they produced a multimillion-dollar show on Broadway. Seeking a balance between what children need and what artists want, Ken Cerniglia, Lisa Mitchell and David Scott, Senior Manager of Theatrical Licensing, calculated how to construct a script and musical score to ensure kids' successful performances, based on their reading levels and emotional maturity at different ages (Cerniglia and Mitchell 2014: 139). They worked closely with each musical's composer, lyricist and librettist to maintain the spirit and message of the original show or live action or animated movie. Nothing was released to the public until it had been tested repeatedly through years of development: multiple table readings, workshops and pilot productions at selected schools (Cerniglia et al. 2013). Given that scripts and scores go out into the world with all of live performance's uncertainties, the education team did everything they could to ensure success – and, of course, to regulate their product.

A 60-minute Disney JR. or 30-minute Disney KIDS version differs from an adult full-length version in a number of ways.[7] First, unlike a typical musical's libretto, in which all of the sheet music appears at the end, these scripts place spoken text and sheet music with lyrics in the show's order, so that children can easily follow the play and know when they're supposed to enter, speak and sing. Second, the music is transposed to accommodate young voices and the harmonies are simpler to master. Third, the adaptations answer the practical, material demands of children's shows: they have bigger casts with flexible casting. Because teachers and directors try to involve as many children as possible and give them opportunities to shine and feel valued, they look for shows with more characters – especially individualized characters with names – more speaking parts, more opportunities for individual children to sing a lyric or dance solo and more expandable chorus parts. Finally, and crucially, JR. shows are shorter so that the musical can fit into a school day performance as well as hold young children's limited attention.

The time, effort and money dedicated to creating the JR. and KIDS versions have paid off in spades. Not only is youth adaptations' licensing a self-sustaining business, but more money returns in Broadway and touring company ticket sales. As Schumacher (2015) said, 'If you play Gaston then you want to see the show'. In this way, Disney works its way into the everyday lives of communities and schools and also allows kids to perform roles from movies they know and love.

Production Support: The Disney ShowKits

The breathtaking, coast-to-coast success of licensing Disney JR. and Disney KIDS titles makes it more than clear that kids all over America want to do musicals – that is, Disney musicals. In many communities, however, though the desire is there, the expertise and experience are not. To enable anyone to produce a musical and, again, to maintain control over the product, Disney Theatrical Group crafted ShowKits: 'step-by-step materials that will help you create your production', which are included with the licence of any JR. or KIDS title. As the website explains, 'The Director's Guide offers advice on everything from how to create a rehearsal schedule to fun games to play with your cast to help them develop characters'. It also includes a budget template and ideas for constructing simple, inexpensive costumes and sets. A choreography DVD 'provides suggestions for how to block and choreograph major musical numbers'. A karaoke-style 'Accompaniment & Guide Vocal CD' has full professional orchestral accompaniment as well as tracks with 'reference vocals': kids singing on the CD to help newbies learn their vocal parts (Disney Theatrical Licensing 2015). Like the scripts and scores, the ShowKits are carefully calibrated to deliver just enough (but not too much) information to instil confidence in teachers, directors and kids and to ensure the production's success. Every aspect of the show must be clear and accessible to children, from the young performers to the backstage crew, and to the family, neighbours and friend audiences who attend the show (Cerniglia et al. 2013).

Outreach: Disney Musicals in Schools

The scripts, scores, licensing agreements and ShowKits for *Cinderella KIDS*, *Peter Pan JR.* and all of the other titles are readily available to be purchased by anyone anywhere at any time. But what about communities where musical theatre is not a part of the academic or community landscape? In 2009, Disney Theatrical Group began to reach this population by launching a highly sophisticated, closely monitored and blazingly ambitious outreach programme to support the production of a Disney KIDS show at approximately ten underserved public elementary schools in New York City each year (Disney Musicals in Schools, Frequently Asked Questions 2015).[8] At the time, a 2009 report by the NYC-based 'Center for Arts Education' noted that 'the great majority of the city's public schools were failing to meet the minimum state requirements for arts education as set by the New York State Education Department' (Israel

2009: 3, quoted in Cerniglia and Mitchell 2014: 140). Disney Musicals in Schools was created in part to compensate for this deficiency.

The positive social, emotional and intellectual effects of participation in the arts in general and musical theatre specifically have been well documented, with more studies appearing every day. According to Lisa Mitchell's New York City-based study, participation in theatre develops 'strong self-efficacy concepts', as children gain a sense of themselves in the world and their own agency (quoted in Cerniglia and Mitchell 2014: 141).[9] Furthermore, in the 2009 report, Douglas Israel found that 'children who perform in a school musical ... are more likely to stay in school than their peers without access to the arts' (ibid.).[10] James Catterall observes that 'Students with high level of arts participation outperform "arts poor" students by virtually every measure. Since arts participation is highly correlated with socioeconomic status, which is the most significant predictor of academic performance, this comes as little surprise' (ibid.: 140–1).[11] While all children benefit from engagement with the arts, Catterall argues, those from lower socioeconomic backgrounds profit even more (ibid.: 141).

Disney Musicals in Schools' gift to participating schools consists of three parts: first, free licensing rights to one of the 30-minute Disney KIDS titles, which includes scripts and scores for the whole cast; second, the ShowKit with Director's Guide and all the other bells and whistles; and third, the semester-long presence of Disney teaching artists to work with classroom teachers to produce the show. From the start, the Disney Theatrical Group education team prioritized all three components: licensing, informational materials and people with expertise were all necessary for a school to produce its first musical. But the programme has higher aspirations. More than just produce one show, DMIS aims to seed self-sustaining musical theatre programs in schools, that is, 'to develop a culture of theater production within high-need urban elementary schools' (Cerniglia and Mitchell 2014: 140). Thus Disney decreases its support in subsequent years, which forces each school to harness local resources and find ingenious ways to sustain its production of a yearly musical. Remarkably, almost every school initially funded by DMIS has continued to produce shows.

New York City, with its intense concentration of theatrical energy, arts philanthropy and a population of students who live right next door to Broadway but had never been there, was the perfect place to launch such a programme, yet this was a blip on the screen of Disney Theatrical Group's ambitions, as they wanted to help start musical theatre programmes all over the country. In 2010, they began Nashville's programme, and by 2015 Disney Musicals in Schools had expanded to seven additional cities: the Bay Area, CA, Cleveland, OH, East Lansing, MI, Las Vegas, NV, Newark, NJ, Seattle,

WA and Orange County, CA, with new sites being added each year (Disney Musicals in Schools Find Us 2015).

Disney's wide reach and visibility across every communication platform make it the ideal – and perhaps the only – artistic enterprise that could pull off such a bold and wide-ranging initiative. Although musical theatre production is an intimate, local practice that requires on-the-ground oversight, Disney's brand is global and ubiquitous. Even children who have never seen a live play are familiar with Disney characters and have seen the animated movies on which the Disney KIDS shows are based. 'Disney is the gateway art', said Kristin Horsley of the Tennessee Performing Arts Centre (Horsley 2015). Most DMIS schools choose for their first play a musical that the kids already know, especially because many have never seen a play and don't know what theatre is (Ashby 2015a). DMIS, then, builds on pre-existing knowledge, at once benefitting kids in underserved communities and generating a future base of consumers, potential theatre goers and even possibly artists, all with loyalty to the Disney brand. More than that, this programme imagines a radically diverse musical theatre future, ethnically, racially and socioeconomically. With this project, Disney knits corporate profits into philanthropy.

TPAC: Acquiring Cultural Capital

For its first out-of-NYC venture in 2010, Disney chose Nashville and the Tennessee Performing Arts Center (TPAC) as its local partner (TPAC Disney 2015). Disney designed a 'unique blend of a commercial theater producer, nonprofit arts center, school district, and corporate charity partnering to bolster arts-education' (Cerniglia and Mitchell 2014: 141). They model a team approach with each of the various stakeholders contributing. First, Disney provides the materials as well as advice and support for the sponsoring local performing arts centre, especially in the programme's first year. 'I was calling New York every five minutes', said the extraordinarily smart and energetic Roberta Ciuffo West, Tennessee Performing Arts Center's Executive Vice President for Education & Outreach, who oversees Nashville's programme. She was only half-joking, well aware that Disney had worked out many of the kinks in New York and that the home office had clear goals and expectations for the programme (Ciuffo West 2015). Operations and oversight are the responsibility of the local performing arts centre staff, who vet and select the schools, disperse the materials, hire the teaching artists, and answer questions and support the schools from auditions through rehearsals and performance. TPAC also produces the end-of-year Student Share, a celebratory performance in which each first-year school performs one musical number from its production in the 2,472-seat Andrew Jackson Hall in downtown Nashville for family, teachers and students from other sponsored schools. This 'professional debut' adds a layer of glossiness to the hard work of doing a show, trains the students as spectators of their peers, and allows the students, teachers and families to see the larger community of DMIS participants across the city. The teachers at each school, of course, do the bulk of the work.

Once Disney selected TPAC to pilot its nationwide venture, Ciuffo West sought applications from elementary schools in the Metropolitan Nashville Public Schools, visited a number of finalist schools and, in consultation with MNPS Coordinator of Visual and Performing Arts Nola Jones, chose five schools for the programme's first year.[12] They looked for 'need and readiness': evidence that producing a musical would be impossible without DMIS's resources and that the school's administrators, teachers and staff were prepared to dedicate the enormous time and energy necessary to pull it off (Ciuffo West 2015). In addition, they sponsored schools in different neighbourhoods across the city, though all had a significant percentage of students receiving free or reduced lunch. DMIS's purpose is 'to primarily serve public-school students living at or below the federal poverty level' (Cerniglia and Mitchell 2014: 140). Amy Kramer, a fourth grade teacher at Buena Vista Enhanced Option Elementary School, said, 'Most of our students have never had any experience like this before, any performing, [any] extracurricular activities. Many of them ... aren't involved in anything after school' (Kramer 2015). In 2014–15, 1,100 students in twenty schools across Nashville participated in the programme,[13] and 43 per cent of the seventy-one elementary schools in the MNPS had applied. Ciuffo West hopes that all Nashville public schools will be funded in time (Ciuffo West 2015; MNPS 2015). A few months later, teachers from the selected schools gathered at TPAC downtown for an orientation day, which included a detailed overview of the program, budget and tech recommendations, and a display of all of the Disney KIDS materials for them to examine and, by the end of the day, choose their show to take back to their school with much excitement and anticipation.

The group of adults who collaborate on each school's production possess complementary expertise: the teaching artists have considerable musical theatre experience, while the teachers know their school, its culture and the children. DTG's Mitchell and her team designed a seventeen-week, 90-minute bi-weekly rehearsal schedule in which teaching artists – two per school who visit once a week – take the lead for the first third of the rehearsal process; then they and the team of teachers partner evenly for the second third; then the teaching artists step back and the teachers oversee the production's final rehearsals, tech, dress rehearsals and performances. Ciuffo West hires teaching artists who are 'artists first', many of whom are local professional musicians, dancers or actors (Ciuffo West 2015), and they all participate in an intensive three-day training to learn the Disney way. The school gathers a team of at least three to five teachers who volunteer to work on the show, which typically includes the school's arts specialist (every public school in Nashville has an arts specialist on staff, with expertise in music or art or theatre) and others who may or may not have any previous musical theatre experience. The teachers quickly learn the ropes of theatrical production, while the teaching artists figure out the idiosyncrasies of the school and the children. Susan Scoby, a teacher at Gower Elementary said, 'Our TAs have been wonderful and probably the most valuable they've been to us was through the audition process [when 150 children auditioned] because they had done that before.' She added that the teaching artists were also able to see performance potential in students that teachers who know the kids might miss. 'I would have never picked the boy playing Bagheera for a lead role and he's phenomenal', she said (Scoby 2015). From the other side, the teaching artists benefit from and build on the learning and behaviour practices already in place at the school. At Buena Vista, for example, the Disney musical process began as all classes do at the start of the school year, with students articulating the 'norms' – that is, the rules and expectations that they themselves propose and that all agree to follow, which included 'Be brave' (meaning don't be shy), 'Respect', 'Try our best' and 'Keep practicing at home' (Buena Vista 2015).

The adults aim to create an atmosphere that is both serious and fun, creative and disciplined. Teaching artist Ginger Newman explained that she holds a 'workshop' and plays theatre games rather than calling what they are doing 'auditions'. 'You say the word audition and they stiffen', she said (Newman 2015). During rehearsals, though, the kids learn and get accustomed to an expectation of 'professionalism', including hearing theatre terms like 'blocking' and 'house right'. When I visited Gower, teaching artist Marci Murphree gave the students a pep talk: 'This is a dress rehearsal. Bring your best stuff: your best singing, dancing', and later she told them, 'I love the way it sounds in here. It's so professional' (Gower Elementary School 2015). Later in the same day's rehearsal, drama teacher Miya Robertson coached a student, 'Use your mother's voice when she can't find you. Use your acting skills' (ibid.). Some lessons are learned the hard way. Master teacher Kathy Hull, who piloted *The Lion King KIDS* as well as Disney's accompanying elementary school curriculum,[14] told me this story:

One of my kids, he skipped a line or something and it caused someone to miss their cue. Evidently the child that missed her cue was his cousin. So she slaps him – backstage after the show was over. I put her out of the show. [I said], 'This is not right, not here, ever in any theater in the country, you would not be allowed to behave that way.' (Hull 2015)

While the production is taken on with the utmost seriousness and highest expectations of the performance's quality, every adult to whom I spoke stressed the importance of 'process over product' and the fun and growth-fulness of the children's experience above all. To be sure, every child's answer to 'What did you think about doing the Disney show?' was 'It was fun!' 'We got to learn new dances, we got to sing fun stuff', said a fourth-grade girl (Ashby 2015b). Here lies yet another contradiction in Disney's engagement with musical theatre and kids. On the one hand, every aspect of the Disney Musicals in Schools programme is designed to allow Disney to control its product. On the other, the Disney Theatrical Group home office knows that theatre is messy and each production entirely unique. Moreover, for many children, it's a steep learning curve of both performance skills and theatrical culture. The teachers at Buena Vista explained that their students knew the story and songs from the movie of *The Jungle Book*, which was their first play in 2014, but that none had ever been to the theatre or knew what a live play was.[15] They didn't know what it meant to learn lines or blocking, portray a character or wear a costume especially made for them in front of an audience. Team leader and teacher Joe Ashby found another school's (possibly illegally recorded) production on YouTube, which the teachers watched with the children before starting rehearsals, and each student followed along in his or her script. By the second year's auditions for *Aladdin KIDS*, though, the whole school had experienced *The Jungle Book KIDS* and had seen their first play (Buena Vista Enhanced Option Elementary 2015). This is how cultural capital is acquired.

Nashville: The Transformative Experience of DMIS

Each school in Nashville navigates a balance among generating enthusiasm for the play, encouraging many students' participation and dealing with inevitable attrition. Teachers at every school I visited shared stories about the number of kids who auditioned compared to how many performed in the end. In the first year, they might lose half the cast along the way as kids learn that being in a play is hard work. It's not unusual for a role to be re-cast during the rehearsal process, even a day before the performance, as

I witnessed at one school. A nine-year-old boy playing a leading role had missed a number of rehearsals and didn't know the choreography. He was unceremoniously replaced by a girl who knew the part well. 'You should be relieved', a teacher told the crying boy. 'You looked like you didn't know what you were doing.' Within 10 minutes, the same boy was hamming it up in the chorus (Gower 2015). At another school 75 per cent of the population is transient (many of them homeless), which means that three-quarters of the students who start the school year are gone by the spring, and around 270 children enter the school mid-year. To manage the school's demographics, the adult team casts the leading roles with students who are likely to still be there in May, and welcomes all students to rehearse for as long as they attend the school, or join the cast or crew whenever they arrive (Ashby 2015a). In the Nashville schools, no casts have had fewer than thirty students, and some schools feature more than 100 performers, plus fifty more helping backstage. From the moment the show is announced to the final curtain call and enthusiastic applause, the adults underline team work and the importance of each and every character, of each and every student's contribution, which is supported by the numerous named characters in the Disney KIDS scripts.

Some Nashville schools also adapt Disney's materials to the particularities of their population and resources. For example, many of the students at Harris-Hillman Special Education School are in wheelchairs or are non-communicative, so for their 2014 production of *The Aristocats KIDS*, their caregivers, tutors or teachers stood behind and manoeuvred wheelchairs, moved their limbs or sang their parts. 'They respond tremendously during rehearsal. I see a difference in the kids', observed teacher Stacy Subero, and teaching artist Ginger Newman enthused, 'I've never encountered fearlessness like I have here ... that's the one quality that we can't teach. And to walk into an environment and it's right there? It's been unbelievable' (Disney Musicals in Schools | Nashville: Harris-Hillman Special Education School 2014). Though licensing forbids changing lines, DMIS allows roles to be cast in any way and for the chorus to be infinitely expanded. At Wright Middle Prep's 2015 production of *Alice in Wonderland JR.*, three differently sized girls played Alice at the different stages of her adventure, and three other girls were cast as the Cheshire Cat(s), with the lines divided among them, as they formed a kind of harmonious girl group.[16] At Buena Vista, they incorporated a step routine to the choreography of 'Prince Ali', as Joe Ashby explained, so they could 'bring some of the things they like to do into the world of Agrabah' (Ashby 2015a). In the end, all theatre, even when it's produced and overseen by a huge multi-national corporation, is local.

Teaching artists, who, as visitors, work with the children once a week over the course of four months, observe remarkable changes, especially in the kids' confidence, expressiveness and ability to articulate their ideas clearly. Tonya Pewitt, a Nashville teaching artist at Wright Middle School, explained, 'The students are also getting to use their imagination. And instead of sitting at home they are at school being active. This is also giving them a way to express themselves through art, singing and dancing. If they are struggling at home this is a great outlet for them' (Pewitt 2015).

The teachers who see the children every day in class note academic and behavioural improvement. For the children, 'doing Disney' is a privilege. Natalie Affinito, a maths teacher who was Creswell's *The Little Mermaid JR.*'s musical director, explained,

> I get to see the kids in two very different realms: in the math classroom and in rehearsal … These two worlds are almost colliding now … you start to see some of these students open up more in the classroom, and you start to see the kids that maybe were a little bit too rowdy in the classroom, now they have an outlet to do that, they start to become more focused in the classroom … You can see a real balance with the students and it's just been such a joy to witness. (Disney Musicals in Schools | Nashville: I. T. Creswell Arts Magnet Middle School 2014)

Kathy Hull said of Hull-Jackson Montessori Magnet School's 2012 production of *Aladdin KIDS*, 'They are so proud of themselves. And I think that they have come to realize their potential. They never really realized that they could pull off something like this' (Disney Musicals in Schools | Nashville: Hull-Jackson Montessori Maget School 2012). Sara Cottrill-Carlo, from Lakeview Elementary Design Center, said about their production of *Aladdin KIDS* in 2014,

> I've seen them feel connected to the school in a way that I don't think they did before. And I think some that maybe whose grades aren't fantastic, who aren't getting a lot of praise in other ways, they're getting it here, and so they're having, you know, a higher sense of self-worth because they're part of something bigger. (Disney Musicals in Schools | Nashville: Lakeview Elementary Design Center 2014)

Every teacher told stories of specific children who 'blossomed' during the production. A teacher at Gower said of one very quiet and shy boy, 'This has just been the first time he has been able to shine. He's in the fourth grade now and I've never seen him do what he's doing now' (Gower Elementary School 2015).

The experience of doing a Disney musical is profoundly transformative for virtually every child. A fourth-grade boy who performed in *Aladdin KIDS* said, 'I stopped being afraid. I'm thinking to myself, Yea, this is going to be awesome!' (Disney Musicals in Schools | Nashville: Lakeview Elementary Design Center 2014). A third-grade girl from Buena Vista's *Aladdin KIDS* said that she enjoyed 'the costumes and how we worked together to do it' (Ashby 2015b). Teaching artist Tonya Pewitt recounted a conversation with the mother of a boy who was a last-minute replacement for a leading role and was 'extremely nervous':

> I told her how much I think he has grown and how much more outgoing he has become. She told me, 'I can see a difference too, and I am so thankful that he is getting to do this. I know he has it in him, but I don't have the money to put him in anything like this. I am so grateful the school is offering something like this'. (Pewitt 2015)

One Creswell student, a boy who worked on *The Little Mermaid JR.*, exclaimed, 'It's amazing, just the magic of theatre, how you can take a book and' – he raised his arms in a kind of invocation – 'just bring it to life and …' – he paused – 'it's magical!' (Disney Musicals in Schools | Nashville: I. T. Creswell Arts Magnet Middle School 2014).

While the performance is a big occasion for every school, some have been able to draw in parents or other members of the neighbourhood to help out. Kathy Hull, for example, schedules several Saturday afternoons for families to come to the school to help. She sets up different stations, and parents and children make masks, sew costumes and paint flats. Even though parents might belong to opposing local gangs, they put their differences aside to work on the show (Hull 2015). In this way, Disney Musicals in Schools fosters a collaboration between the school and the community. The production adapts to the community's norms, and families and neighbours are more likely to get involved because they recognize the Disney brand.

The Student Share, which is the 'professional debut' culmination of a school's first year in the programme, reproduces the contradiction between process and product that weaves through the entire Disney Musicals in Schools enterprise. Students look forward to performing on the big performing arts centre's stage in their city, and the teachers and teaching artists polish one musical number that inevitably highlights their skill as directors as well as the kids' talents (as much as no one wants to talk about talent) and perseverance. Nashville's 2015 Student Share was hosted by rising star country music duo, Maddie and Tae, and 300 children from six schools performed (TPAC Spotlight 2015).

New York's 2015 Student Share was held at the New Amsterdam Theatre, where *Aladdin* was playing at 97 per cent capacity, having grossed $1.5 million that week (Broadway World Grosses 2015). NYC's Student Share was an expertly managed affair, with hundreds of kids, their teachers, family members and friends, and invited guests from Disney, MTI, the New York City Department of Education and other stakeholders. Hosted by a Broadway performer – Bonita Hamilton, who played Shenzi in *The Lion King* – the afternoon event featured each first year DMIS school performing a musical number from their show, punctuated with patter from the host and a beautifully produced, tear-jerking video about the programme and its effects all over the country. Each group was introduced by two teachers and that school's teaching artists, who testified to the impact of the show on the students and the school.

From Thomas Schumacher, who opened and closed the event, through the host and the video, to the adults' introductions to their school's performance, 'You're making your Broadway debut' was the mantra. This showcase takes the students and their performances out of the local context and into the theatre district, connecting what they've been doing with the larger world of Broadway. When kids enter the theatre, they're overwhelmed. 'Are you serious?!' exclaimed one girl in a bright yellow flower costume as she looked up and around the Smith Centre, the location of Las Vegas' Student Share. 'This stage is so big!' said a boy in a cap with raccoon ears (The Smith Centre's Disney Musicals In Schools 2015). If rehearsals at school emphasize good and responsible behaviour, expressiveness and cooperation, the Student Share opens up the possibility of a future as a Broadway star.

Conclusions

Seeing fifteen different student groups at the each of the several Student Share performances that I attended allowed me to understand more clearly how teachers and teaching artists are able to wrangle eighty ten-year-olds and make a performance that is not only coherent but also charming and engaging for the audience. The general choreographic template was unified, simple movements for the very large chorus and basic blocking for the featured characters. A few schools had more complex choreography, such as two different groups doing different movements all at once, or a gesture that was passed down the line. The featured performers tended to be children with bold expressiveness and undeniable charisma on stage – kids of all sizes and shapes and races and personality types – who had all mastered the skill of seeming to speak to their scene partner while remaining physically open to the audience. Gower Elementary's production of *The Jungle Book*, whose dress rehearsal I observed, had two sets of risers on the floors in front of the stage, on which all the children sat, in full view of the audience, when they were 'offstage'. The show, as most KIDS' scripts, has many ensemble numbers, and the kids gestured or stood to perform simple, unified choreography from the risers. For other numbers, they came down off the risers on to the cafeteria floor to dance in the big group songs. In this way, the whole cast was involved during the entire 30 minutes of the musical, and the ensemble performed as observers of the action, as audience members when they weren't singing or dancing. The show – as the numbers repeated in the Student Share – was conceived to make everyone look good, and it did.

Disney Musicals in Schools has been astonishingly successful so far, balancing 'quality control' of the brand with the idiosyncrasies of each locale. Each performing arts centre operates under its city's structures and rules, each school system differs, each arts' scene differs. 'We were surprised and delighted to see how much each city's DMIS program takes on its own local flavour,' said Mitchell. 'In Nashville, many of the teaching artists are musicians, so the music is fantastic; Seattle has a kind of cool grunge feel; and in Las Vegas, the kids are doing complex, undulating choreography since there are so many dancers and many of the teaching artists have been performers in Cirque du Soleil style shows' (Mitchell 2015). Almost all of the participating schools have continued to do musicals, though some performing arts centres have elected to supplement Disney's decreasing support. Cities are added each year with ever expansive plans, but Disney's national ambitions for this inspirational and aspirational project are the polar opposite of standardized testing. At the same time, what are the bigger social, economic and theatrical implications of this programme? At once generously philanthropic and also colonizing – they only do Disney musicals, after all – Disney Musicals in Schools advertises the company, glossy with generosity and good will. It's clear that Disney Musicals in Schools is working on a grassroots level. Will these plays change the children later in their lives? Will these children change theatre? Only time will tell.

In addition, the gender stereotypes that prevail in many Disney products haunt these shows too. Even in elementary schools, more girls than boys participate in theatre. Many of the shows that were first developed as KIDS' vehicles, including *The Jungle Book*, *101 Dalmatians* and *Aristocats*, feature many characters that aren't explicitly gendered. But other titles, like *Sleeping Beauty*, *Cinderella* and the more recently released *Aladdin* and *The Lion King* have stories that not only rely fundamentally on gendered roles but also track a heterosexual romance.[17] The promise of Disney musicals' progressive political potential lies in part in the flexibility of gender in casting, especially because the newer and soon-to-be more popular titles star male characters. Will elementary schools in far-flung locations be brave enough to cast a girl as Aladdin? Several teachers at Gower told me that they were happy to be doing *The Jungle Book KIDS* because 'at least it doesn't have princesses', one said. 'Or a girl being saved by a man,' said another (Gower Elementary 2015).

In terms of race, though, this programme is undeniably and impressively progressive. The racial population of the Nashville DMIS schools – and this is the case for all of the Disney Musical in Schools cities – leans heavily towards students of colour and so ensures multi-racial and 'colour-blind' casting, dominated by kids of colour. Though critics may fret over the urban stereotype of the hyenas in *The Lion King*, such a view is irrelevant in this context, where every character in every musical is likely to be played a child of colour: a refreshing and moving vision of the twenty-first-century musical theatre stage.[18] From licensing to developing supplementary materials to creating a national philanthropic musical theatre programme, Disney Theatrical Group has gradually expanded from corporation to church, from content to method, from providing product that is already desired to creating desire by introducing musical theatre to an ever more diverse population.

As for *The Little Mermaid*, it didn't return to Broadway, but was success-fully altered and revised by director Glenn Casale for a Dutch production in 2012, which he reworked again at the Paper Mill Playhouse in New Jersey, followed by a three-city 'mini-tour' and a 2014 acclaimed production at the North Shore Music Theater in Beverly, MA (Hill 2014). The now frequently produced (by both professionals and amateurs), licensable script is new and improved, thanks to the alterations instigated by the JR. adaptation. But I doubt if any production will be as engaging or impressive as the one at I. T. Creswell Arts Magnet Middle School.

References

Ashby, J. (2015a). Personal communication, 7 May.
Ashby, J. (2015b). Personal communication, 29 May.
Box Office Mojo (2015). Available online: http://www.boxofficemojo.com/movies/?page=releases&id=littlemermaid.htm (accessed 8 June 2015).
Broadway World Grosses (2015). Available online: https://www.broadwayworld.com/grosses.cfm (accessed 14 August 2015).
Bruni, F. (2015). 'The Sunny Side of Greed.' *New York Times*, 1 July: A29.
Buena Vista (2015). Personal communication, 7 May.

Byena Vista Enhanced option Elementary (2015). Personal communication, 7 May.

Cerniglia, K. and L. Mitchell (2012). Personal communication, 28 September.

Cerniglia, K. and L. Mitchell (2014). 'The Business of Children in Disney's Theater'. In G. Arrighi and V. Emeljanow (eds), *Entertaining Children: The Participation of Youth in the Entertainment Industry*. London: Palgrave Macmillan.

Cerniglia, K., L. Mitchell and D. Scott (2013). Personal communication, 15 March.

Ciuffo West, R. (2015) Personal communication, 6 May.

Disney Musicals in Schools (2015). Available online: http://disneymusicalsinschools.com/about (accessed 5 June 2015).

Disney Musicals in Schools (2015). Find Us. Available online: http://disneymusicalsinschools.com/find-us (accessed 17 August 2015).

Disney Musicals in Schools (2015). Frequently Asked Questions. Available online: http://disneymusicalsinschools.com/about/faqs (accessed 19 July 2015).

Disney Musicals in Schools | Nashville: Harris-Hillman Special Education School (2014). Available online: https://www.youtube.com/watch?v=eRrnPK ZNTxs&feature=youtu.be (accessed 8 June 2015).

Disney Musicals in Schools | Nashville: Hull-Jackson Montessori Magnet School (2012). Available online: https://www.youtube.com/watch?v=Bz-1XBL4L4g (accessed 11 August 2015).

Disney Musicals in Schools | Nashville: I. T. Creswell Arts Magnet Middle School (2014). Available online: https://www.youtube.com/watch?v=ijmmd4 DluPo&feature=youtu.be (accessed 11 August 2015).

Disney Musicals in Schools | Nashville: Lakeview Elementary Design Center (2014). Available online: https://www.youtube.com/watch?v=0Hbv0zU_RSU (accessed 11 August 2015).

Disney Theatrical Licensing (2015). Available online: http://www.disneytheatricallicensing.com/addmagic (accessed 5 June 2015).

Disney Theatrical Licensing Elementary (2015). Available online: http://disneytheatricallicensing.com/elementary (accessed 13 August 2015).

Disney Theatrical Licensing Middle (2015). Available online: http://disneytheatricallicensing.com/middle (accessed 13 August 2015).

Fiske, Edward B. (ed.) (1999). *Champions of Change: The Impact of the Arts on Learning*. Washington, DC: Arts Education Partnership.

Forbes (2015). 'The World's Biggest Public Companies'. Available online: http://www.forbes.com/companies/walt-disney/ (accessed 8 June 2015).

Gower Elementary School (2015). Personal observation, 6 May.

Hill, J. (2014), 'How Glenn Casale Helped *The Little Mermaid* Find Her Feet After This Disney Stage Show Stumbled on Broadway'. *Huffington Post Blog*, 23 July. Available online: http://www.huffingtonpost.com/jim-hill/how-glenn-casale-helped-t_b_5612802.html (accessed 9 August 2015).

Horsley, K. (2015). Personal communications, 5 May.

Hull, K. (2015). Personal communication, 6 May.

Israel, D. (2009). 'Staying in School, Arts Education and New York City High School Graduation Rates.' Report. New York: The Center for Arts Education, 3.

Kramer, A. (2015). Personal communication, 7 May.

The Little Mermaid (2014). DVD. I. T. Creswell Middle School, Nashville, TN.

Metro Nashville Public Schools (2016). Available online: http://www.mnps.org/dynimg/_HLAAA_/docid/0x7AC106B6F3B9D054/2/Facts201415_web.pdf (accessed 11 August 2015).

Mitchell, L. (2015). Personal communication, 2 June.

Music Theatre International Shows (2016). Available online: http://www.mtishows.com/show_detail.asp?showid=000378 (accessed 31 December 2016).

Nashville School Finder (2015). Available online: http://nashvilleschoolfinder.org/school/isaiah-t-creswell-middle-arts-magnet/ (accessed 11 August 2015).

Newman, G. (2015). Personal communivations, 7 May.

Pewitt, T. (2015). Personal communication, 22 May.

Schumacher, T. (2015). 'Disney and Broadway Musicals.' Lecture in Gender and Musicals Class at Princeton University, 7 April.

Scoby, S. (2015). Personal communication, 6 May.

Smith Center's Disney Musicals In Schools (2015). Available online: https://www.youtube.com/watch?v=0fXSMyaLxwQ (accessed 14 August 2015).

Spotlight (2015). Available online: http://www.tpac.org/spotlight/country-duo-maddie-tae-to-host-disney-musicals-in-schools-student-share-on-may-14-at-tpac/ (accessed 19 July 2015).

Tams-Witmark (2015). Available online: http://www.tamswitmark.com/about/ (accessed 9 June 2015).

TPAC Disney (2015). Available online: http://www.tpac.org/disney/ (accessed 9 August 2015).

Part Three

Disney Musicals:
Gender and Race

Dancing toward Masculinity:
Newsies, Gender and Desire

Aaron C. Thomas

As the story goes, the 1992 film *Newsies*, directed by Kenny Ortega and starring Christian Bale, was an attempt by Disney to revitalize the live-action movie-musical genre with a story based on real events from 1899. Impoverished orphan children selling newspapers in New York City went on strike when the price of the papers they were selling was raised by media moguls William Randolph Hearst and Joseph Pulitzer during the Spanish–American War. The boys sing, dance and fight for organized labour, finally prevailing over the greed of their employers. *Newsies* was a resounding flop on the big screen – the *New York Times'* Janet Maslin called it 'joyless', 'pointless' and 'bungled' (1992: C17) – but the picture gained enormous popularity on the expanding Disney channel, which needed content it could air, and then later on home video, becoming a kind of cult classic.[1] Nearly twenty years later, the movie was crafted into a stage musical by book writer Harvey Fierstein, original composer Alan Menken and original lyricist Jack Feldman. Directed by Jeff Calhoun, *Newsies* premiered at Paper Mill Playhouse in New Jersey. The production team claims that, fearing a repeat of the movie's flop, they were not planning for the show to go to Broadway. But to Broadway it went: *Newsies the Musical* had its first preview on 15 March 2012 and ran until August 2014, clocking over 1,000 performances at the Nederlander Theatre on West 41st Street. The show was nominated for eight Tony awards and six Drama Desk awards, winning at both ceremonies in the categories of best choreography and best score.

A family-oriented show (almost all reviews of *Newsies* remark on this), perhaps the most notable thing about the cast of *Newsies* is the number of men it contains. There are two significant female characters in the show, young reporter Katherine Plumber and wise chanteuse Medda Larkin. The cast also includes two other women, and women play nuns and other ensemble roles. The entirety of the rest of the cast is male. But if its overwhelming maleness is what immediately strikes one about *Newsies*, what is most memorable about the show is its dancing.

The young men in the show – most spectacularly in the number 'Seize the Day' – outdo themselves, performing extraordinary feats of terpsichorean athleticism. In the first important review of *Newsies* at Paper Mill, the *New York Times'* David Rooney was delighted by the company's 'spring-loaded backflips, airborne spins, rambunctious kicks and balletic pivots', noting the 'irrepressible physicality' of 'the athletic ensemble' (2011: C5). Just before the show opened on Broadway the *New York Post* reported that during previews 'there were three midshow standing ovations, triggered in each case by Christopher Gattelli's buoyant choreography' (Riedel 2012: 36). In the *Daily News*, Joe Dziemianowicz praised the fact that 'Gattelli's awesome athletic choreography never quits. He keeps the young dancers flipping, tapping and twirling across the urban landscape' (2012: 50). More descriptively, perhaps, Wayman Wong described the 'athletic and dynamic dances' as 'pay[ing] homage to [Kenny] Ortega, Michael Kidd and Gene Kelly' (2011: 13). The *Times'* Ben Brantley, who was decidedly less charmed by *Newsies*, compared the dancing young men to 'toddlers on a sugar high at a birthday party', but his review still focused on the dancers' energy and athleticism: 'they keep coming at us in full-speed-ahead phalanxes, fortified by every step in a Broadway-by-the-numbers dance book. There are back flips, cartwheels, somersaults and kick lines galore, not to mention enough pirouettes to fill a whole season of *Swan Lake*' (2012: C1). There will be more to say later about the excess Brantley describes, but for now I want simply to note the way critics, almost without exception, describe Gattelli's choreography as energetic, athletic and most importantly possessing a kind of stamina or relentlessness.

Gattelli won both the Tony award and the Drama Desk award for his choreography, and since then the 'Seize the Day' dance number has become *Newsies'* calling card: the chorus of dancing newsies made rousing appearances on television, demonstrating Gattelli's athletic choreography not only on the broadcast of the Tony awards but also on the daytime talk show *The View* and the primetime variety programme *Dancing with the Stars*. Further, Disney's education and outreach team taught the 'Seize the Day' choreography to visiting groups of adolescents. These visits from schools proved extraordinarily popular: as the programme's director Lisa Mitchell notes, 'We taught twice as many kids *Newsies* in half a year as we did for *Mary Poppins* and *The Lion King* combined for all of 2012' (in Cerniglia 2013: 129). As part of a fitness programme called '*Newsies* Get up and Go!' Gattelli and dancers Jacob Guzman and Michael Fatica even appeared in an instructional video on YouTube, teaching a version of the 'Seize the Day' choreography intended to 'encourage active lifestyles through dance'. This video was released as a part of First Lady Michelle Obama's 'Let's Move' campaign, an initiative designed to combat childhood obesity and promote children's health. The choreography for the show's hit song was modified specifically for children between twelve and eighteen.

It makes sense that the *Newsies* publicity team would lead with dance. Many of the artistic contributors to the show refer to dance as the reason they connected with the original 1992 film. Lyricist Jack Feldman has said:

> nothing was as moving to me as the conversations I had with a number of the young actors who told me that it was the movie of *Newsies* that gave them the courage to go to dance class – a socially risky and possibly dangerous decision for a boy even today – and dare to dream of a career in the arts. (in Cerniglia 2013: 45)

Casting director Justin Huff adds that the movie

> challenged my belief that musicals weren't cool. Finall[y] there was something that allowed me to believe that cool guys do musicals. Christian Bale's rough-and-tumble Jack Kelly [...] gave permission for boys like me to follow their dreams of performing. (in Cerniglia 2013: 36)

Associate director Ricky Hinds notes that even though he had already decided upon a career in musical theatre at age eleven 'it wasn't until [he] saw those newsboys dancing their hearts out that [he] realized it was okay to be a boy in the performing arts' (in Cerniglia 2013: 148). Gattelli's own story mirrors these: 'I remember sitting in the movie theater and being blown away seeing that many guys my age dancing like that. [...] I just remember sitting there and being so inspired. I saw that it was possible to be a guy and be able to dance like that' (in Cerniglia 2013: 34). The dancing male body, in other words, was a figure with whom many of *Newsies*' contributing artists identified when they were young men. The athletic, rebellious newsboy who fought for his rights, joined a union and stood up to capitalist greed while also singing and dancing was a figure not merely of inspiration but of identity, reassurance and desire. The men describe seeing the film, recognizing themselves as identical in many ways to the dancing young men, and subsequently feeling more comfortable, more confident about their own desires to sing and dance.

Disney's *Newsies* is intriguing for many reasons, but I want to focus here on the way that the musical aims for this identification with young men and boys. I am less interested in the show's apparent messages of labour-solidarity and generational struggle than I am in the ways that Gattelli's choreography and Fierstein's book attempt to recreate an identificatory experience with maleness. I want to argue that the *Newsies* version of maleness is a reinvented one, a maleness that expands in order to include the chorus boy teased by his schoolmates for preferring the athleticism of dance to the fancy footwork and fluidity of football and basketball, a maleness that welcomes the musical theatre kid into its fold. This chapter will examine the new masculinity offered by the men who created *Newsies*. It is my argument that the show realigns maleness in relation to three other figures from the turn of the twentieth century when *Newsies* is set: the child, the woman and the fairy. Understanding that *Newsies* is aimed chiefly at families and given its extraordinary popularity, an analysis of the way it imagines or reimagines a turn-of-the-twentieth-century masculinity is crucial to thinking about how the show works in today's society and what effects it will be able to have on its twenty-first-century audiences and in the future.

Children of the City: Boyhood and Masculinity

In *The Male Dancer*, Ramsay Burt's important foray into discussions of masculinity in dance, one finds a curious axis of comparison: although Burt describes an interest in the 'male dancer', his text is 'primarily concerned [...] with images of men in twentieth-century theatre dance' (1995: 2). The book finds itself describing men and masculinity in contrast, in the first place, to women and, later in the book, to gay men. What Burt most conspicuously leaves out of his discussion are male dancers who are *not* men. In fact, Burt consistently describes masculinity as though it is only legible when contrasted with femininity. He also invariably conflates male homosexuality with femininity; there is no gay male masculinity in *The Male Dancer* (see 104, 110, 127). Burt avoids altogether an entirely different yet common axis along which men describe their own maleness: boyhood. As Michael Kimmel argues in his discussion of US American masculinity in the eighteenth century, 'Being a man meant also not being a boy. A man was independent, self-controlled, responsible; a boy was dependent, irresponsible, and lacked control' (2006: 14). As Kimmel makes clear, definitions of masculinity and manhood would shift numerous times over the ensuing centuries, but being a man never only means not being a woman; it also means not being a boy (among other things). Masculinity need not only contrast with femininity; it is often described in contrast to juvenility.

The most significant feature of New York's newsboys in contemporary discussions of labour, poverty and criminality was the fact of their minority. Jacob Riis's famous exposés *How the Other Half Lives* (1890) and *The Children of the Poor* (1892) describe abandoned, impoverished adolescents, fending for themselves on the streets, and often sleeping in alleyways, huddled together for warmth. He reports that 'Three-fourths of the young men called on to plead to generally petty offences in the courts are under twenty years of age, poorly clad, and without means' (2010: 51). The street urchin, Riis says, 'is as much an institution in New York as Newspaper Row, to which he gravitates naturally', and Riis feelingly describes the typical child:

> Crowded out of the tenements to shift for himself, and quite ready to do it, he meets [on Newspaper Row] the host of adventurous runaways from every State in the Union and from across the sea, whom New York attracts with a queer fascination, as it attracts the older emigrants from all parts of the world. (111)

Riis's photographs of these boys capture children as young as five years old clutching piles of newspapers and hawking them on the street. Some of the boys are older, a few are teenaged, but they are quite obviously children, and there are thousands of them.

Jack Kelly, the main character in *Newsies the Musical,* is seventeen years old ('trapped where there ain't no future, / even at seventeen', he sings) and he is surrounded by boys of indeterminate age whom the musical asks us to assume are Jack's juniors. He refers to the other newsboys as 'kids' after the violent crackdown in Newsies Square; Katherine and Davey, too, both refer to the young men as 'kids', and Katherine titles her article about the strike 'The Children's Crusade' (see Fierstein 2012: 74, 53, 72, 90). *Newsies* is insistent about its characters' youth. The show's educational packet, which is aimed at student groups visiting the show, features photographs by contemporary reformer Lewis Hine of children who are obviously under the age of ten, and under the heading 'Child Labor!' the packet defines *newsie* as

> a term for a *child* who sold newspapers on the streets at the turn of the century. The newsies of New York City were popularly admired as 'little merchants', for, unlike *children* working for a company in factories, the newsboys were seen as business people. (Disney Theatrical Group Education Department 2012: 21)

Critics writing about *Newsies,* too, take the characters' minority for granted. Nearly all reviews of the musical compare the show to either *Annie* or *Oliver!* and, more often than not, to both of them.[2] *Oliver!* and *Annie* are both musicals about large numbers of scruffy, scrappy, orphaned children, but it is worth noting that these shows are also usually performed by child-actors.

Newsies, however, is not performed by boys. The child-actors employed by the show at any given time were alternates for the role of Les, Davey's ten-year-old brother; the other actors were seventeen or older. Although

Christian Bale, for example, was seventeen when he played Jack Kelly in the 1992 film, Jeremy Jordan, who originated the role onstage and later became famous on the NBC series *Smash* (2012–13), was nearly twenty-seven when the show premiered in 2011. Ben Fankhauser, who played Davey (age seventeen in the script), was a relatively young twenty-one during the Paper Mill run, but Andrew-Keenan Bolger, who played Crutchie (age fifteen), was twenty-six. In its Paper Mill and Broadway runs *Newsies* was almost uniformly performed by adults in their twenties.[3]

Popular criticism almost uniformly ignored this age discrepancy. In *Variety*, after the requisite mentions of *Oliver!* and *Annie*, Steven Suskin described the choreography as '16 boys jumping, bounding and comporting themselves like a gang of Jets on a West Side playground' (2012: 23),[4] and Elisabeth Vincentelli in the *New York Post* said that the newsies are 'so adorable, you want to pinch their cheeks and give them whatever they want' (2012: 44). The term *newsboys* might seem natural enough when referring to the characters, of course, but pinching cheeks and boys on playgrounds? The show unabashedly treats these adult men as objects of desire. The newsies are even introduced in the bathroom at the top of 'Carrying the Banner': two shirtless newsies enter first, and then another group comes onstage in undershirts, arms exposed, biceps bulging. These are 'boys' who apparently also find time to hit the gym.

If Disney Theatricals and popular newsmedia were invested in referring to the adult male actors as kids or boys, they simultaneously laid no small stress on Jeremy Jordan's masculinity and power in the lead role of Jack Kelly. Chris Montan, Disney Theatricals' executive music producer, was glad 'to have a guy like Jeremy, who could be masculine in the part and still sing a lot of numbers. It was like the old John Raitt days', he said, 'where these really handsome guys enter and bang out these songs with self-confidence. Jeremy helped galvanize the whole cast around a strong, masculine Jack Kelly' (in Cerniglia 2013: 86). In the same review in which she reports wanting to pinch the actors' cheeks, Elisabeth Vincentelli calls Jordan a 'hunk' and says he 'hits a good balance of sexiness and humor' (2012: 44). Several other reviewers refer to Jordan's sex-appeal and masculinity, but descriptions of this sort were also common among the show's main collaborators: the *Daily News*, for example, quotes Alan Menken as saying 'Jeremy is a dream. In his looks and his acting, he's like a young Marlon Brando' (in Wong 2012: 4). Menken's comment is both typical and intriguing: he refers to Jordan as both masculine and young. Brando, in fact, was three years *younger* than Jordan when he was on Broadway in *A Streetcar Named Desire* and twenty-six when he made the iconic film version, the same age as Jordan at the time of his debut in *Newsies*. To put it another way, Disney and the popular press described Jordan as a masculine *boy*, and in this way they created an extraordinary slippage between the men onstage and the children they were portraying, not only as beings capable of achieving and demonstrating masculinity, but also as objects of desire and identification for audience members.

Feminine Power: Women and Masculinity

The most important script change from the original 1992 *Newsies* was Fierstein's decision to insert a love story. The love story in the film, between Jack and Davey's sister, is mostly an afterthought, not at all central to the plot. But in Fierstein's retooled book, love, while still taking a back seat to the chorus's dance moves, is much more important. The courageous reporter played by Bill Pullman in the movie has been transformed into a beautiful eighteen-year-old writer named Katherine (played by Kara Lindsay), unhappily stuck in the society pages. This gender-switch necessitates the delightful lyric 'Am-scray punk, / She's the King of New York!' and what it means for the plot is that the love story becomes a prominent feature of the show (Fierstein 2012: 69). What it also means is that the number of likable adult men in *Newsies* is significantly reduced.

With the exception of Theodore Roosevelt there is, in fact, no adult male role-model in the show. Joseph Pulitzer and William Randolph Hearst are the show's villains, and the other adults in the show include Snyder, the evil proprietor of The Refuge, the cruel Wiesel, the strike-breaking Delancey brothers and a group of policemen who beat up the newsies when they try to go on strike. Even the adult men who don't appear in the show function as poor models for the boys as they aim toward some kind of adult behaviour. Jack's dad was destroyed by New York City, and Davey and Les's dad is out of work, made disposable by his employers and dependent on the boys so that the family can eat (2, 24). The rest of the men the newsies discuss are either referred to with derision ('Try any banker, bum or barber. / They almost all knows how to read'), fear ('Me father's gonna kill me anyway!') or reflect a lack of care or even outright neglect ('Wait 'til my old man gets a load of dis. I won't be last in line for the tub tonight'). Katherine does mention reformer and anti-racist liberal Horace Greeley – the man who said 'Go West, young man, and grow up with the country' – as a possible model in Act II, but Jack dismisses Greeley quickly as someone who was crushed by the city (6, 61, 66).

To be sure, the musical is not completely without an adult male hero. Teddy Roosevelt charges in at the end of the show to save the day (a kind of *gubernator ex machina*), and he was indeed a voice for social reform, as well as a close friend of Jacob Riis's. Michael Kimmel, in fact, describes Roosevelt as 'the perfect embodiment of American-as-adolescent boy-man. His definition of manhood was […] a relentless test to be proved constantly and in every arena in which men find themselves' (2006: 124). But this is not *Newsies'* version of the governor. Roosevelt's interaction with the newsboys is limited to a handshake and a short word or two of advice. 'Keep your eyes on the star[s] and your feet on the ground,' he tells Jack. A bit later, and more significantly, Roosevelt asserts one of the important themes of the show itself: 'Each generation must, at the height of its power, step aside and invite the young to share the day,' he tells the group of assembled newsies. 'You have laid claim to our world, and I believe the future, in your hands, will be bright and prosperous' (Fierstein 2012: 104, 107). Rather than espousing a maleness that needs to prove itself around other men, Roosevelt might more precisely be described as following the lead of the most important female voice in the show, Katherine, who, in act one, sings the lyrics:

> Just look around
> At the world we're inheriting,
> And think of the one we'll create.
> Their mistake is they got old.
> That is not a mistake we'll be making,
> No, sir, we'll stay young forever!
> Give those kids and me
> The brand new century
> And watch what happens! (53)

Following Katherine's lead becomes a thematic trend throughout the rest of the show. After beginning the tap number 'King of New York' and showing off their innovative dance skills using the props available to them – spoons, chairs, table – Race, Albert, Elmer and the other young men invite Katherine to join the dance. They scoff at her first few moves, but the dance quickly becomes a call and response with Katherine leading and the other dancers following. This culminates in Katherine doing a leg extension, a dance movement typically performed by women. This movement, which extends the leg up to the dancer's head, also emphasizes the dancer's body as female, since it necessitates lifting her skirt. The femininity of this particular dance move is further underlined by the choreography: this time the other dancers don't copy Katherine's movement; instead, the characters scream with apparent pleasure and astonishment. Next, Katherine does a cross with the same props the young men have used – the spoon, the chair, the broom – doing riffs on the choreography the boys have done. After this they all dance together: now she's one of the boys.[5] What I am noting here is the way the choreography of the young men's movement physically incorporates the woman's moves. Narratively, the young men accept Katherine as one of their own, and this story is told through Gattelli's choreography. Whether the young men precisely mimic Katherine's feminine leg extension or not, then, this movement functions as a powerful and virtuosic flourish that works to incorporate traditionally feminine phrases into the range of choreographic possibilities available to these young men.

Jack, for his part, also follows Katherine's lead, taking very seriously her advice that 'Being [the] boss doesn't mean you have all the answers. Just the brains to recognize the right one when you hear it' (90). Katherine's advice to Jack in this sequence is a calm, reasoned attack on traditional masculinity. Jack does not need to be a person who does everything on his own. Katherine reminds him: 'The strike was your idea. The rally was Davey's. And now my plan will take us to the finish line. Deal with it' (90). She advocates teamwork over the posturing, solitary masculinity of the adult men in the show. Jack agrees and adopts this alternate masculinity for himself so much so that he repeats Katherine's line in the play's penultimate scene. When Pulitzer declares with conviction that 'Anyone who does not act in his own self-interest is a fool,' Jack responds by telling Davey that 'Guys like Joe don't talk with nothin's like us. But a very wise reporter told me a real boss don't need the answers. Just the smarts to snatch the right one when he hears it' (101). The young men, in other words, are not without role-models; it just happens that the primary role-models in *Newsies* are women.

She's the King of New York: Drag, the Third Sex and Masculinity

The most spectacular of the newsies' role-models is, of course, the chanteuse and entrepreneur Medda Larkin, played by white actress Helen Anker in the Paper Mill production. Capathia Jenkins took over the role on Broadway, and reviews began stating that the role was loosely based on black vaude-villian Aida Overton Walker.[6] In the lyrics to her song 'That's Rich', however, Medda tells us that 'some guys give me ermine, chinchilla and mink / And some give me diamonds as big as a sink', and if her reference to diamonds doesn't immediately recall the Mae West of *She Done Him Wrong*, her double entendre in the same song – 'seems whatever I touch starts to rise' – ought surely to make us think of 'is that a pistol in your pocket or are you just happy to see me?' (28–9). Fierstein drives home the comparison in *Newsies*' final scene, in which Medda exits on Roosevelt's arm saying 'Come along,

Governor[,] and show me the back seat I've been hearing so much about'
(109). Mae West flourishes like this abound in *Newsies,* and they drop hints
(hairpins, if you will) to the audience about the existence of a different New
York from the one on which this family-oriented show focuses, an adult
world with which real newsies in 1899 would likely have been quite familiar.

I refer, of course, to the bourgeoning gay male world detailed by historian
George Chauncey in the seminal book *Gay New York,* which describes a
highly visible subculture of men prior to the invention of 'homosexuality',
a subculture that was 'participating in and expanding a street culture
already developed by working-class youths seeking freedom from their
families' supervision' in New York City's tenements (1994: 202). One of
the most colourful figures from 1890s New York was the *fairy*: the word
described persons with recognizably male anatomy who adopted 'effeminate
mannerisms' as 'a deliberate cultural strategy' that allowed them to 'negotiate
their relationship with other men' (56). There are, to be sure, no 'fairies' in
Newsies, but in 1899 New York City they were a fixture in places like Paresis
Hall and other Bowery 'resorts' in Manhattan's Lower East Side. The newsies'
colourful handles both in history (Kid Blink, Crazy Arborn, Barney Peanuts,
Scabutch) and the musical (Race, Crutchie, Romeo, Specs, Buttons) certainly
align them with the delightfully disreputable world of prostitutes, fairies
and drag queens, who have always given themselves *noms de guerre* (Violet,
Blossom, Edna May, Big Tess, Loop-to-Loop). Even the real-life vaudevillian
performers on whom Medda Larkin is based were known for their gender-
bending performances: Mae West was a great friend of drag queens in 1920s
New York, and her persona was partially based on well-known turn-of-
the-century female-impersonator Julian Eltinge; Aida Overton Walker, too,
became famous as a brilliant comedienne, but she was also a male imper-
sonator who sensationally stood in for a role her husband George usually
played, and male drag numbers became one of Walker's specialties.

In the period in New York City before homosexuality caught on as a way
of classifying sexual desire, a fairy was a type of man who populated this
turn-of-the-century world. Fairies were men who wanted to have sex with
men and who, in order better to accomplish this, presented themselves as
effeminate – as sharing identity with women. Chauncey says that because of
this 'the fairy, so long as he abided by the conventions of this cultural script,
was tolerated in much of working-class society'. Perhaps even more intrigu-
ingly, the fairy

> was so obviously a 'third-sexer', a different species of human being,
> that his very effeminacy served to confirm rather than threaten the
> masculinity of other men, particularly since it often exaggerated the

conventions of deference and gender difference between men and women. (57)

Turn-of-the-century maleness, in other words, was shaped not only by men wishing to present as masculine, but also by men wishing to present as feminine. In many ways, the borders of masculinity were shored up by these queer men, men who saw masculinity as a desirable feature in a sexual object but not a feature they wished to adopt in their own gender performance.

As Menken, Feldman, Fierstein, Calhoun and Gattelli have fashioned *Newsies*, maleness has been decoupled – as, indeed, it would have been in 1899 New York – from any ideas about so-called 'sexual orientation'. At the same time, masculinity in *Newsies* has become attached to, even combined with, a figure against which it is traditionally placed in contrast: the boy. And if we see masculine power in the figures of these newsboys, working to make a living like little men in the city, *Newsies* also asks us to see power in the women who function as these young men's role-models. The show finds strength in both femininity *and* masculinity, and it gives the newsies and those who identify with them access to both.

Extra! New Masculinities

Two fairly recent articles about masculinity and dance in musical theatre are worth noting in conclusion. Both George Rodosthenous (2007) and Judith Sebesta (2013) have chosen to discuss masculinity in dance by analysing musicals about boys rather than men, primarily *Billy Elliot* and *Spring Awakening*. Scholars have turned their attention to boys attempting to perform a masculinity that they do not possess, as though one might better be able to visualize masculinity *tout court* if it is removed from the bodies of men as such (this is an argument carefully outlined by J. Halberstam in *Female Masculinity* [1998: 2]). Both scholars refer to aggressive movements and athleticism in the boys' dances. They see masculinity as re-written in *Billy Elliot* and *Spring Awakening*, and Sebesta (following Rodosthenous) suggests the possibility that dance might 'offe[r] the real potential for material change in our perception of, and constitution of, masculine identities' (158).

I want also to return to Ben Brantley's curmudgeonly but right-on-target *New York Times* review of the show. One of the things that bothered the critic about *Newsies* was that it didn't know 'when to quit'. Brantley was referring to Gattelli's choreography, which for him was excessive and insistent: 'just when you think a number is over, it starts up again, and no sooner are you recovering from that one, then there's another one, with all the same darn back flips, pirouettes, etc' (2012: C1). Brantley is, no doubt, quite correct, but if the newsboys dance more than is necessary, working hard to demonstrate their agility, energy, athleticism and stamina, in this way they reflect a fundamental trait of masculinity itself as gratuitous performance, dependent on what Robert McRuer has called 'compulsory able-bodiedness' (2006: 2). Masculinity is always excessive, a performance (simultaneously) of identity and individuality designed to stave off fears 'that others will see [one] as weak, timid, frightened', but that also works to compete with and dominate others (Kimmel 2006: 4). By emphasizing the extraordinary effort involved in executing the *Newsies* choreography Gattelli, in fact, makes the theatrical element of masculinity abundantly clear. In this way the show critiques masculinity, not by calling it bad but by calling masculinity out as performance.

Newsies not only makes colourable the theatrical aspect of masculinity, but expands its own version of masculinity so that, for the newsies, desirable ways of moving in the world also include traditionally feminine movements. What is important about this is that *Newsies the Musical* is not aimed primarily at men and women but at children and adolescents. One could accurately describe a majority of the characters onstage as minor, and the key audience for whom they are performing is minor as well. What is intriguing about *Newsies*, however, is that though the characters are boys the actors who played them on Broadway were men. The feats of ability the dancers perform in 'Seize the Day' demonstrate a virtuosity and skill that cannot be achieved by a majority of the show's intended audience ... yet. As I argued before, *Newsies* actively courts identification between the newsies and the 'fansies' as kids. Young people in the audience, particularly boys, are asked to identify with, and aspire to be, as athletic, powerful, graceful and happy as the 'boys' onstage. *Newsies*, in other words, does not attempt to remake, refashion or subvert (whatever that might mean) masculinity for adults. What it does instead is attempt to expand the range of possibilities of acceptable gender performance for the boys and girls identifying with these characters. And when they grow up – when, that is, they transition to adult men, women, transmen or transwomen – they might perhaps understand their own bodies as less constrained by masculinity than the generation previous.

As I noted earlier, *Newsies* actively hails this younger generation in the audience, underlining the generation gap between Pulitzer and the newsboys numerous times. The most anthemic musical phrase in the entire show (from the eleven o'clock number 'Once and for All') is accompanied by the lyrics 'There's change comin' once and for all. / You're gettin' too old, / Too weak to keep holdin' on. / A new world is gunnin' for you,' and this generational shift signals not only a new world (of labour-equity, justice, teamwork), but also a different type of male being-in-the-world, a new world with a new type of adult to inhabitant it (99).

As a marker of its historical moment, Fierstein was writing the book for *Newsies* during the height of the 'It Gets Better' campaign, an internet-based movement that attempted to provide teens and adolescents with models with whom they could identify. Hundreds of YouTube videos surfaced on the internet featuring adults who encouraged young people using the phrase *It gets better*. *Newsies* uses choreography, lyrics, music, to share a similar message, physically enacting the possibilities held by this new world gunning for its audience. For if the boys in the show have no male role-models for their onstage version of masculinity, the men playing those boys serve as precisely that for a new generation of boys and girls who won't be afraid to dance – who will feel more comfortable moving, in other words, in ways that are traditionally considered feminine.

References

Brantley, B. (2012). 'Urchins with Punctuation.' *New York Times*, 30 March, C1.
Burt, R. (1995). *The Male Dancer: Bodies, Spectacle, Sexualities.* London: Routledge.
Cerniglia, K. (ed.) (2013). *Newsies: Stories of the Unlikely Broadway Hit.* Glendale, CA: Disney Editions.
Cerniglia, K. and L. Mitchell (2014). 'The Business of Children in Disney's Theater.' In G. Arrighi and V. Emeljanow (eds), *Entertaining Children: The Participation of Youth in the Entertainment Industry.* London: Palgrave, 139–45.
Chauncey, G. (1994). *Gay New York: Gender, Urban Culture, and the Making of the Gay Male World 1890–1940.* New York: Basic.
Disney on Broadway (2014). Available online: https://www.youtube.com/watch?v=LSEUR2gZUFc (accessed 2 January 2 2016).
Disney Theatrical Group Education Department (2012). *Newsies the Musical Study Guide.* Available online: http://newsiesthemusical.com/pdf/NewsiesStudyGuide.pdf (accessed 2 January 2016).
Dziemianowicz, J. (2011). 'It's Terrific "News"! Disney Musical Makes Headlines in New Jersey.' *Daily News*, 28 September, p. 37.
Dziemianowicz, J. (2012). *Newsies a Doozie. Daily News*, 30 March, p. 50.
Fierstein, H. (2012). *Newsies the Musical.* Unpublished Broadway opening night script. Revised 29 March.
Halberstam, J. (1998). *Female Masculinity.* Durham, NC: Duke University Press.
Herrera, B. (2012). 'Compiling *West Side Story's* Parahistories, 1949–2009.' *Theatre Journal* 64 (2): 231–47.

Kimmel, M. (2006). *Manhood in America: A Cultural History*, 2nd edn. New York: Oxford University Press.

Maslin, J. (1992). 'They Sing, They Dance, They Go on Strike'. *New York Times*, 8 April, C17.

McRuer, R. (2006). *Crip Theory: Cultural Signs of Queerness and Disability*. New York: New York University Press.

Riedel, M. (2012). 'Good *Newsies* for Disney.' *New York Post*, 28 March, p. 36.

Riis, J. (2010). *How the Other Half Lives*, ed. Hasia R. Diner. New York: W. W. Norton.

Rodosthenous, G. (2007). '*Billy Elliot the Musical*: Visual Respresentations of Working-Class Masculinity and the All-Singing, All-Dancing Bo(d)y'. *Studies in Musical Theatre* 1 (3): 275–92.

Rooney, D. (2011). 'Theater Review: *Newsies the Musical*.' *New York Times*, 28 September, C5.

Scheck, F. (2011). 'Song and Star Scoop *Newsies* Story.' *New York Post*, 27 September, p. 36.

Sebesta, J. (2013). 'Angry Dance: Postmodern Innovation, Masculinities, and Gender Subversion.' In D. Symonds and M. Taylor (eds), *Gestures of Music Theater: The Performativity of Song and Dance*. New York: Oxford University Press, 146–58.

Sommers, M. (2011). 'Good *Newsies*: Disney's Crowd-Pleaser Delivers.' 3 October, p. 53.

Suskin, S. (2012). '*Newsies: The Musical*.' *Variety*, 30 March, p. 23.

Takiff, J. (2014). 'Bristol Stomp: *Newsies* Winning Choreographer Hails from Bucks.' *Philadelphia Daily News*, 29 October. Available online: http://articles.philly.com/2014-10-29/news/55402110_1_newsies-jack-feldman-bob-tzudiker (accessed 2 January 2016).

Vincentelli, E. (2012). 'Striking Ensemble is on Tap.' *New York Post*, 30 March, p. 44.

Wong, W. (2011). 'Making *Newsies*: How a Disney Flop Became a Stage Hit.' *Daily News*, 2 October, p. 13.

Wong, W. (2012). 'Read All About It: Meet Jeremy Jordan, Broadway Star of Disney's *Newsies*.' *Daily News*, 25 March, p. 4.

'We're All in This Together': Being Girls and Boys in *High School Musical* (2006)

Dominic Symonds

The impact of the TV movie *High School Musical* on its first screening in January 2006 was phenomenal. Carefully planned by the Disney Channel to benefit from four separate screenings over three days (see Rudisill 2009: 255; Potter 2011: 124), it attracted over 35 million US viewers over that opening period and has since been watched by an estimated 295 million people worldwide, grossing around $500 million from an investment of just $4.2 million. Two sequels followed, and then a live stage version of the musical in a number of countries. A schools' version was quickly licensed for amateur availability, and a slew of competitions across Asia ('My School Rocks') capitalized on the popularity of TV talent shows, promising global youngsters the chance to become not only their own high school's musical star, but potentially a musical star as international as Zac Efron and Vanessa Hudgens had become before them.

With reach and influence on this scale, Disney's responsibility to its audience is significant. Of course, the organization has a reputation for being squeaky clean, eschewing overly sexualized content in its productions and maintaining standards of modesty that suit various audiences and cultures. Even so, its production of a movie like *High School Musical* on such a global scale 'raises questions about the nature of children's programs, the audience which consumes them, and media policies which have nurtured [...] children's programs since the 1970s', writes Anna Potter (2011: 122). Given the school setting and a storyline with which children the world over can associate, *High School Musical* carries particular weight in the way it potentially influences fans. But with moral messages that 'embody feelings of acceptance, inclusion, unity and generosity' (ibid. – voiced in musical numbers such as the finale, 'We're All In This Together') it seems on the surface to be treating that responsibility with care. On the other hand, as these and other critiques have noted, Disney's ideals can also be reinterpreted to expose conservative and even problematic politics, especially with regard to identity, and for the purposes of this consideration in regard to gender.

The gender politics of the Disney films has come under fire for a number of reasons over the years, with Kay Stone offering an early critique in 'Things Walt Disney Never Told Us' (1975), Elizabeth Bell, Lynda Haas and Laura Sells focussing their book *From Mouse to Mermaid* (1995) on 'The Politics of Film, Gender and Culture' and Leah R. Vande Berg editing a special issue of *Women's Studies in Communication* on 'Gender and the World of Disney' (1996). For many, the magic of Disney is unbreakable, yet, as these accounts reveal, there are behind the family friendly, entertaining surfaces of the Disney products some concerning assumptions about identity, and particularly gender. In the main, these have been explored with reference to the animated constructions of gender in Disney's comics, cartoons and films; yet Disney has also released a wealth of live-action material on its many TV channels and in cinemas. Although gender construction may be more obvious in the animations, it is just as much encoded in the live-action narratives, and arguably more ideological, since the depictions appear more true to life.

In addition to the *High School Musical* franchise there have been other high-profile live-action Disney vehicles that have achieved global success, not least *The Suite Life of Zack and Cody* (with its spin-offs) (2005–11) and the *Hannah Montana* phenomenon (2006–11) (and it is interesting to consider in gender terms how this particular character, Hannah Montana, has grown up as her alter-ego Miley Cyrus). But the proliferation of channels available nowadays means that these examples are just the tip of an iceberg of gender depictions targeted at impressionable children in the eight- to fourteen-year age bracket; the contemporary child is presented with and influenced by an almost wall-to-wall saturation of 'suite life' role-models. As those children grow up, these already-formed gender expectations are reinforced by further programmes and models aimed at an older age bracket.

Of the many role models constructed by such vehicles, it is arguably the teenage girl models that carry most influence, not just because they are the most direct influences on impressionable teenage audiences, but because, according to feminist thinkers, it is in the character of the 'girl' that post-feminism has articulated its most damaging backlash against the gains of second-wave feminism. In this 'girl' guise (the guise of The Spice Girls and 'girl power'), the media has constructed an image of successful womanhood in 'girlie culture', a lifestyle whose icons have achieved the gains of feminism yet maintained the 'weaknesses' of femininity. Even while making claims to empowerment and emancipation, critics argue, the character of the 'girl' betrays the 'commodification and *containment* of feminism – the triumph of "image power" over "political power"' (Munford 2007: 274). Alongside characters such as Buffy, Disney's contemporary heroines provide model 'girls' who are womanly in many ways (in maturity, in looks and in proto-sexual knowingness), yet who are still depicted as vulnerable children; figures who are 'independent', 'successful' and 'unafraid' yet who are also 'in emotional turmoil' (Gorton 2007: 213–14). In fashioning what Meenakshi Gigi Durham calls the 'new girl hero', Disney and other media corporations have been able to update the role modelling of their protagonists to satisfy gender developments whilst still keeping to an ideological agenda in promoting traditional, conservative values. 'Implicitly, the "new girl hero" could function as a solution to the presumed crisis of girls' adolescence but still function as a commodified figure marketed to the commodified girl audience and in turn marketed to advertisers' writes Sarah Projansky (2007: 44). This Kristyn Gorton sees epitomized in the character of Ally McBeal, who articulates that show's 'general premise' and the general premise, one might say, of post-feminism *per se*: 'that a successful career woman […] cannot be fully satisfied without a man' (Gorton 2007: 213–14). *High School Musical*'s Gabriella – the romantic love interest-cum-brainiac heroine of the movie musical franchise – is another example of the 'new girl hero'. And in purveying this archetype globally to its impressionable audiences, Disney plays a major role in imprinting that post-feminist ideal as the aspirational model for young girls as they grow up.

This chapter explores the representation of gender in *High School Musical*. First, I will consider it in relation to its stated influence *Grease*; then, I will take a look at the way that both male and female teenagers are represented in the movie. I am going to focus on the thematic use of song as a drama-turgical tool, and on three particular numbers: 'Get'cha Head in the Game', in which we first meet the boys, a group of basketball jocks preparing for the all-important championship match; 'Stick to the Status Quo', a lively company number ambivalently flirting with the idea of conformity and independence; and 'When There Was Me and You', the heroine Gabriella's lament for Troy, the boy she thinks she has lost. I'll suggest throughout this chapter that the Disney mantra of firmly entrenched conservative ideologies is still writ large in *High School Musical*, even if on the surface it presents a post-millennial, post-feminist utopia. In East High School, Albuquerque, if nowhere else, the values of 'about, oh, 1954' are still guiding the gender game (Morford 2006).

Disney and the 'New Girl Hero': Re-imagining Him and Her

Conceived as a retelling of the Romeo and Juliet story, *High School Musical* was the brainchild of Disney producer Bill Borden. He wanted to create a movie that, like *Grease* did for a previous generation, would capture the spirit of the new millennium, 'spreading its uplifting message to audiences of all ages and attracting a new generation':

> Beyond the show's catchy songs, the cool costumes, and the typical high school dramas, their stories are ones to which everyone can relate. *High School Musical* demonstrates how it's possible for young people to achieve their goals by having faith in themselves, pursuing their passions and working together to support their friends. ('Disney *High School Musical* Live on Stage Study Guide', Disney Theatrical Group Education Department)

High School Musical bears lots of thematic similarities to *Grease*, which also sets its storyline around a group of junior high schoolers at the beginning of a new term. Both films begin their stories during the vacation, with young couples Danny and Sandy (*Grease*), and Troy and Gabriella (*HSM*) falling head over heels with each other while holidaying. When they return to school after the vacation, the boys are astonished to discover that the girls have enrolled at their respective schools, Rydell High, Los Angeles and East High, Albuquerque. Plunged into this new context, the budding relationships must compete with the existing dynamics of status and popularity already entrenched within the school communities. Both Danny and Troy are characterized at school within social groupings that are rigidly gender-defined: Danny is the leader of the T-Birds, a gang of greasers interested only in their cars (and whose members are exclusively male); Troy is the captain of the Wildcats, the school basketball team whose members are only interested in sports (and whose members are exclusively male).[1] In these clearly demarcated masculine contexts, it is the interruption of a feminizing influence that in both stories drives the drama.

In *Grease*, the pretty-in-pastel Sandy ends up winning her man by reinventing herself entirely on his terms. Dispensing with a decade and more of women's liberation and second-wave feminist politics in one quick change, Sandy appears in the final scene dressed in tight-fitting leather pants, her image totally sexualized for the benefit of Danny's (literally) drooling gaze. Popular though the film has been with a family audience, it hardly offers a progressive message in terms of gender. Thirty years later, even if the gender politics has matured with *High School Musical*'s new-millennium take on an old theme, the dramaturgical interplay of the movie is still rooted in assumptions about gender. Indeed, though it may not be as obviously encoded as *Grease* in troublesome politics, it is nevertheless deeply committed to gender ideologies from the past, and central to these is the rigidly demarcated way in which males and females within this school environment are ascribed activities.

In *High School Musical*, men are encoded as sports stars, and women as 'brainiacs', a clear divide between the virile activity of masculinity and the intellectual affinity of women. True, the girls are not relegated to the role of cheerleaders, as may so easily have been the case, supporting their male idols with a display of the female body and a performative worship of male prowess.[2] It is fair to say also that, superficially at least, the balance between male brawn and female brains may seem at least to level the gender playing field whilst maintaining a gendered difference: in this post-millennium battle of the sexes, women have (scholarly) girl power and respectable claims to an identity of their own, balancing the more literal power of the boys.

Yet the playing field is not really level: the boys are driven by winning team glory in an athletic contest whose parameters are understood – a basketball game. Here, codes of team playing and leadership are evidently virtuous, the ethics of dedication and commitment are carefully laid out, we see a rigorous training regime being pursued, and the skills of focus and communication are well drummed in throughout the film. But for the girls the situation is somewhat different: although they are intent on winning their 'Scholastic Decathlon', the parameters of their goal are not well defined, the rules of the competition unclear and what is at stake unexplored. Indeed, the girls' abilities (Gabriella aside) are not shown to be mathematical talent or intellectual intelligence and their ethics are not even to work as a team or develop qualities like the boys. The Scholastic Decathlon is just a means to an end, and the end is to define the girls as willing stooges for the boys.

Too Cool for School: 'I Haven't Quite Told Them about the Singing Thing'

At the heart of *High School Musical* is an attempt by everyone to dissuade Troy and Gabriella from participating in the school show, which would be not only a social *faux pas* in status terms, but also a crippling impediment to the school's athletic success. The interest in musical theatre starts right from the beginning of the movie, quickly establishing song as the meta-theatrical key that unlocks the film's mechanics. Trapped on New Year's Eve at a children's disco up a mountain, neither Troy Burton nor Gabriella Montez is remotely interested in New Year, discos, the ski resort or each other, but they are selected to perform a karaoke duet and it is during this number that they capture each other's hearts and awaken a passion for Broadway. The film is hardly subtle about the way this plot point is established, and the performance of this song – despite being sung spontaneously by grudging teenagers disinterested in engaging – is extraordinary: beautifully sung and heavily produced with complex harmonies and a perfect vocal match, there is no sense of irony about the instant way they fall in love. Perhaps to pre-teen viewers at whom this film is targeted, the unlikely virtuosity of the characters doesn't jar, but to adult audiences the obviousness of this exposition highlights if nothing else the movie's deliberate fetishization of song and the power of the voice. Even through the first verse, which he sings by himself, Troy seems blithely disinterested in the beautiful girl standing beside him; he only notices her when she sings the second verse and on hearing her voice he is instantly smitten. From that point on, it is the voice, the music and the song that become the talismanic drivers of the relationship between them.

Troy's interest in singing is seen by the boys as a travesty, something that will jeopardize the team's chances of winning the basketball championship. Singing for Troy and his friends is clearly a humiliating activity, pitched in the script in contrast to sport (basketball, snowboarding) and (surely with some irony) condemned as the height of depravity. Troy himself reveals concerns about his penchant: 'my friends know about the snowboarding; I haven't quite told them about the singing thing' he admits; meanwhile, his best friend Chad (Troy's 'second' on the basketball team) acknowledges certain musical styles that pass, but, as he scoffs, 'the music in those shows [musicals] isn't hip-hop or rock, or anything essential to culture; it's, like, show music'. Chad and the boys, with the help of the Brainiacs, proceed to find every ruse in the book to sabotage Troy and Gabriella's chances of getting into the school musical.

What is at stake in the trade-off between Troy's commitment to basketball and his newly found interest in the musical is team gold, and what is at stake for the boys is that a crucial element of their team dynamic will be missing if Troy is distracted by either the show or the girl. Troy is depicted as the leader who is being taken away by an outside threat (the musical/the girl). Without his leadership, the team will fail, so the onus in the boys' plotting is to refocus their leader and 'get [his] head in the game'. In this scenario, the choice is mutually exclusive: there is no possibility of juggling the commitments to both the basketball team and the musical/the girl.

But, while the boys are depicted as having a clear focus in their concern for Troy, the motives of the girls in their concern for Gabriella are seen as no more than a response to the demands made by Chad and his colleagues. Taylor (the leader of the Brainiacs) is in thrall to Chad. Once Chad issues the directive to the girls to lure Troy and Gabriella back to their appropriate pursuits (which is really a directive to ensure that Troy is returned to his position as team leader), the girls employ all sorts of underhand machinations to fulfil the boys' demands. Where the boys' skills are framed as worthy qualities of teamwork and respect, the girls' propensities throughout the film are to win by conniving and manipulative means.

In the first example of this, the girls rig up technology to allow Gabriella to listen in on a private conversation; at the end of the movie, they literally disrupt fair play by sabotaging the power supply to the game and gassing the science lab so their plan can be put into effect. Their intentions at this stage are more honourable – to overcome the even more devious shenanigans of the evil musical theatre triumvirate of Sharpay, Ryan and Ms Darbus, and ensure Troy and Gabriella are cast as the leads in the high school musical; yet although Sharpay may be the obvious manipulative witch character to Gabriella's princess, Taylor and her Brainiacs are shown to be no less macchiavellian in serving their princes through deceit. As Henry A. Giroux remarks, 'Disney's negative stereotypes about women and girls gain force through the way in which similar messages are consistently circulated and reproduced' (1999: 100). In this Disney film, to succeed as a girl is to play on codes of deceit and manipulation.

To Troy, Gabriella is a distraction, and the recurring motif throughout the movie is that it is this distraction that is preventing him from his proper leadership duties as captain of the team. 'Get'cha Head in the Game' is the second song of the show, introducing the boys in the team, and staging an athletic dance routine around the physicality of a warm-up session in the gym. The palette of the song makes liberal use of concrete sounds such as the bounce of the balls, the squeak of sneakers on the gym floor and the breathy repetition of the ensemble lyrics, which give the impression the boys are working hard physically as they sing.

Of course they do sing, revealing the central irony in the film, which is, after all, a musical built around the conceit of how uncool musicals are. In one of the few really integrated moments of the film, the set-piece of the song is interrupted by Troy's vocalized internal monologue. The concrete sounds of the song's hip hop rhythms give way to a lilting, feminine lament, with Troy pictured in a spotlight in the centre of the stage (gym): 'Why am I feeling so wrong? / My head's in the game / But my heart's in the song', he sings. How interesting that it is music, the song, that is associated here with the lure of the feminine, both in terms of the vocal style and Troy's muse Gabriella. This emphasizes the fact that the game is sited as the masculine domain, the rhythmic and embodied codes of hip hop articulating the testosterone of the boys as they play. It also emphasizes the link between the musical/the girl and encodes the use of song as a feminine expression. Chad's remarks about musical theatre and hip-hop come back to mind, and we are able to accept the contradiction of his attitude towards singing even while he sings because of this stylistic framing.

This device – the use of different styles of music as a gendering tool – is something that re-emerges in the TV series *Glee* (2009–15), which followed *High School Musical*, trading off many of its features. As Jessica Sternfeld has noted, despite the series ostensibly being an example of the TV musical form, the use of musical theatre songs as opposed to pop and rock songs is limited to just two characters (Kurt and Rachel), who themselves are defined as gendered outsiders (the gay boy and the diva): 'Broadway songs and singing become marginalized, rendered both powerful for their ability to express earnest emotion at peak times, as well as dangerous in their cultural implications and therefore carefully boxed off', she writes (2013: 128). In this sense, suggests Katherine J. Wolfenden, programmes such as *Glee* (and, one assumes, *High School Musical*) project what she terms 'neoliberal flexibility', a device of including marginalized or minority characters whilst leaving the 'gender/sex binary and biological essentialism unchallenged' (2013: 1). Yet, of course, 'Get'cha Head in the Game' is not the only song performed by the team; only a short while later, along with everyone in the school canteen, they join in the spirited whole company routine of 'Stick to the Status Quo', a song reminiscent of a set piece from the *Kids from Fame* in its shameless celebration of musical theatre.

The distrust of singing – or of doing anything outside the activities sanctioned by the behaviour of the social group – becomes almost pathological in 'Stick to the Status Quo'. Here, we learn that the school is (apparently) entirely divided into subcultures defined by their identity: we've met the 'Brainiacs' and the 'Jocks', and in passing we have encountered the 'Cheerleaders' and 'Drama Club'; in this song we also come across the 'Skater Dudes'. One of these five identities defines every individual within the school, and codes of behaviour are strictly policed, often along gender lines, within these group identities.

The song occurs just as the news is announced that Troy and Gabriella have call-backs to audition for the musical. This is news that Troy's teammates take particularly badly. Chad is the ringleader of the naysayers: 'You missed free-period workout to audition for a heinous musical', he spits, 'and now suddenly people are confessing ...' Indeed, another member of the team,

Zeke, takes an opportunity to confess, 'coming out' himself as a keen chef who loves to bake crème brûlée. A wave of admissions follows around the school canteen, with one Brainiac claiming that hip-hop dance is 'cooler than homework', and a Skater Dude owning up to playing the cello. In moments, the ordered society of the school has broken down and chaos erupts, stylistically reflected in a feverish song-and-dance routine (and culminating in Gabriella's lunch being thrown all over Sharpay). 'Something's not right', sings the crowd – 'We've gotta get things back where they belong'. The suggestions here are interesting, both in terms of the language used and the way in which order is seen so quickly to collapse. On one level, what breaks out is a mass hysteria invoked by the slightest deviation from socially normative behaviour.

The excessive responses in this scene are undoubtedly exaggerated for comic value; yet even seeing these entirely unproblematic activities as indiscretions (singing, baking, playing the cello) is so fundamental to the guided behaviour implied by *High School Musical* that one wonders whether this song is intended ironically or not. In fact, these activities are not merely seen as indiscretions, but as almost criminal within the school context: singing is 'heinous'; individuals are 'confessing'. In wider terms, this might be seen to reflect the sort of widespread panic that periodically erupts in American society in relation to unsanctioned activity (say, communism). The fear that a minor breach of expected social behaviour will lead to a major breakdown of societal order speaks volumes about the state-fuelled paranoia that controls American society. Historically, it is this fear that has justified extreme enactments of the repressive state apparatus (segregation), protectivist articulations of violent self-defence (gun ownership) and a societally sanctioned normalization of rigid behaviour control in cultural practices (the pledge of allegiance). In *High School Musical*, an Althusserian encoding of these ideologies, this early determinism is imprinted on audiences through carefully selected language about status and conformity: 'If you wanna be cool, follow one simple rule'. What a simple device for indoctrinating conformity in an impressionable audience.

Interestingly, the Study Guide circulated by Disney Theatrical for use with the live stage production of *High School Musical* emphasizes these social groupings ('Jocks', 'Brainiacs', 'Skater Dudes', 'Cheerleaders', 'Drama Club') by way of exploring the benefits of 'community building'. In such a way the repressions of behavioural control are ideologically reinterpreted as positive values. 'To help build community in your classroom', one exercise suggests, 'create a class contract to articulate the group's collective goals' ('Disney *High School Musical* Live on Stage Study Guide', Disney Theatrical Group Education Department: 15). This is one of a number of Study Guides prepared by Disney that contain practical ideas and exercises explicitly aimed at the target audience of the production.

In this case (this is the UK guide), the exercises 'relate to a range of subjects and courses studied at Key Stages 3 and 4' (that is, children aged 11–14 and 14–16).[3] The guide suggests picking up on community values such as 'support one another', 'listen and respect other's opinions' and 'focus', all of which seem admirable directions (15); it also acknowledges with the question 'How might stereotypes be limiting?' that the exercises and subcultures represented here may be superficial and perhaps problematic. Yet despite these balancing measures, there is an underlying sense that Disney – through the film and its tools such as this guide – is advocating a social organization of individuals into rigidly defined behaviour groups, thereby stage-managing conformity, especially in gender terms.

Certainly, some of the other questions and comments in the guide direct children's thoughts towards assumptions not about how people *might* behave, but about how they *should* behave ('If you wanna be cool, follow one simple rule'): so, although the guide asks the apparently innocuous question, 'What are the stereotypes, reputations and expectations associated with each role?', it also asks, 'Do the characters accept their respective roles?' (15). This begins to hint at the sort of indoctrination that cultural products risk with careless (or deliberate) handling of language, and – more problematically – the sort of propaganda that might be accused with language that rigidly asserts certain expectations. True, children of these ages may be sophisticated enough to read these social groupings as simply superficial, stereotyped roles at which they might temporarily 'play', but on the other hand – especially if these roles are gender-labelled – the notion of role-play can become socially, psychologically or even civically binding to impressionable individuals (in this case, children).

So, we finally come to the princess character of this post-millennial Disney fairy tale. In some ways it is evident how far Disney has progressed in depicting a story of contemporary teenagers in the real world. Conventional wisdom has it that the typical Disney heroine 'represents royalty, lives in a male-dominated world, and ultimately finds fulfilment through marriage to a prince' (Wasko 2002: 135). East High seems a world apart. But is it really? Has the modern princess Gabriella really overcome her gender-defined expectations?

Gabriella is certainly a girl with her own personality, a certain independence and some admirable qualities. When she first arrives at the school, she seems visibly different from the other girls in class and in the corridors, repeatedly asserting the fact that she wants to concentrate on her studies and that she isn't interested in joining cliques. She views the pretensions of Sharpay with contained amusement and isn't even remotely attracted to the cheerleaders. Yet she does eventually gravitate towards the Brainiacs through developing a friendship with Taylor; in this, we begin to see a side to Gabriella's character just like that of any other girl – in other words, conformist, cliquey and stereotypical. The gossipy conversations she has with Taylor betray her adolescent superficiality, especially when they encounter the cheerleaders in the school grounds.

Gabriella	What do you know about Troy Bolton?
Taylor	Troy? Hmm, I'm not an expert on that particular sub-species, however, unless you speak cheerleader, as in, 'Oh, my gosh! Isn't Troy Bolton just the hottie super-bum?'
Cheerleader	Oh, he's so beautiful.
Taylor	Ha-ha, See what I mean?

And shortly afterwards:

Taylor	Watch how it works tomorrow when you have lunch with us. Unless you'd rather sit with the cheerleaders and discuss firm nail beds.
Gabriella	My nail beds are history!
Taylor	Sister!

This is a conversation that reveals some of the tensions between social groups. Taylor's line 'Oh, my gosh! Isn't Troy Bolton just the hottie super-bum?' is delivered as she walks through a gaggle of cheerleader girls, mocking them by role-playing their conversational style. Taylor is claiming Gabriella as a colleague for the Brainiacs, implicitly elevating their group status above that of the cheerleaders and also above that of the Jocks ('that particular sub-species'). By joining in with Taylor's status game when she subsequently *speaks cheerleader* herself ('My nail beds are history!'), Gabriella confirms her distance from one social group while falling into the gender-defined expectations of the film (that girls are 'bitchy'). Taylor's reply ('Sister!') is both a continuation of the mockery and a gesture of affiliation coded into the implied language of (all) female teenagers. Although the Brainiacs may have a different set of characteristics and social codes from the Cheerleaders, their persona is still derivative and socially performed.

Indeed, Gabriella's behaviour, like Troy's, seems least contrived and performative when they are alone together, perhaps emphasising to audiences how well matched they are, and how prepared they are for a mature, adult relationship. Aside from the moments in which they are goaded by friends to act ungraciously, they treat one another with the utmost respect. In fact, many of these encounters are distinguished from the social play of the group scenes because of gender signifiers on the part of Troy that slip ambiguously towards the feminine: his private sanctuary is the rooftop garden bedecked with flowers; his reconciliatory gesture after falling out with Gabriella is to visit her domestic space and speak with her mother; and when they sing, his voice is feminized in its aesthetic. The high, breathy head-voice notable particularly at the beginning of 'Start of Something New' and 'What I've Been Looking For' trades on a contemporary vocal sound privileging the feminine sound of the male voice. This underlines a stylistic trait of recent pop culture and is a world away from the deep-voiced princes of Disney's yesteryear (think of Prince Philip singing 'Once Upon a Dream' in *Sleeping Beauty* [1959]). Thus the very act of singing becomes something laced with connotations of romance, intimacy and gender ambiguity; metaphorically, it is their closest expressive engagement with each other, a replacement in this sexless world for the intimacy of a physical relationship.

Later in the movie, when Gabriella sings her torch song for Troy, 'When There Was Me and You', she returns to this metaphor: 'I swore I knew the melody / That I heard you singing.' This reference, whose meta-theatricality is the mythologizing glue that holds *High School Musical* together, is interspersed with nods to other romantic clichés, each one turned on its head to express the bittersweet poignancy of the moment: 'I thought you were a fairy tale', she sings, 'A dream when I'm not sleeping.' And, in a direct reference to Disney's role in establishing these mythologizing credos, she concludes with the most poignant shattering of the Disney myth once and for all: 'Wishes on a star / Just don't come true', a reference to 'When You Wish Upon a Star' from *Pinocchio* (1940). In a final lament, she brings back the metaphor: 'I'm only left with used-to-bes / And once upon a song.'

Gabriella's general tone during this lament is another articulation of her coded identity as female, in the sense that her sentiments are sorrowful and that she expresses them in (feminized) song. Yet it is in the visual imagery of this song that the most striking gender expressions are displayed. Shot like a pop video, this features Gabriella alone in the school. The first verse and refrain show her gazing wistfully off-camera as she sings to herself in the classroom. When she moves into the corridor, though, the artificiality of this sequence begins to emerge. She walks slowly through the corridor with measured steps, easing her hands into her pockets in an expression of casual melancholia. By the second refrain these mannered movements have become classic articulations of the indulgence of gendered distress: she is captured backlit on an upper balcony, her hair framed in a halo of light; she caresses the railing of the balcony tenderly, and the camera gives a close up of her fingers sensuously touching its metalwork; she clutches her fist to her bosom and then gives a provocative flick of her hair and body, her body distorting in gratuitous emotion. In the third refrain, as she moves down the staircase to the line 'and wishes on a star just don't come true', she is pictured in a series of stock manoeuvres common from pop video imagery and evoking previous gendered displays deriving from artists such as Madonna.[4] These are very contrived: her body contorts, swivelling at the hips and bending at the knees, emphasising the silhouette of her figure and her lithe femininity. On the word 'true', her hand returns to her body and traces a line round the contour of her face, down her neck and across her shoulder to play with her hair. (Being Disney, she refrains from continuing the caress over her breasts as many more adult versions of this imagery would.)

In this video, Gabriella is seen to be submissive, sensuous and sexually desiring, all traits of typical post-feminist representations of girl power (i.e. disempowering herself to the male gaze). As with much pop imagery, the voice becomes complicit in the rhetoric as an additional layer of the gendered attraction. The poses she strikes are so commonplace that it is unlikely young audiences will see them as out of place; yet they invite audiences, both male and female, to see Gabriella as a body to be looked at and to replicate and further normalize these presentations of gendered display in their own lives. Indeed, a number of the poses Gabriella strikes in this video are among those explored by Erving Goffman in his book *Gender Advertisements*, in which he picks up on repetitive traits in the portrayal of gender in advertising: 'Women, more than men', for example, 'are pictured using their fingers and hands to trace the outlines of an object or to cradle it or to caress its surface', he remarks (Goffman 1987: 29); 'Self-touching can also be involved, readable as conveying a sense of one's body being a delicate and precious thing' (31). Goffman does not so much interpret these gendered conventions as he acknowledges their prevalence in media images; however, as he says, 'That a multitude of "genderisms" point convergently in the same direction might only tell us how these signs function socially, namely, to support belief that there is an underlying reality to gender' (9); in this case, the reality of the 'new girl hero' is that she is every bit the objectified girl of the 1950s – updated to a contemporary milieu, perhaps, and newly energized with a proto-sexual self-awareness, but nevertheless emotional, vulnerable and incomplete without the presence of a man. And the 'underlying reality' is that Disney is impressing upon its young female audiences ways they *should* behave ('If you wanna be cool, follow one simple rule'): girls *should* be submissive, sensuous and sexually desiring, *should* succeed through manipulation and deceit whilst being bitchy to one another and *should* become distressed as the default response to losing a man.

Gabriella ends up standing by a supersize poster of Troy, who stares defiantly straight into the camera. This is male assertion writ large, and it is a theme that continues: in the final audition scene, when Gabriella voices her anxiety about performing in front of the whole of the school, it is Troy – the man – who 'rescues' her by singing the first verse himself ('function ranking', as Goffman calls it [34]). In his most masculine voice yet, Troy sings his opening lines directly to Gabriella, who gazes up at him and responds in a meek, little, plaintive voice as she takes his hand for support: 'If we're trying, so we're breaking free', she whines. Not so free that you'd call her success emancipation, however.

Championing Independence but Sticking with the Status Quo

Indeed, *High School Musical* is, throughout, Troy's story: his relationship with his father is far more pronounced than Gabriella's with her mother; his tussle between captaining the team and singing on stage seems to have far more at stake than Gabriella's between singing and being part of the Scholastic Decathlon. At the very end of the movie, the dramatic action plays out in the juxtaposition of a gripping basketball game and the equally gripping audition scene; the third event – Gabriella's moment of glory in the Scholastic Decathlon – is here relegated to the off-screen space, the assumption that it has been happening at the same time, and the message delivered in passing by Gabriella herself – that 'we won that too'.

High School Musical purports to be a movie championing independence, then, especially independence for girls, yet it is does this by consolidating and reinforcing traditional gender values about need, desire, strength and behaviour. At the same time, its deliberately generic projection of time and location – this takes place more-or-less in the present day and in the undefined some-place of an American High School – allows it to adopt a universality that undermines the specificity of personalized third-wave politics. The fact that the musical has become more globally circulated than any other Disney product to date emphasizes the homogenous values it presents and the universalizing tendencies of this apparent story of success. But for all the success that is achieved by any of these kids in their scholarly, sporting and performance exploits, the real question is one of access, which is a common concern in terms of gender in the Disney canon:[5] girls can achieve, can have a voice and can gain independence (we are told), but the only way they will achieve access to those rewards is if they conform to the 'inhibitions' of their gender.

References

Bell, Elizabeth, Lynda Haas and Laura Sells (1995). *From Mouse to Mermaid: The Politics of Film, Gender and Culture*. Bloomington and Indianapolis: Indiana University Press.

'Disney *High School Musical* Live on Stage Study Guide', Disney Theatrical Group Education Department, http://www.aberdeenperformingarts.com/uploads/high%20school%20musical%20-%20pt%201.pdf (accessed 11 January 2017).

Durham, Meenakshi Gigi (2003). 'The Girling of America: Critical Reflections on Gender and Popular Communication.' *Popular Communication* 1 (1): 23–31.

Giroux, Henry A. (1999). *The Mouse That Roared: Disney and the End of Innocence*. Lanham, and Boulder, New York and Oxford: Rowman & Littlefield.

Goffman, Erving (1987). *Gender Advertisments*. New York: Harper & Row.

Gorton, Kristyn (2007). '(Un)Fashionable Feminists: The Media and Ally McBeal.' In Stacy Gillis, Gillian Howie and Rebecca Munford (eds), *Third Wave Feminism: A Critical Exploration*. Houndmills: Palgrave Macmillan, 212–23.

Leadbeater, Bonnie J. and Gloria Lodato-Wilson (1993). 'Flipping their Fins for a Place to Stand: 19th- and 20th-Century Mermaids.' *Youth and Society* 27 (4): 466–86.

Lotz, Amanda D. (2007). 'Theorizing the Intermezzo: The Contributions of Postfeminism and Third Wave Feminism.' In Stacy Gillis, Gillian Howie and Rebecca Munford (eds), *Third Wave Feminism: A Critical Exploration*. Houndmills: Palgrave Macmillan, 75–85.

Morford, Mark (2006). 'American Teens, Perky as Candy: Disney's Dorky Smash Hit "High School Musical" Proves Teens Aren't What You Think. Are They?' *San Francisco Gate*, 22 March. Available online: http://www.sfgate.com/entertainment/morford/article/American-Teens-Perky-As-Candy-Disney-s-dorky-2539010.php (accessed 7 July 2015).

Munford, Rebecca (2007). '"Wake Up and Smell the Lipgloss": Gender, Generation and the (A)politics of Girl Power.' In Stacy Gillis, Gillian Howie and Rebecca Munford (eds), *Third Wave Feminism: A Critical Exploration*. Houndmills: Palgrave Macmillan, 266–79.

Potter, Anna (2011). 'It's a Small World After All: New Media Constellations and Disney's Rising Star – the Global Success of *High School Musical*.' *International Journal of Cultural Studies* 15 (2): 117–30.

Projansky, Sarah (2007). 'Mass Magazine Cover Girls: Some Reflections on Postfeminist Girls and Postfeminism's Daughters.' In Yvonne Tasker and Diane Negra (eds), *Interrogating Postfeminism: Gender and the Politics of Popular Culture*. Durham and London: Duke University Press.

Rudisill, Kristin (2009). '"My School Rocks!" Dancing Disney's *High School Musical* in India.' *Studies in Musical Theatre* 3 (3): 253–71.

Sanday, P. (1990). *Fraternity Gang Rape: Sex, Brotherhood and Privilege on Campus*. New York: New York University Press.

Sells, Laura (1995). '"Where do the Mermaids Stand?" Voice and Body in *The Little Mermaid*'. In Elizabeth Bell, Lynda Haas and Laura Sells, *From Mouse to Mermaid: The Politics of Film, Gender and Culture*. Bloomington and Indianapolis: Indiana University Press, 175–92.

Sternfeld, Jessica (2013). '"Everything's Coming Up Kurt": The Broadway Song in *Glee*.' In Dominic Symonds and Millie Taylor, *Gestures of Music Theater: The Performativity of Song and Dance*. New York: Oxford University Press, 128–45.

Stone, Kay (1975). 'Things Walt Disney Never Told Us.' *The Journal of American Folklore* 88 (347): 42–50.

Vande Berg, Leah R. (ed.) (1996). 'Gender and the World of Disney' (special issue) *Women's Studies in Communication* 19 (2).

Wasko, Janet (2002). *Understanding Disney: The Manufacture of Fantasy*. Cambridge: Polity Press.

Whiteley, Sheila (2000). *Women and Popular Music: Sexuality, Identity and Subjectivity*. London: Routledge.

Wolfenden, Katherine J. (2013). 'Challenging Stereotypes in Glee, or Not? Exploring Masculinity and Neoliberal Flexibility.' *Student Pulse* 5 (2): 1–2.

'I Wanna Be Like You': Negotiating Race, Racism and Orientalism in *The Jungle Book* on Stage

Emily Clark, Donatella Galella, Stefanie A. Jones and
Catherine Young

Academic reviews and popular articles frame the racial politics of the new stage musical adaptation of *The Jungle Book* as curable, a liberal stance that mistakes institutional racism for mere ailment (Williams 2014; Cash 2013). In this chapter we frame *The Jungle Book* within structures of power to analyse the political, pleasurable and profitable work that this cultural production performs. Striving to make 'everyone' leave the theatre 'feeling very good' is a central project for producers and for Chicago-based avant-garde director Mary Zimmerman in this staging of one of Disney's highly lucrative properties (Gantz 2013), connecting this production to an economy of pleasure and exploitation that defines musical theatre.

From the Titipu in Gilbert and Sullivan's *The Mikado* (1885) to the Siam of Rodgers and Hammerstein's *The King and I* (1951) to the Bombay of producer Lloyd Webber's *Bombay Dreams* (2002),[1] musical creators and consumers have imagined 'Asia' as an escapist, Orientalist fantasy for more than a century, and this musical tradition intersects in important ways with US popular theatre's capitalization on the tropes of blackface minstrelsy. Through interplay between desire and disavowal, these intersections manifest in and around *The Jungle Book*, co-produced by Disney Theatrical Productions, the Huntington Theatre in Boston and the Goodman Theatre in Chicago, where the musical premiered in 2013. This contemporary stage production existed within a race-conscious discourse used to disavow its racist performative ideology and its implication in systemic racism, producing profit through seduction and pleasure rather than outright domination.

The Jungle Book is based on the Disney animated film and the story collection by Rudyard Kipling. A white Englishman born in India, Kipling is perhaps most infamous for his poem 'The White Man's Burden', which justifies white supremacist imperialism and colonialism, specifically of the Philippines. In *The Jungle Book* (1893) Kipling narrates the adventures of Mowgli, an Indian boy, as well as other charismatic animals that navigate the perils of the jungle and the British Empire. Focusing on a few of Kipling's stories, Disney's 1967 animated musical film adaptation cultivates the jungle as a mostly fun-filled, liminal space for children to explore until they must mature and enter proper civilization, further imbuing the tale with hierarchized distinctions of bodies and knowledges. The new stage production builds on these stories and sensibilities, complicating them with the presence of real bodies on stage.

In this chapter we argue that in staging *The Jungle Book* Disney and Zimmerman capitalize upon white supremacy by carefully producing and delimiting acceptable Orientalist and minstrel 'pleasures' and simultaneously disavowing institutional and structural racism. We begin by situating our terms and this production historically. We highlight the unequal creative relationships at the site of production as well as the rhetorical manoeuvres on race and power mobilized as part of *The Jungle Book*'s distribution. We explore the distinctions between Zimmerman's denial of implication in structural racism and the show's politics of racial representation, particularly through a close reading of African-American actor André De Shields performing 'I Wanna Be Like You'. We conclude with critical consumption as a measure of our analysis, finding that critics continue to defend the white supremacist projects in which Disney and Zimmerman engage. These economic, discursive and artistic exchanges demonstrate the producers' and artists' participation in social reproductions of racism and open up opportunities for guilt-free profit and pleasure derived from the relationship between the non-profit clime, Orientalism and minstrelsy.

Theorizing Racial Hierarchy

When we cite race, racism, white supremacy, Orientalism and minstrelsy, we are pointing to specific historical and material edifices. We begin from racial formation, a changing process of socially constructed categories with which to apprehend and value varying bodies; 'race' within it is both construct and reality, not in the sense of biological essence but in the myriad ways that macro laws and micro encounters continuously interpolate bodies in measurably patterned ways (Omi and Winant 1994). 'Racism' is this pattern of racial material inequalities that hierarchically sort and govern bodies. Our currently existing order of racial hierarchy is 'white supremacy', which is also the governing principle of that field of power (Swartz 1998). Instead of being an individual institution, white supremacy is a structure that orders many institutions, and allows those institutions to continue to reshape themselves for the maintenance of existing racial hierarchy (Davis 2012). Thus, while institutions distribute resources unevenly according to the differing racialization of bodies, the rules and practices of white supremacy craft *the means by which* such resources are unevenly distributed, with whites as a class accruing and maintaining dominance if not hegemony since at least the modern era.

In the realm of middlebrow theatrical production, two such means of inequitable distribution are particularly important: Orientalism and minstrelsy. More than just cultural forms, Orientalism is a logic of white supremacy that produces representations of 'the Orient' broadly functioning to racialize East and Southeast Asians, as well as Arab Muslims, as exotic and threatening yet inferior Others. For the largely, although not exclusively, white producers and consumers of middlebrow theatre, Orientalist representations can be pleasurable precisely because they maintain white supremacy and material inequality. Joy and comfort in exotic fantasies of Asianness depend on not only constructions of purported Asian inferiority, but also the idea that Asians supposedly deserve this subjection (Said 1978). At the same time, the purportedly authentic characteristics used to subjugate those racialized as Asian fuel the industry for 'exotic' cultural productions.

The other major theatrical legacy of racial hierarchization with which *The Jungle Book* engages is minstrelsy. An antebellum US performance mode that was globally popular for more than a century, blackface minstrelsy commodifies degrading performative stereotypes of blackness as excessive and uncontainable. It haunts contemporary black performance, especially the racially marked traditions of jazz and tap. Minstrelsy positions blackness as, variously, comic and tragic, stupid and sly, nostalgic for plantation life, beastly, over- and de-sexualized. Minstrelsy also requires a pleasurable virtuosity because talent and pleasure are central to disavowing the capital accrual and hierarchizing associated with the form.

Although it operates differently from Orientalism, minstrelsy likewise profits from the 'celebration and exploitation' of its racial representations (Lott 2013: 6). Both minstrelsy and Orientalism allege unmediated encounters with 'Others', who are 'authentically' represented in cultural productions. And both of these representations generate pleasure as they distribute power and capital according to white supremacy, creating hierarchized differences in who knows versus who is known, who is marked and who unmarked, and who must continue to be subjugated for others to thrive. When these dynamics are openly critiqued, US middlebrow cultural producers often call for abstract ideals such as humanity, universalism and artistry to control interpretations and defuse the salience of power imbalances. This defensiveness is a stark reminder that the production of Orientalism and minstrelsy actually reveals more about white supremacy than it does of Asianness or blackness, despite the Asian and black bodies (among others) who must labour to produce these representational logics. By contextualizing the creation, distribution and consumption of cultural productions, we examine racialized desire and disavowal in *The Jungle Book* as part of this white supremacist order.

Situating *The Jungle Book*: Disney's History of Racial Hierarchy

The stage is set for André De Shields' performance as the orangutan King Louie in *The Jungle Book* by Disney's long history of racializing as black sidekick and ne'er-do-well animal characters. Such characters include the crows in *Dumbo* (1941), Br'er Fox in *Song of the South* (1946), Scat Cat in *The Aristocats* (1970), Sebastian the Crab in *The Little Mermaid* (1991) and Mushu in *Mulan* (1998). Disney also deploys racially marked jazz/swing numbers that foster chaotic revelry, like *Dumbo*'s 'When I See an Elephant Fly', *The AristoCats*' 'Everybody Wants to Be a Cat' (voiced by Scatman Crothers) and *Tarzan*'s 'Trashin' the Camp' (1999). In the last two examples, Disney's creative teams were directly inspired by the earlier successful musical style and composition of 'I Wanna Be Like You' from the 1967 *Jungle Book* film. Logics of racial representation, created in animation through tone, setting, accent, language, racialized voicecasting, performance, musical styles, context and intertexuality, precipitate more explicitly when Disney's animated films are adapted into live theatrical productions cast with human performers.[2]

Disney has adapted six animated films for Broadway. The 'Disneyfication' of Times Square has been well documented by theatres scholars, urban planners and globalization experts. The process began in 1994 with the stage production of *Beauty and the Beast*. However, it was Disney's massive renovation of the New Amsterdam Theatre for Julie Taymor's *The Lion King* (1997) that became the anchor of Mayor Rudy Giuliani's strategic plan to clean up Times Square and rebrand it as a family friendly international destination (Wollman 2002). Disney has since produced *Aida* (2000–4), *Tarzan* (2006–7), *The Little Mermaid* (2008–9) and *Aladdin* (2014). As Giroux and Pollock maintain,

Disney, like every other multinational corporation, has a major interest in seeking out new markets and securing lifetime consumers in already established markets. Making profits for shareholders, creating a market base that continues to buy, and shaping culture towards consumption, then, are its main corporate goals. (2010: 159)

Disney celebrates its enormous global theatre presence, proclaiming, 'a Disney musical is being performed professionally somewhere on the planet virtually every hour of the day. Worldwide, its eight Broadway titles have been seen by over 124 million theatergoers and have, cumulatively, run a staggering 195 years' (Chicago Goes Wild 2013: n.p.). Moreover, the corporation is careful to keep *The Jungle Book* from disturbing the ongoing success of its most profitable theatre property and one of its most successful franchises, *The Lion King*, because of their similar stagings of multiracial casts as animal–human hybrids helmed by white avant-garde women directors.[3]

In an attempt to address popular anxieties about the racialization of bodies and music, the musical theatre creative team of *The Jungle Book* sought Indian authenticity. With Disney's financial support, Zimmerman and most of her white collaborators (including composer Doug Peck, scenic designer Daniel Ostling, costume designer Mara Blumenfeld and lighting designer TJ Gerckens) toured India for two and a half weeks to witness for themselves the culture they were to depict on stage (Sullivan 2013). Zimmerman, reflecting on the trip, noted that the team 'saw and felt things you just can't get by going online' such as 'the animals – especially the monkeys, who are everywhere, some friendly and some not. We even visited a tiger park' (Weiss 2013). Taking photographs, buying fabric from the markets and interacting with indigenous animals came to represent encountering an authentic India from which the creative team could begin to imagine their story as real (Huntington Theatre n.d.). Zimmerman replicates the dynamic that black feminist critic bell hooks decries in 'Eating the Other', with the already fictional Orient functioning as spice to enliven dull white culture. hooks warns, 'the commodification of difference promotes paradigms of consumption wherein whatever difference the Other inhabits is eradicated, *via* exchange, by a consumer cannibalism that not only displaces the Other but denies the significance of that Other's history through a process of decontextualization' (hooks 1992: 31). Indeed, Zimmerman and her team positioned themselves as above and outside the culture they observed (Brandon 1989), in a manner reminiscent of the origin stories justifying racist musical performance on the popular US stage since TD Rice learned to 'Jump Jim Crow'. In this formula, cursory contact with racial 'Others' becomes part of the artists' claims to authentic representation.

The artistic team's trip, along with their blending of American and Indian music and their choreographic collaboration with Hema Rajagopalan, the artistic director of the Natya Dance Theatre in Chicago, provided fodder that reviewers used to defend this Orientalist project as 'authentic'.

In addition to Disney's history of racialized production and the creative team's research on Indian culture, the origins of *The Jungle Book* musical brought together for-profit producers with non-profit regional theatres. Zimmerman named the aesthetics of this unexpected union: 'I was very frank about wanting to take the elements of Indian music and dance seriously, without losing the great joy of the animated version' (Weiss 2013: n.p.). The political and racial projects of the film were essential for a multi-cultural and multiracial update for the stage. According to Disney Theatricals CEO Thomas Schumacher, European partners particularly wanted this property to be adapted for the stage, likely for the profitable potential of its memorable songs 'I Wanna Be Like You' and 'Bare Necessities' as well as Europe's particular relationship with a romanticized history of imperialism and colonization. The production opened at the Goodman on 21 June 2013 and transferred to the Huntington three months later (Jones 2013b). Although these non-profit theatres were the lead producers, Disney's contribution of hundreds of thousands of dollars of enhancement money meant that the corporation retained rights for future commercial productions. This arrangement provided the regional theatres with funding and a popular, high-quality product; it provided Disney with a built-in subscriber-base audience, non-profit cultural capital and a safe testing ground away from the critical gaze of New York, as well as a certain distance from the risks of staging such a historically controversial property.

For Zimmerman, the evocative improvisatory potential of jazz supported her interest in interweaving Indian and US cultural forms. Jazz is a distinctly American form, associated with a legacy of important African-American performance modes. The New Orleans style conjures an iconic city known for its majority black population and as the birthplace of Louis Armstrong. Taking their cue from the Sherman brothers' film score, Zimmerman's creative team was specific in its turn to New Orleans-style jazz featuring trombones, trumpets with mutes and tuba. While *The Jungle Book*'s marketing materials need not name the Americanness of jazz, they erased the complicated specificities of Hindustani and Carnatic music that influenced the production. As a consequence, a generalized national 'Indian music' emerged as a viable counterpart to more specific Dixieland jazz. A Goodman promotional video depicts a joyous jam session as Peck lists the many instruments that represent the encounter: 'Our orchestra is half Indian instruments and half jazz instruments. We have clarinets, saxophones, flutes, piano, bass, and drums, mixing with harmoniums, tablas, sitars, veenas, ghatams, all the beautiful sounds of India fusing together with the jazz' ('Behind the Scenes' 2013). Peck's 'half-and-half' formula suggests an even cultural exchange that elides the imbalance of capital in the Disney/Zimmerman/Goodman/Huntington enterprise; this imbalance persists despite the agency of or even the pleasure experienced by individual musicians. Many of the Indian musicians are part of the *mise-en-scène* in Zimmerman's *The Jungle Book*. Being on stage is not an uncommon performance practice for East and South Asian musicians, nor for jazz musicians. Nonetheless, within the Western performance context of *The Jungle Book*, the musicians, like the instruments that make the soundscape 'exotic', play a part in granting visibility and authority to the alleged authenticity and antiracism of the production, which we explore in more depth below.

In Chandra Talpade Mohanty's classic formula (2003), Zimmerman has developed much of her substantial oeuvre 'under western eyes'. Within the Chicago–Broadway theatre matrix, she has differentiated herself among other white women directors coming from ensemble backgrounds such as Tina Landau and Anna Shapiro by adapting and interpreting Eastern texts that facilitate working on an epic scale in terms of *mise-en-scène* and movement. As Khoury (2013) argues, Zimmerman has produced many theatrical works drawn from Asian cultures that treat performers, characters and narratives as beautifully stylized stage pictures, such as *The Arabian Nights*, *The White Snake* and *Mirror of the Invisible World*. Scenic designer Daniel Ostling's 'sensual and gorgeous ... florally infused designs' (Jones 2013c) built a beguiling world of opulent pleasure that organically interweaves with the bright and meticulous work of costume designer Mara Blumenfeld. The aesthetic appeal of the production design has the potential to bolster audience pleasure and mute political critique of Zimmerman's creative choices, even as it is Zimmerman's penchant for highly decorative Orientalism that requires critique. A key facet of Orientalism is the aestheticization of the 'East' in contrast to the alleged substantive nature of the 'West', and Zimmerman's directorial vision troublingly reproduces this objectification.

In fact, the Chicago-based production team enacted an extremely uneven relationship of Western first-world consumption throughout the creative development. Marketing materials and reviews repeatedly evoked this Orient as a consumable exotic (for example, Isherwood 2013; Vitello 2013; Gantz 2013). The *Boston Globe* notes that Zimmerman 'envisioned *Indian-flavored* sets, costumes, music and dance', and quotes a songwriter as modifying a description of a remarkably pretty song by noting it has 'an Indian flavor to it'. Peck indicates the artistic intention to add Indian elements to enhance (or, dare we say, spice up) a genuine Disney original that forms the basis for the show; the Huntington's blog also centres the Disney movie while positioning the musical as more distinguished and thus worth the ticket: 'Though the Jungle Book sprang out of a familiar film with iconic animation and music, this new version promises its own unforgettable experience, alive with the spirit of its inspiration and saturated with the sights and sounds of India' (Huntington Theatre n.d.). The stage version is unique because Zimmerman adds 'just the right amount of Indian influence' (Oxman 2013). The show is worth the ticket price because it strives for a particular version of India: 'a world where you are one with nature and the animals – even with all its dangers and troubles. And also [the audience should experience] the recognition that you can't stay there' (Huntington Theatre n.d.). This is a distinctly Saidian Orientalism that posits India as generic and ahistorical, exotic and inferior (particularly through connecting humans to animals), and a threat as well as a political impossibility.

Race-based Hierarchies of Cultural Capital: Close-up on Choreographers

This chapter is not meant to be a recommendation for how to stage *The Jungle Book* 'correctly'; artists participate in racial hierarchy and capitalism regardless of their intentions. In short, it is the material consequences of racial inequality, not the eye of the beholder that matters. The unequal power relationship between Zimmerman/Disney and the racialized others they create exists at all levels of the production from the songs to the costumes, and this is mediated and largely replicated by journalistic responses to the piece. While Zimmerman and a number of news sources disavow this power imbalance, they are revealed despite the production team's intentions. The choreography, like the rest of the production aesthetics, centres white Western perspective with just enough Indian exoticism for authorization. This permits the artists to retain and expand their existing capitals while maintaining existing structures of domination.

Christopher Gattelli, the Tony Award-winning choreographer for Disney's stage version of *Newsies* (2012), was hired to choreograph the musical and local Chicago 'choreographer–dancer Hema Rajagopalan acted as a consultant' (Aucoin 2013), as some pre-opening materials are careful to note. Rajagopalan is a proponent of Classical Indian dance and is the recipient of numerous awards including one from the National Endowment for the Arts and an Emmy award for choreography ('Hema's Story' n.d.).

Nonetheless, her name and title are not found in most of the promotional material or reviews after the show opened in Chicago, and she is not listed in the Huntington's programme. Centring on Gattelli but retaining Rajagopalan as a consultant allows the production to treat Bharatanatyam dance form as Indian spice enhancing the substantively American musical theatre style of the production. Zimmerman's work is 'authenticated' by an Indian expert, thereby maintaining and disavowing her engagement with white supremacy.

Despite Rajagopalan's knowledge, experience and accolades, her participation in the musical appears to have been to legitimize Gattelli's artistic choices. When discussing his work on the production, Gattelli says, 'I'll have ideas and I'll come up with movements, and I'll ask Hema, "is this appropriate?" and it's great to have someone there who will say, "Yes" or, "We would really use this hand gesture for this." I want to stay true to the culture and the form' (Arndt 2013). Gattelli's choreography certainly uses Bharatanatyam *mudras*, and, under the observance of Rajagopalan, they were used fittingly when possible, but Gattelli does not speak the language of the movement and has never trained in the form. Yet with his assertion 'Oh, I'm not really far from this at all' Gattelli dismisses the decades of rehearsal and study that practitioners of Bharatanatyam, like Rajagopalan, have dedicated to the art form, to say nothing of the hundreds of years of cultural tradition that such performers honour (Weinert-Kendt 2013).

Rajagopalan's inclusion nevertheless permits the denial of Orientalism. Simultaneously, Rajagopalan was not hired as the choreographer for the show, confirming the distinctly material inequity of her adjunct position. Gattelli's cultural capital both from his work with Lincoln Centre (including other depictions of the Orient such as the 2009 revival of *South Pacific*) and his work on *Newsies* could be converted easily into economic capital and additional cultural capital. Rajagopalan's cultural capital, while invaluable for its purported authenticity, continues to be dominated within the already racially hierarchized field. This is an example of how white supremacy is continually rebuilt, including through this production. Independent of their intentions or labour, Gattelli is authorized as the figure who can decide how to represent Indianness, while Rajagopalan is tokenized to protect Zimmerman's production by legitimizing this representation. Like Broadway as a whole, *The Jungle Book* is a collusion between for-profit and non-profits, and connects this profit to both multiracial productions and to racial hierarchy.

(Not) Talking about Racism

Director Mary Zimmerman's artistic and discursive negotiations around *The Jungle Book* both acknowledge and deny imperialism, Orientalism and minstrelsy. The producers scrambled to defend their positions around this production after Zimmerman was interviewed by *Chicago* magazine and the founding artistic director of Silk Road Rising, Jamil Khoury, responded critically to the director's disavowal of historic colonial and continuing racial material inequality (Khoury 2013). We quote Zimmerman in both her initial interview and her follow-up interview with Khoury in order to illustrate the power structures revealed by her strategies of disavowal, and to counter the myriad articles that work to redeem the director as unambiguously *not racist* (Stevens 2014).[4] When asked whether critiques of King Louie as a racial stereotype (Metcalf 1991) concerned her, the director replied:

> Yeah, it was a concern. But I've decided to make it not a concern. I know what the lyrics say and how squeamish you can get about that. But we've done some things with casting that I'm not going to give away, but that I think will remove that element. I know what the lyrics of ['I Wanna Be Like You'] say, but look at the original – it's sung by Louis Prima. He's the King of the Swingers. It's something I think where the racism is in the eye of the beholder, you know? If you look at that as racist, doesn't that say more about what you're projecting on to the character? There's clearly politics in the [British] accents Disney used, but I don't think we'll be using accents at all.
>
> Having been in India I realize most of the stuff we know about India is from books written by Westerners. But you go over there and you see that the British occupation was so short in the history of the country. No one is sitting around moping about the raj. You have to remember the past, but you don't have to live in it. (Sullivan 2013)

Zimmerman acknowledges oppression historically only to disavow it as a continued material reality. She acknowledges 'concern' of replicating stereotypes and doing symbolic violence through the performance of King Louie and his song 'I Wanna Be Like You'. Then she dehistoricizes and thus dematerializes that concern by citing her casting, the original vocal performance for the animated film and the lack of British accents. In so doing, she erases how King Louie was originally imagined with black performer Louis Armstrong in mind (Weinert-Kendt 2013), and how American accents and American histories of imperialism are far from neutral (Pao 2004; Davé 2013). Her frequent vacillation betrays an intense anxiety and the persistent salience of race and racism despite her disavowals. Because she argues that 'racism is in the eye of the beholder', grounding systemic oppression in personal perspective, racial material inequality is, to her, handily solved by certain ahistorical artistic decisions, specifically those that demonstrate that her own personal perspective does not see racism. Zimmerman uses her professed familiarity with India to acknowledge Orientalist knowledge production but also to make light of a long, impactful history of British and US imperialism and colonialism. By minimizing racism and locating it in the distant past, Zimmerman demands that the oppressed move beyond historical and continuing inequities (Bonilla-Silva 2010). Zimmerman's strategic denials reflect what Brandi Wilkins Catanese identifies as 'racial transcendence [which] exacts disavowal of our racially mediated reality as the price of progress toward resolving American society's racial conflicts' (2011: 21).

In the interview with *Chicago* magazine as well as in the follow-up with Khoury, Zimmerman continues to practice disavowal, racial transcendence and personalization. Speaking to her quip 'racism is in the eye of the beholder', she clarifies, 'I was attempting to locate the act of racism, in this single specific example, in the observer and not the observed object – not to deny the fact of it' (Khoury and Zimmerman 2013). She at once implies that racism writ large exists yet reasserts that the 'real' racist is the person who perceives a history of minstrelsy. She does not alter her original dehistoricization project when she explains

> My understanding of the term 'orientalism' is as a kind of fetishized and objectifying drive towards a culture different from one's own. While it is certainly possible to have such fetishes, I also believe that one can love a text from another culture as one can love a person from another culture.
> (Khoury and Zimmerman 2013)

By generalizing Orientalism as if it is a universal process that could be applied to all cultures, and personalizing this knowledge production by comparing it to a loving relationship, she appeals to liberal humanism and erases material inequality between oppressors and the oppressed including, perhaps ironically, the material power differentials of who can critique Orientalism: Zimmerman or Khoury?

The Jungle Book's multiracial cast offered multiple possible interpretations of the meaning of race and racial hierarchy (Pao 2010). While such interpretations have the potential to disrupt or reify traditional understandings of race and racial hierarchy, various figures in the fields of theatrical and cultural production struggled over the show's meaning. The cast for *The Jungle Book* read as diverse, with slightly more than half people of colour who were legible as seven South Asian performers, three black performers and eight white performers. On the one hand, providing much needed opportunities for actors of colour is cause for some celebration, given that approximately 80 per cent of professional roles on Broadway and off-Broadway go to whites (Asian American Performers Action Coalition 2012). Nevertheless, actors of any race can participate in white supremacist patterns of representation. Anjali Bhimani, the actress who originated the role of the Mother Wolf and 'the daughter of Indian immigrants', dismisses Kipling's imperialism, noting '"The Jungle Book" was simply a story from my childhood that let me access adult themes through animals' (Weiss 2013). Regardless of how true this is for Bhimani, this depoliticization serves as a model for reviewers to respond to critiques of imperialism. In addition, the audience enters the story through Mowgli, providing room for critical empathy with an Indian character. Yet he is also a cypher reducible to his brown body. As the *Chicago Tribune*'s Mark Caro notes, the episodic structure of a 'little kid ... being passed off from [this] animal group to [this] animal group' shapes Mowgli as a passive character (2013). Because the villains, Shere Khan and Kaa, and the elephants, which represent British colonial order, were played by mostly white actors, Zimmerman's casting suggests attentiveness to certain white regimes of domination. At the same time, the racialization of the characters relies upon a history of racist representation and inequitable resource distribution. Furthermore, the mix of actors suggests that spectators should not read race closely for dramaturgical and historical logic: we are beyond race in this multiracial version of India, an extremely pernicious ideology in an era when most Americans deny structural racism (Galella 2015). For example, De Shields first appears as Akela, the magisterial Lone Wolf, and subsequently as King Louie amidst a multiracial ensemble as if to raise and then neutralize questions of racial meaning, framing race as mutable and thus immaterial.

Actor, Director, Producer, Audience: The Political Economic Stakes of 'I Wanna Be Like You'

Although Zimmerman would identify us as the real racists, we continue to see racist and antiracist dynamics ghosted by minstrelsy in a close reading of the musical's big number 'I Wanna Be Like You'. In this performance, De Shields replicates a Jazz Age template in which virtuosic technique is presented within a plot and *mise-en-scène* tinged with social Darwinism and eugenic logic. As King Louie, De Shields holds court in the mode of Cab Calloway leading 'Jumpin' Jive', and, like Calloway, he appears to be enjoying every minute of it. De Shields even seems to exaggerate the racialized connotations of the role by choosing to insert subject–verb disagreement where none exists in the original lyric, singing for example 'I *wants* to be like you', as a strategy to differentiate performer from character. With a precise twitch of his shoulder, swivel in his hips and a swing of his cane, De Shields masterfully performs showmanship. His expertise creates potential for spectators to simultaneously celebrate King Louie and transcend race and racism through the dehistoricization of black representation. Chris Jones of the *Chicago Tribune* found De Shields' performance so virtuosic that it obliterated the historical controversy of the song:

> De Shields does what only great actors know how to do: Stuff the history, ignore the naysayers, take charge as an artist, dig deep into the truth of the character of King Louie and the aspirational lyric and sell the entire package to the back row. By the end of this number, all the racially complex cobwebs have been swept away. It is the highlight of the night. (Jones 2013a)

But the song is more complex than this, with the meaning changing during the course of the performance. At first, King Louie addresses Mowgli. Because he stands nattily attired in a marigold-hued sherwani and zoot suit pants next to the nearly nude Mowgli (played alternately by Roni Akurati or Akash Chopra), the thought that imperious and playful King Louie might want to be anything like the vulnerable, inexperienced Mowgli seems far-fetched. At the same time, the actors are not subsumed by the characters they play. The audience sees a black man telling a brown boy that he hopes to emulate him. This replicates a social Darwinist racial hierarchy that puts blacks at the bottom, whites at the top, and non-black people of colour within an indeterminate middle. Moreover, animals are linked to racialized bodies and placed below humans, who are linked to white subjectivity. De Shields' costume, cut to reveal his pectorals, connects King Louie to the lesser monkey characters whose costumes reveal the skin of their arms and torsos, aligning the bare body with primate characters while other animal groups such as wolves, vultures, elephants and butterflies don full-coverage costumes. The 'you' of the song shifts toward the end of the number as King Louie acknowledges and playfully upturns the racial hierarchies of British colonialism. Joshua Williams (2014) notes De Shields 'aped the mannered formality of a tea party – a gesture, perhaps, toward Homi Bhabha's concept of mimicry as anti-colonial critique', suggesting that race is performative and De Shields a masterful performer. And De Shields's virtuosity sparkles during his final enunciations of 'I wanna be like you': as he turns to address the audience, spitting out the words, daring spectators to defy him, he holds a tremendously long note. Why would he want to be like us when he is the top? By changing who he addresses throughout the performance, De Shields takes turns in replicating, challenging and transcending racial hierarchy to both disrupt and produce the racial order, encouraging the audience to applaud his virtuosic performance as both representative of and an exception to racial hierarchy.

While De Shields's performance engaged multi-dimensionally with contemporary racial hierarchy, Zimmerman dealt with these complications by asserting that her casting practices solved the racist legacy of *The Jungle Book* and in particular the blackface baggage of King Louie (Miller and Rode 1995). De Shields's skill and participation functioned to authorize Zimmerman and *The Jungle Book* as not racist, as if institutional racism could so easily be solved. Zimmerman recalled that De Shields chose to audition for the role of King Louie and explained, '[I]f I hadn't cast him, it would have been because he is African–American. That would have been the only reason – the fear of the past, of the historical discourse, of the stereotypes of the past' (Isaacs 2013). In this account, Zimmerman is caught in a contradiction the result of a false racist/not-racist binary created by imagining that any production decision (such as casting) could cure white supremacy. Aptly recognizing that it would be troubling to deny De Shields the part because of stereotypes, Zimmerman must defend her authority on racial politics by arguing that the only *real* racism would be to deny De Shields the part because of his race, thus defending from critique the Orientalism that is the foundation of her career. Yet the above quotation illustrates how her colourblind proclamations achieve the exact opposite of what she claims: she needed to permit race to be a factor in this casting decision in order to be colourblind, reflecting how allegedly colourblind casting often reinforces racial categories and hierarchies rather than disrupts them.

To retain her capital despite the limits of her solution for racial hierarchy, she positions De Shields as a free agent and virtuosic performer and herself as a bold, colourblind artist moving forward unburdened by racism. The casting of King Louie with De Shields is indeed 'really layered' as Zimmerman observes (Isaacs 2013). Choosing a black actor rather than a white one in part redresses the original, vocally blacked-up casting, but the performance of this jazzy, swinging orangutan by an African–American performer remains haunted by the legacy of blackface minstrelsy that cannot be broken by a simple opposition between past and present casting decisions (Lott 2013; Catanese 2011; Robinson 2007; Lee 2003; Lhamon, Jr 2000; Metcalf 1991). Zimmerman's production spectacularizes blackness as well as the Orient, regardless of the individual 'eye of the beholder' because the reception that the 'eye' represents is itself structured in and by power. By emphasizing De Shields's artistry and the audience's receipt of it as separate and separable from politics, and using such anti-political inclusion to dismiss critiques that challenge her Orientalist vision and practice, Zimmerman advances a troublingly post-racial view that obscures and upholds racial hierarchy.

Conclusions

The Jungle Book stage musical continues a long history of Orientalist, minstrel and Disney productions whose racial politics cannot be easily dismissed. Yet the artistic production team labours to do just this by cultivating myths of authenticity, exoticism and exchange. While Zimmerman's own interviews reveal the contradictions of this in practice, critical consumption also affirms the racial politics we describe. One such review makes explicit the political consequences of Zimmerman's racial project. In the *Chicago Reader* Tony Adler focuses on the very negotiations around racism that we have explored throughout this chapter. Adler clearly favours Zimmerman, whom he finds 'soothing', over Khoury, whose response is a 'screed' (2013). Reflecting that Zimmerman has not changed her original position on race and racism, Adler notes that she is merely 'going about her business – with maybe just the slightest thumb of the nose in the thrown in'. After Khoury's confrontation, Zimmerman continued unabated her disavowal of the material racial hierarchy in which she was comfortably situating herself.

Critical reception reveals the politics that are obscured by the extensive project of disavowal launched around *The Jungle Book*. Adler proclaims that, for Zimmerman, 'there's no such thing as purity when it comes to culture', and that this is what marks her as not-Orientalist, as though critiques of the 'ruthless conquest and exploitation' of Orientalism are about protecting a now-impossible cultural purity instead of struggles against future white supremacist harms. Adler emphasizes that certain key qualities of *The Jungle Book*'s production are Zimmerman's best answer to accusations of racism: the show's diversity (in the variety of musical animals present on stage as well as the variety of musical instruments), 'tolerance' (because Mowgli is accepted by those animals) and cultural 'mix of everything from everywhere all the time'. Tolerance, involving an empowered party aligned with dominant interests who is authorized to permit the survival of that which/ who is tolerated, is a form of political action that is not just amenable to but already ridden with hierarchy. In addition, critical theorist Wendy Brown's exploration of tolerance revealing it as a liberal project that 'is an exercise of hegemony that requires extensive political transformation of the cultures and subjects it would govern' is apt (Brown 2006: 202). The conditions of a tolerant relation grant the person(s) doing the tolerating moral legitimacy, while requiring the tolerated be subjugated to, at the very least, the tolerator's symbolic order. A critic, producer, director or audience that is tolerant is affirmed as an authority who deigns to read and not-kill a tolerated performer; a tolerant production is anything but an anti-racist political goal. While tolerance is a different logic propelling the formation of race and racial hierarchy than that of 1893 or 1967, and while it is today coupled with a certain celebration of the pleasures of diversity, this particular recipe for 'cultural mixing' produces the same hierarchies in symbolic, economic and cultural capital as other modern forms of white supremacy. Tolerance, superficial diversity and cultural mixing are the end game of Zimmerman's racial politics, yet absolutely compatible with white supremacy. Zimmerman's stance on race and racism and her production of *The Jungle Book* aligned with contemporary hegemonic interests and specifically Disney's long history of capitalizing upon racial hierarchies in performance. Those hierarchies, though vigorously disavowed, remain significantly profitable.

References

Adler, T. (2013). 'The *Jungle Book* Wars, Onstage: Mary Zimmerman's Best Answer to Her Critics is This Flawed, Defiant Show,' 3 July. Available online: http://www.chicagoreader.com/chicago/mary-zimmerman-jungle-book-goodman-theatre/Content?oid=10213978 (accessed 30 June 2015).

Arndt, N. (2013). 'The Jungle Sings and Sways: Music and Dance in *The Jungle Book*,' June. Available online: https://www.goodmantheatre.org/Documents/OnStage/1213/1213Onstage_5.pdf (accessed 18 February 2015).

Asian American Performers Action Coalition (2012). 'Ethnic Representation on New York City Stages 2006/07-2010-11 Seasons,' February. Available online: http://www.aapacnyc.org/uploads/1/1/9/4/11949532/ethnic_representation_nyc.pdf (accessed 9 April 2015).

Aucoin, D. (2013), 'André De Shields to star in Mary Zimmerman's "Jungle Book" at the Huntington,' 24 April. Available online: http://www.boston.com/culturedesk/2013/04/24/andre-shields-star-mary-zimmerman-jungle-book-the-huntington/tDgXyITECf7bVS7Jv7MQUO/story.html (accessed 27 June 2015).

Bonilla-Silva, E. (2010). *Racism without Racists: Color-Blind Racism and Racial Inequality in Contemporary America*, 3rd edn. Plymouth: Rowman & Littlefield.

Brandon, J. R. (1989). 'A New World: Asian Theatre in the West Today.' *The Drama Review* 33 (2): 25–50.

Brater, J., J. Del Vecchio, A. Friedman, B. Holmstrom, E. Laine, D. Levit, H. Miller, D. Savran, C. Griffin Smith, K. Watt, C. Young and P. Zazzali (2010). '"Let Our Freak Flags Fly": *Shrek the Musical* and the Branding of Diversity.' *Theatre Journal* 62 (2) (May): 151–72.

Brown, W. (2006). *Regulating Aversion: Tolerance in the Age of Identity and Empire*. Princeton, NJ: Princeton University Press.

Caro, M. (2013). 'Goodman's Jungle Book: "Visually Beautiful".' Available online: https://www.youtube.com/watch?v=lXbO6Pnh8_c (accessed 30 June 2015).

Cash, D. (2013). 'How to Adapt *The Jungle Book* (and Not Make it Racist).' *Atlantic*, 7 October. Available online: http://www.theatlantic.com/ entertainment/archive/2013/10/how-to-adapt-em-the-jungle-book-em-and-not-make-it-racist/280292/ (accessed 25 June 2015).

Catanese, B. W. (2011). *The Problem of the Color[blind]: Racial Transgression and the Politics of Black Performance*. Ann Arbor: University of Michigan Press.

Davé, S. (2013). *Indian Accents: Brown Voice and Racial Performance in American Television and Film*. Urbana: University of Illinois Press.

Davis, A. Y. (2012). 'Recognizing Racism in the Era of Neoliberalism'. In *The Meaning of Freedom: And Other Difficult Dialogues*. San Francisco: City Lights.

Galella, D. (2015). 'Redefining America, Arena Stage, and Territory Folks in a Multiracial *Oklahoma!*' *Theatre Journal* 67 (2) (May): 213–33.

Gantz, J. (2013). 'Giving "Jungle Book" its Beat.' *Boston Globe*, 1 October. Available online: https://www.bostonglobe.com/arts/theater-art/2013/09/30/ musical-fusion-gives-jungle-book-its-beat/Fmw97m09rdoVCMWejMY1kL/ story.html (accessed 25 June 2015).

Giroux, H. A. and G. Pollock (2010). *The Mouse That Roared: Disney and the End of Innocence*. Lanham, MD: Rowman & Littlefield.

Goodman Press (2013). 'Chicago Goes Wild for *The Jungle Book*: An Unprecedented Third Extension Week Just Added, Must Close August 18,' 15 July. Goodman Theatre press release. Available online: thttp://pressroom. goodmantheatre.org/PressArt/LinkClick.aspx?fileticket=68ye-9yX_ Uo%3D&tabid=39&mid=562 (accessed 27 June 2015).

Goodman Theatre (2013). '*The Jungle Book*: Behind the Scenes.' Available online: https://www.youtube.com/watch?v=v2bhBMNqErY (accessed 28 June 2015).

'Hema's Story' (n.d.). Available online: www.natya.com/hemas-story/ (accessed 30 March 2015).

hooks, b. (1992). 'Eating the Other: Desire and Resistance'. In *Black Looks: Race and Representation*. Boston, MA: South End Press.

Huntington Theatre (n.d.). 'The Sights and Sounds of India: Reimagining the Jungle Book.' Available online: http://www.huntingtontheatre.org/mobile/ Blog/?depth=1&srcid=5521 (accessed 25 June 2015).

Isaacs, D. (2013). "'That Felt Wrong": Mary Zimmerman on *The Jungle Book*.' *Chicago Reader*, 8 July. Available online: http://www.chicagoreader.com/ Bleader/archives/2013/07/08/that-felt-wrong-mary-zimmerman-on-the-jungle-book (accessed 30 June 2015).

Isherwood, C. (2013). 'Indian Music Meets Jazz in Kipling's Wild World.' *New York Times*, 7 August. Available online: http://www.nytimes. com/2013/08/07/theater/reviews/the-jungle-book-opens-at-the-goodman-theater.html (accessed 25 June 2015).

Jones, C. (2013a). 'André De Shields' Road to King Louie.' *Chicago Tribune*, 17 July. Available online: http://www.chicagotribune.com/entertainment/ct-ott-0719-jones-loop-20130717-story.html (accessed 12 June 2015).

Jones, C. (2013b). "'The Jungle Book" at Goodman Theatre: When Mary met Walt (and Rudyard).' *Chicago Tribune*, 14 June. Available online: http:// articles.chicagotribune.com/2013-06-14/entertainment/ct-ae-0616-jungle-book-preview-20130614_1_jungle-book-shere-khan-disney-theatricals/2 (accessed 25 June 2015).

Jones, C. (2013c). 'Review: "The Jungle Book" at Goodman Theatre.' *Chicago Tribune*, 1 July. Available online: http://articles.chicagotribune.com/ 2013-07-01/entertainment/ct-ent-0702-jungle-book-review-20130701_1_ the-jungle-book-baloo-mowgli (accessed 25 June 2015).

Khoury, J. (2013). 'The Trouble With Mary,' 11 June. Available online: http:// www.silkroadrising.org/news/the-trouble-with-mary (accessed 24 June 2015).

Khoury, J. and M. Zimmerman (2013). 'Mary Responds: My Interview with Mary Zimmerman,' 14 June. Available online: http://www.silkroadrising.org/ news/mary-responds-my-interview-with-mary-zimmerman (accessed 14 June 2013).

Lee, Josephine (2003). 'Racial Actors, Liberal Myths.' *XCP: Cross Cultural Politics* 13: 88–110.

Lhamon, Jr, W. T. (2000). *Raising Cain: Blackface Performance from Jim Crow to Hip-Hop*. Cambridge: Harvard University Press.

Lott, E. (2013). *Love and Theft: Blackface Minstrelsy and the American Working Class*. Oxford: Oxford University Press.

Lowe, L. (1996). *Immigrant Acts: On Asian American Cultural Politics*. Durham, NC: Duke University Press.

Metcalf, G. (1991). "'It's a Jungle Book Out There, Kid!": The Sixties in Walt Disney's "The Jungle Book".' *Studies in Popular Culture* 14 (1): 85–97.

Mohanty, C. P. (2003). *Feminism without Borders: Decolonizing Theory, Practicing Solidarity*. Durham, NC: Duke University Press.

Omi, M. and H. Winant (1994). *Racial Formation in the United States: From the 1960s to the 1990s*. New York: Routledge.

Oxman, S. (2013). 'Theater Review: "The Jungle Book".' *Variety*, 1 July. Available online: http://variety.com/2013/legit/reviews/legit-review-the-jungle-book-1200503587/ (accessed 25 June 2015).

Pao, A. (2004). 'False Accents: Embodied Dialects and the Characterization of Ethnicity and Nationality.' *Theatre Topics* 14 (1): 353–72.

Pao, A. (2010). *No Safe Spaces: Re-casting Race, Ethnicity, and Nationality in American Theater.* Ann Arbor: University of Michigan Press.

PBS (2004). *Broadway: The American Musical,* Episode Six: 'Putting it Together (1980–Present).' Thirteen/WNET New York Public Broadcasting.

Robinson, C. (2007). *Forgeries of Memory and Meaning: Blacks and the Regimes of Race in American Theater and Film before World War II.* Chapel Hill: University of North Carolina Press.

Said, E. (1978). *Orientalism.* New York: Vintage.

Stevens, R. (2014). 'Stomping on Eggshells: An Honest Discussion of Race, Identity, and Intent in the American Theater,' 2 February. Available online: http://howlround.com/stomping-on-eggshells-an-honest-discussion-of-race-identity-and-intent-in-the-american-theater (accessed 16 June 2015).

Sullivan, C. (2013). 'Here's How Mary Zimmerman Created Goodman Theatre's "The Jungle Book".' *Chicago,* 15 May. Available online: http://www.chicagomag.com/Chicago-Magazine/June-2013/How-Mary-Zimmerman-Created-Goodman-Theatres-Jungle-Book-Musical/ (accessed 25 June 2015).

Swartz, D. (1998). *Culture and Power: The Sociology of Pierre Bourdieu.* Chicago: University of Chicago Press.

Vitello, B. (2013). 'Goodman's enchanting "Jungle Book" delights the ears and eyes.' *Chicago Daily Herald,* 5 July. Available at http://www.dailyherald.com/article/20130705/entlife/707059975/ (accessed 25 June 2015).

Weinert-Kendt, R. (2013). 'Cutting Through a Cultural Thicket: "The Jungle Book" Comes to the Stage.' *New York Times,* 20 June. Available online: http://www.nytimes.com/2013/06/23/theater/the-jungle-book-comes-to-the-stage.html?_r=0 (accessed 18 February 2015).

Weiss, H. (2013). 'East Meets West in Goodman Theatre's "The Jungle Book".' *Chicago Sun Times,* 15 July. Available online: http://voices.suntimes.com/arts-entertainment/the-daily-sizzle/east-meets-west-in-goodman-theatres-the-jungle-book/ (accessed 25 June 2015).

Williams, J. (2014). '*The Jungle Book* directed by Mary Zimmerman.' *Theatre Journal* 66 (2) May: 276–8.

Wollman E. L. (2002). 'The Economic Development of the "New" Times Square and its Impact on the Broadway Musical.' *American Music* 20 (4) (Winter): 445–65.

Ashman's *Aladdin* Archive: Queer Orientalism in the Disney Renaissance

Sam Baltimore

Howard Ashman (1950–91) was a Baltimore-born lyricist, librettist and director. He first became known as a writer of musicals with his adaptation, in collaboration with composer Alan Menken, of Kurt Vonnegut's *God Bless You, Mr. Rosewater* in 1979. Shortly thereafter, in 1982, Ashman and Menken surged to international fame with their off-Broadway smash hit *Little Shop of Horrors*. For *Little Shop*, as for most of Ashman's stage work, he developed the concept (an adaptation of a Roger Corman B-movie), wrote the script and lyrics, and directed the initial production.

Ashman and Menken's first production with Disney was *The Little Mermaid*, a film widely considered the harbinger of the Disney renaissance, the 1980s–1990s run of musicals from a new generation of animators that reinvigorated the studio's animation division. Fresh off the success of the *Little Shop* film (1986), Ashman and Menken were courted by Disney to take *Mermaid* on board – Peter Schneider, the president of the animation division, sent the first drafts of the script to Ashman in the fall of 1986, offering to fly *Mermaid*'s writers to Baltimore to meet with Ashman.[1] The courting was successful, and the team helped usher in a run of successes that the studio hadn't seen in decades.

Largely due to Ashman's involvement, the first three films of the Disney renaissance – *Mermaid*, *Beauty and the Beast* and *Aladdin* – are replete with gay signifiers. Ashman, assisted by other queer employees at Disney, hid gay Easter eggs throughout what would be the final three major projects of his career, playfully relying on (adult) gay audience members to recognize them and other audience members to remain blissfully unaware.[2] This time-honoured camp tradition is part of what links the Ashman–Menken collaborations to the queer history of both film and stage musicals, rather than including any explicitly gay characters, whom Ashman largely avoided, and who would have been taboo in children's entertainment at the height of the AIDS epidemic, regardless of whether or not Ashman wanted to include them.

After the studio released *Mermaid*, but before *Beauty* or *Aladdin* were completed, Ashman died of AIDS. His final days, confined to a hospital in the Bronx, included significant correspondence with Disney personnel working on *Beauty*. As had been the case five years earlier, at the beginning of his Disney career, Ashman's involvement was so important to the studio that despite his location, materials and collaborators were shipped across the country for his approval and consultation. Disney dedicated *Beauty and the Beast* to his memory, though they did not mention on screen what had cut his life so short.

Disney produced *Aladdin* after *Beauty*, hiring lyricist Tim Rice to write additional songs with Alan Menken to replace some of the Ashman and Menken numbers for which the evolving script no longer had a place (see below). The success of Ashman's Disney cartoons, as well as the stage adaptation of *Beauty* (1994), made the 1990s Ashman's most critically acclaimed decade. His posthumous projects often built upon his camp aesthetic, while leaving behind, for better and for worse, some of his ideas about race.

This chapter explores versions of Disney's *Aladdin*, from its proposal to the studio in the 1980s through its film incarnation in the 1990s to its stage version in the 2010s, through the contributions of Howard Ashman, its first lyricist and the driving force behind its adoption by Disney for production. By comparing Ashman's initial proposal to the film and to the stage show, I demonstrate that *Aladdin* developed within a tradition of queer Orientalism that has marked musical comedy throughout the twentieth century. Further, I demonstrate that this queer Orientalist tradition, often intended as a gesture of solidarity between white queer writers and their Orientalized subjects, has been used to exoticize and eroticize Asian and black performers in ways that are, in Ashman's words, 'an ethical mess'.

One Night in Baghdad: Broadway Orientalisms in 2014

On 19 July 2014, I saw two Broadway musicals: *Aladdin* and *Hedwig and the Angry Inch*. A prop distributed at *Hedwig* highlights a surprising connection between shows that seem, at first glance, at opposite ends of the musical theatre spectrum. A candy-coated Disney extravaganza for children and a profanity-laced, sexually explicit rock concert for queers meet in the Playbill for *Hurt Locker: The Musical*, written by *Hedwig* author John Cameron Mitchell. There is, thankfully, no musical version of Kathryn Bigelow's 2008 film about an American bomb disposal team in Iraq, but the mock Playbill elucidates a number of current and longstanding trends in Broadway musicals that inform the stage production of *Aladdin*.

The centrepiece of the Playbill is a 'Director's Note' by fictional director Kip Buckner:

> I had just locked picture on *Man Cave* ... when I got the call to direct *Hurt Locker: The Musical* ... The most bankable blockbuster director working today? Direct a *musical*? Aren't musicals for women and dudes who act like them?
>
> ... 'What do DUDES want to *see*?' Explosions, negligible storytelling, camouflage and tits. And tits are attached to what? Cartilage ...
>
> So I turned to my wife, Tanyaa, who is 1/8 Iranian ... And from this deeply personal primordial soup rose ... Malá ...
>
> *What is the combination to a locker full of hurt?*
>
> ... elements of late 90's post-metal, early 80's catch phrases like 'Where's the beef?', Balinese puppetry, Chechen dentistry, Ultimate Fighting, Arab stuff, dubstep and twerking ...
>
> *(Hurt Locker: The Musical* Playbill: 5)

Buckner's Note skewers contemporary trends in Broadway marketing – 'Apparently there's a brand new movement to get bros to Broadway' – and composition, with its parade of unlikely musical and movement styles combined into an unintelligible mishmash. Simultaneously, it satirizes centuries-old practices of Orientalist writing: 'Malá ... has been enslaved, partitioned, attacked, pillaged, slandered, badly reviewed and unfairly sued. I am Malá. We are all Malá.' The hyper-Orientalized woman is envisioned as geographic feature ripe for penetration while also, somehow, standing in for and shaping the author himself.

This brutal depiction of an (almost) impossibly misogynist and racist white director and his teenaged wife, 'passed out on Ambien ... in her baby tee and thong', highlights the tension between comedy and violence that so often marks the cultural productions and lived experiences of marginalized queer people. The Note exaggerates the racial violence underlying Orientalist entertainment and gendered violence underlying homophobic straight male attitudes toward musicals and 'women and dudes who act like them'. By so extravagantly inflating this violence, it simultaneously diffuses (and, if you'll pardon the bomb-disposal pun, defuses) the impact of that violence through comedy and indicts *Hedwig*'s Broadway neighbours – including *Aladdin* – for participating in similar violence, however carefully disguised.

Aladdin negotiates between the Orientalist violence Mitchell satirizes and the culture of 'women and dudes who act like them' he depicts as the object of that violence. It is liberatory and colonialist, a positive force for the expression of alternative sexuality and an oppressive example of how marginalized groups often perpetuate the subjugation of other, further marginalized populations.

Homoerotic Orientalism: Musicals' Queer Foundations

Many scholars and fans have demonstrated the queerness at the historical and creative heart of the musical comedy. John Clum's *Something for the Boys*, Stacy Wolf's *A Problem Like Maria* and D. A. Miller's *Place for Us*, among other books, explore the connection between queer people and the musical as performers, writers and fans. Miller illustrates the complicated relationship between gay male fans and the golden age musical in *Place for Us*, painting a portrait of the importance of the musical to gay community both pre- and post-Stonewall. Clum, in a similar vein, demonstrates how diva worship, among other factors, is a sign of both gay male influence on and gay male attraction to the genre. Wolf's *A Problem Like Maria*, an important corrective to this male-centric focus, demonstrates the ample room the musical leaves for lesbian fandoms and readings. While these explorations of musicals' reception are important to the genre's queer identity, musicals go far beyond allowing for a gay audience.

As Wolf points out, musicals' plots are '"about" heterosexual romance ... but that doesn't describe what is actually performed on stage ... [musicals] may, ironically, spend more stage time revealing how thoroughly incompatible the couple is' (Wolf 2011: 219). D. A. Miller's queer readings of show tunes, what he describes as 'releas[ing], thus rubbed, a gay genie who had always been lying cramped inside it, but [who] now wafts vaporously, to more or less mischievous effect, over every line' (Miller 2000: 35), demonstrate that musicals frequently welcome their queer audience because the material they contain is legibly, demonstrably queer. Raymond Knapp, Mitchell Morris and many other scholars have read the queer texts and subtexts that exist in musicals prior to their enthusiastic queer fandoms.

Finally, the musical is marked as queer because of the overwhelming presence of queer artists in the genre. As George Chauncey notes in *Gay New York*, in the 1910s a 'gay enclave had quietly developed in Times Square ... because the theater ... attracted large numbers of gay men who worked as chorus boys, actors, stagehands, costume designers and publicity people' (Chauncey 1994: 301–2). Many of the most successful composers, lyricists,

writers, choreographers, directors and performers are queer, from Stephen
Sondheim to Neil Patrick Harris, by way of Leonard Bernstein and the
2015 Tony winner for her book and lyrics for *Fun Home*, Lisa Kron. Even
those creators who are not themselves sexually queer, like Kron's *Fun Home*
collaborator Jeanine Tesori or Bernstein's *On the Town* collaborators Betty
Comden and Adolph Green, nevertheless remain queer in Eve Kosofsky
Sedgwick's explosive definition that includes 'people able to relish, learn
from, or identify with' sexually queer people (Sedgwick 1993: 8).

As *Aladdin* demonstrates, however, this queerness has often expressed
itself through an Orientalist lens that, while opening the stage to many queer
performers of colour, nonetheless reinscribes notions of the static, exotic
and sexually perverse east on the bodies of those performers. This gesture,
far from unique to musicals, has been extensively documented in literature
by Joseph Allen Boone, in his 2014 book *The Homoerotics of Orientalism*.
Boone notes:

> the large number of Anglo-European (and later US) ... men who over
> the centuries have found themselves gripped by and compelled to
> attempt to represent what, to their eyes, has seemed to be the relative
> openness, to say nothing of abundance, of erotic relationships between
> men in the Islamicate world. (2015: xxi)

As Boone points out, this homoerotic undercurrent 'has covertly under-
written much of the appeal and practice of the phenomenon we now call
Orientalism', and the connection between Orientalist imagery and something
resembling homosexuality 'is not simply a case of establishing unidirectional
domination over or penetration of [the] Orient, [but] also tacitly signifies
one's willingness to offer oneself up to unsuspected, multiple ways of being'
(2015: xxxiv). As in Cole Porter's *Aladdin* before it, as in *The King And I*, as
in *Thoroughly Modern Millie*, as in dozens of other musicals from throughout
the twentieth and twenty-first centuries, Ashman's *Aladdin's* willing self-
identification with Orientalist subjects allows queer creators, characters
and audiences to recognize ourselves on stage and screen, to inhabit the
homoexotic ideal represented by Aladdin himself.

Of course, the availability of that subject position – choosing to identify
with the Other – rests on creators' ability to pass as Not Other. For queer
writers of Orientalist musicals, that means inhabiting, at least in part, the
normative Eurocentric identity at the heart of Orientalism's patriarchal
view of the exotic. The careful positioning of self-as-other is not acceptable
for queer writers whose racial or sexual identity is always already other –
for queers of colour, for queer women, for queers unable or unwilling to
mask their sexuality, the Orientalist gesture of pseudo-solidarity is not an

option. In order to create commercial entertainment that takes advantage of homoexotic Orientalism, the writer must retain the façade of respectable, heterosexual, white maleness that so often serves as a gossamer-thin veil over campy Orientalist fantasy.

This veil is pierced in *The Hurt Locker*'s Playbill:

> Darrîn (Choreographer) Off-Broadway: *Screams of Cher, High Kick!*, *Puppetry of the Naked Penises Singing*, as well as continued work with Ibiza Expressive Flag Corps, The Lavender Players, and the Pizzazz! Therapeutic Theater Company. Darrîn is so grateful to his female wife, Shelli, for her continued self-sacrifice and faith in him throughout his personal life's journey of dance! (*Hurt Locker: The Musical* Playbill: 6)

This satirical biography resonates with a trend in the *Aladdin* Playbill. Aladdin, the Genie, the Sultan, Iago, the standby Jafar/Sultan and a Henchman thank their wives by name and title. Nobody thanks a same-sex partner by any identifying title, despite the Darrîn-level evidence in their bios that such partners are likely. Even Ashman, whose bio states that he 'died in 1991 from complications of AIDS', and who is therefore in no position to choose whom to thank, has his personal life elided to 'Ashman's family'. Queerness is coded, concealed, apparent to those who can read between the lines, but never explicitly stated. The veil of normativity cannot be penetrated, no matter how elaborately the show's Orientalist fantasy performs a queerness that is Ashman's professional signature.

Baghdad of the Imagination: Ashman's *Aladdin*

In January of 1988, even before *The Little Mermaid* had catapulted the Disney Corporation back to the summit of children's entertainment, Ashman proposed *Aladdin* as the next big Disney cartoon musical. He sent his 'treatment' of the story, along with several songs, to Disney executives and to *Mermaid* writer–directors John Musker and Ron Clements.[3] While certain elements of the treatment are now familiar from the finished film, this is a very different *Aladdin*. Ashman's idea is a camp extravaganza, teeming with references to queer cultural objects from throughout the early twentieth century. Importantly, Ashman's vision is not merely gay, but broadly queer, with touchstones for women as well as men, and with a sense of not just men sexually interested in men, but something more akin to Sedgwick's 'open mesh of possibilities'.

In the opening paragraph of his treatment, Ashman paints a picture of what he calls 'Old Baghdad. Well, not *old* Baghdad. This is a zany and fanciful Baghdad of the imagination ... There's a hint of Humphrey Bogart's Casablanca and Marlene Dietrich's Morocco.'⁴ Already, the queer Orientalist signification is coming thick and fast, with a reference to Dietrich's famous lesbian kiss cheek by jowl with the homoerotic subtext often noted between Bogart and Peter Lorre in both *The Maltese Falcon* and *Casablanca.* Subtle hints abound throughout the document, including introducing the main character as 'the youngest Shark in *West* Side Story [*sic*],' an Orientalist conflation of brown-skinned Puerto Ricans with Persians that also recalls the white gay supergroup that constructed that musical – Jerome Robbins, Arthur Laurents, Leonard Bernstein and Stephen Sondheim. Later, Aladdin's dramatic entrance to the Sultan's palace is described as 'not unlike Liz Taylor's in *Cleopatra*', a gender-bent reference to mid-century Orientalist extravaganza films tied to gay audiences not only through the abundant genre connections Boone points out, but also through gay icon Taylor, who a few years prior to Ashman's writing began publicly fighting for treatment and destigmatization of AIDS and HIV.

From a description of one song as 'a Gene Kelly/Donald O'Connor-style Musical Number' that recalls their homosocial-cum-homosexual partnership in *Singin' in the Rain*'⁵ (Knapp 2009: 75) to the entrance of the Genie, 'a cross between Mr. Clean, Cab Calloway, Leon Redbone, and the strutting bandleader (or headwaiter) of a Harlem nightclub circa 1939' that merges the preponderance of queer performers in the Harlem Renaissance and its attendant nightlife with the gay housework genie of the Procter & Gamble corporation, Ashman's 'zany and fanciful Baghdad of the imagi-nation' is a self-conscious illustration of Boone's thesis some twenty-five years before Boone put it to paper. Larded with these in-jokes and winks to queer readers, Ashman's treatment plants its tongue firmly in cheek from the opening sentence and deliberately performs a 1980s camp homage to pre-Stonewall camp culture. One recipient of the treatment, gay Disney VP Charlie Fink, wrote to Ashman a week later, lauding the treatment as 'very funny, wacky, cartoony, and very adult', with the word 'adult' signalling that he had understood at least some of Ashman's historical references.⁶

Beyond the plot as laid out in the treatment, Ashman included a character list with detailed descriptions of nearly everyone. These included not only characters now familiar from the film – Aladdin, the Genie, Jasmine, the Sultan, and the as-yet-unnamed evil Wazir and his talking parrot⁷ – but also a host of others who did not make the final cut – Aladdin's street gang of Babkak, Omar, Kasim and the tomboyish Abbi: Aladdin's mother and a mysterious Narrator. Notably, the cut characters are described in terms that mark all of them as queer: the gang are described as 'The Jets and the Sharks, or Run DMC after a sweet-injection', with Abbi specifically noted as 'in *West*

Side Story, she'd play Anybody's' and as 'Judy Garland to [Aladdin's] Mickey Rooney', connecting Aladdin's friends to musical comedy symbols of both male and female queerness, including the lesbian-coded Anybody's and the rumoured-to-be-bisexual Garland.

Aladdin's mother, Maman, is described as 'crusty [and] wise', and is compared to Geppetto from *Pinocchio*, a solitary elderly figure of the sort often read as queer (see Aunt Eller in *Oklahoma!*) even without his symbolically giving birth to Pinocchio. The Narrator, later revealed to be a second, smaller Genie, is described in terms that mark him as slight and effeminate: 'his turban is bigger than he is', and, 'an elfin creature'. Even the Sultan is compared to Bert Lahr, who famously played a pansy role as the Cowardly Lion in *The Wizard of Oz*. The only important character in the film who is missing from Ashman's treatment is the wordless monkey, Abu. There is, however, a fleeting reference to Sabu, the Indian child actor who played a human named Abu in *The Thief of Baghdad*, a character whom Boone describes as romantically paired with Rock Hudson's and as 'pédérastie fantasy material', and who bears a striking resemblance to Aladdin as he was eventually drawn (Boone 2015: 415). This film, Boone notes, provided much of the plot for Ashman's *Aladdin* – another coded gay reference on Ashman's part, as filtered not only through the homoerotic subtext of that specific film, but also through Rock Hudson's personification, in the 1980s, of Hollywood's AIDS epidemic.

Aladdin after Ashman: The Film

Ashman's *Aladdin* is not what Disney eventually produced, for reasons running from Jeffrey Katzenberg's dissatisfaction with the treatment[8] to the studio's decision to focus on *Beauty and the Beast* as the project after *Mermaid*. Other treatments (by Musker and Clements of *Little Mermaid*, and by Linda Woolverton of *Beauty and the Beast* – heterosexuals all) hover between the 1988 Ashman treatment and the 1992 release. As the film inched its way toward production, first with Ashman's active involvement and then, tragically, without him, it shed queer characters and their songs and jettisoned women. This version of *Aladdin* simultaneously retreated halfway into the closet and focused its remaining queerness strictly on male characters.

Ashman's original treatment featured three women characters in Jasmine, Abbi and Maman. Maman was written out by later writers for purportedly overwhelming her passive son with her forceful personality, a classic mid-century diagnosis of the source of male effeminacy (read:

homosexuality). Meanwhile, tomboy Abbi and petted princess Jasmine collapsed into one another, with the spoiled brat capturing the street urchin's spunk as well as Aladdin's heart. The story that Ashman described in his treatment as 'not a romance' gained after his death 'A Whole New World' of heterosexual drive – a drive that was rewarded when that number ̖beat out Ashman's contributions for all of the awards the score garnered.

The change in romantic motivations matched a change in musical style also occasioned by the loss of Ashman. As Menken said in interviews given before the release of the film in November of 1992, the team had imagined a '40s jazz style' 'Fats Waller type' of score (quoted in Todd Camp, 'Alan Menken changes his tune', *Fort Worth Star-Telegram*: 8). Indeed, in the margin of his original treatment, Ashman noted that though the treatment describes the genie as 'of indeterminate race', the effect of his character 'seems racial; seems too black'. This is hardly a surprise, when the 'indeterminate' Genie, whom Menken in later interviews referred to explicitly as 'a black hipster', introduces himself in the treatment as 'your personal "come and get it day"'. It is amidst this confusion of musical and ethnic signifiers that *Aladdin* steps into the American musical's own particular hue of queer Orientalism.

Ashman's 'zany and fanciful Baghdad of the imagination' is Harlem during its Renaissance, when 'the relative openness, to say nothing of abundance, of erotic relationships between men' that Boone notes in the Islamicate world was on full display in the nightclubs the Genie inhabits. Numerous scholars have noted at length the prevalence of queer sexualities among artists and performers of the Harlem Renaissance, as well as among inhabitants of and visitors to the neighbourhood. As George Chauncey notes in *Gay New York*, 'black gay men … turned Harlem into a homosexual mecca … which in many respects surpassed [Greenwich] Village' (1994: 244).

This deliberate conflation of black, Arab and queer identities is a gesture that simultaneously moves the Orient closer to home and keeps it at arm's length from the straight, white majority audience of the proposed film. This relocation of the homoexotic east into the homoexotic uptown has a long history in the musical, a history that functions here as yet another signifier of *Aladdin*'s roots in queer musical history. Many creators of musicals, both black and white, have used this exoticizing gesture in front of white audiences. When, in 1938, the black creators of *The Swing Mikado* transplanted the Japanese setting of *The Mikado* to an 'imaginary coral island in the Pacific Ocean', Chicago audiences loved the newer, blacker version of the distant Other (Batiste 2011: 127). For white promoters and club owners in 1920s New York, 'the spectacle of black "primitivism"' drew audiences to see queer black performers at clubs in white neighbourhoods, clubs that 'played on their customers' desire to feel they were transgressing the conventional boundaries of race while they resolutely confirmed them' (Chauncey 1994: 2010).⁹ The Genie, as conceived by Ashman and as musicalized by Menken, fits neatly into this long tradition. With the casting of Robin Williams to voice the Genie, and with the removal of most of Ashman and Menken's score, the 1992 film version of *Aladdin* obscures those black roots and trims the queerness inherent in Ashman's treatment down to a particular gayness that remains visible in the finished product.

Joseph Boone notes of the *Aladdin* film that the title character 'has attracted an underground cult gay following' and that Williams' Genie 'embodies the polymorphously perverse gone wild' and introduces 'a note of gay campiness' into the film (he seems unaware of the symphony of gay campiness behind the film). Williams' Genie takes 'several turns in drag', and shows up, he notes, in 'numerous online pornographic cartoon sites', paired with the title character. Boone even includes a flyer for a 'gay porn entrepreneur'-sponsored screening of *Aladdin* as a fundraiser for an AIDS charity in Hollywood in his demonstration of the sexual significance of this children's cartoon for adult gay men (2014: 415–16).

The gay signification of Williams' genie goes far beyond the polymorphous perversity Boone describes. In his famous out-of-controlness, Williams threatens to derail the temporality of the film, recalling what Jack Halberstam terms queer time. Queer time invests in 'a new emphasis on the here, the present, the now'; in the work of Samuel Delany, Halberstam demonstrates 'that queers use space and time in ways that challenge conventional logics of development, maturity, adulthood, and responsibility' (2005: 13). This notion is not exclusively celebratory, but it acknowledges the freedom that abstaining from teleology can grant a queer writer. It is worth noting, however, that Orientalist writing also often depicts a lack of teleology that is imagined upon the static East by the progressive West, a gesture that troubles the notion of queer time as separate from teleology and reinstates a dichotomy that Halberstam wants to avoid. Williams as the queer, Oriental genie confounds time in many ways, from the cessation of narrative that his show-stopping musical numbers entail to the delays in production necessitated when his adlibs needed to be animated long after the film should have been complete.

Importantly, both of his big musical scenes – 'Friend Like Me' and 'Prince Ali' – are Ashman/Menken numbers in the Cab Calloway/Fats Waller vein, numbers written to celebrate the Genie and his fantasy version of Aladdin, to pause any ensuing romance in favour of delighting in fantasy, razzle-dazzle and physical prowess (see below for a discussion of the stage versions of these numbers). In documents contained in Ashman's papers, Jeffrey

Katzenberg complains explicitly that Ashman's and Menken's songs halted forward progress. Menken explained in interviews that 'originally, *Aladdin* was fully a musical', and that this 'song concept' was later dumped in favour of 'a more comedic approach'. Indeed, the Genie's songs, the only remaining Ashman numbers to be included in the film in anything like their original length, are elaborate production numbers that move nothing forward, but move many things around and about, up and down, in and out, and in every other direction but forward.

The gayness of the film, despite its sharply reduced queerness, also comes through in its implied couples. From the camaraderie between Aladdin and Abu, both of them versions of Sabu's Abu in *Thief of Baghdad*, to the aforementioned connection between Aladdin and the Genie, the title character treads dangerously close to Ashman's effeminate, younger version of Aladdin, the one overwhelmed by his domineering mother. The couple least addressed in dialogue, and least commented upon in gay readings of the film, is one drawn into the film – the Sultan and Jafar. Co-director John Musker told the *San Francisco Chronicle* that animators modelled the Sultan on Ronald Reagan and Jafar on Nancy, perhaps a subtle jab at the Reagans' role in the AIDS epidemic that had taken Ashman away from *Aladdin*.

A Whole New World: *Aladdin* on Broadway

The stage musical, a twenty-first-century production far removed from Reagan, returns to Ashman's original treatment in many ways. Several characters and songs were restored, the 'furry creatures' Ashman did not want to include are excised, and homoerotic undertones become far more explicit in the hands of director-choreographer Casey Nicholaw. In addition, the restoration of much of Ashman and Menken's 'an element of … hip jazz of the '40s and … an element that's Arabic' (S25)[10] score allows for a musical restoration of blackness. This blackness is embodied by Marisha Wallace, the chorister who plays the largest and the sassiest of Jasmine's maids, and by James Monroe Iglehart as the Fats Waller-esque Genie. Iglehart's Tony-winning performance anchors 'Friend Like Me', 'Prince Ali' and the show's opening number, a restored version of Ashman and Menken's 'Arabian Nights'.

'Arabian Nights', originally conceived as a framing story told by the narrator and returning in several brief reprises, became the focus of Arab American protest against the film, despite being reduced to a single brief verse. The offensive lyrics 'Where they cut off your ear / If they don't like your face / It's barbaric, but hey, it's home' were just one of several cringe-inducing jokes that Ashman included, in the formula Orientalist-stereotype-followed-by-exculpatory-Jewish-comic-address-to-audience. From his tone in the initial treatment, it is clear that these increasingly over-the-top 'jokes' about the barbarism of Arabs were intended as satire of the very attitudes they depicted, but that satire entirely failed to come through in the final version of the film. Ashman seems to have written these jokes for an insider audience who would understand that stereotypes were outdated, and who would think of him as another insider speaking from a similar marginalized position – a camp audience, in short – but no camp performance or reception could save 'Where they hack off your lips / If they don't like your smile / It's the law / Did I make it? No' in either the early 1990s or the mid-2010s. In the new stage version, as in the home video release of the film, the line about physical violence is replaced, but the 'it's barbaric' remains; the companion 'lips / smile' verse remains absent, as do the reprises, but the rest of the song is restored and it becomes a production number to rival 'Prince Ali' and 'Friend Like Me'.

With Nicholaw at the helm and Iglehart centre stage, the song, which Menken described in 1992 as 'your orthodox Arabic/Middle Eastern style' is a tour-de-force of the queerly enticing Harlem Orient. The 'Middle Eastern style' is expressed in jingling bells, gapped scales, arabesque ornamentation in vocal and woodwind lines, all staples of the 1940s Orientalist films Menken used as a model. The queerness is on display everywhere, from Iglehart's disbelieving falsetto exclamation 'you've never been!?' before introducing the audience to the city of Agrabah to the display of muscled male torsos that contrasts sharply with Gregg Barnes' comparatively chaste costumes for the chorus women. Harlem is harder to find here, but it comes through in Iglehart's Fats Waller-style interjections between dance breaks. Ashman's lyrics, describing Agrabah as 'Unbelievable, yes / And an ethical mess / Nonetheless, no one's very contrite', perfectly encapsulate not only the mythical Orient he depicts, but also the show's attitude towards it.

With Iglehart's broadly vibrating 'even the poor people look *fabulous*' echoing in the audience's ears, the chorus girls conceal themselves behind entirely opaque veils in a reversal of expected heter-Orientalist display of what the Genie calls 'the softer side of Agrabah', a phrase that recalls not 1940s Orientalist film, but 1990s commercials for Sears. As he reminds the audience that everyone in Agrabah has 'a minor in dance' and that 'everybody sings', Iglehart, channelling Waller, plays high camp emcee to a staging that largely moves women to the back and men to the front. This displacement of chorus girls behind chorus boys highlights a surprising gender imbalance in the chorus that reverses the century-old practice in musical comedy of displaying women's bodies as an enticement to straight male viewers. *Aladdin's* chorus is a display for those who want to see men's bodies – 'women and dudes who act like them', in the words of Kip Buckner. In an interview published in the *Hedwig and the Angry Inch* Playbill, Iglehart confides that 'the dancers in our show are among the best on Broadway – but you expect it. When you see those abs, you know they can dance.'[11] This comment not only points out the revealing nature of the chorus men's costumes, but also the afterthought that women seem to be in this production. Nicholaw's vision of *Aladdin*, far more than even the film, is a celebration of male–male desire. Whereas Ashman's version celebrated a queerness that included Maman and Abbi, both familiar representations of female sexual and gendered difference, the stage show follows the path laid out by the film toward a focus on men's relationships. Aladdin's street gang is restored for the Broadway production, allowing the reinsertion of the songs 'Babkak, Omar, Aladdin, Kasim' and 'High Adventure', while Jasmine, the lone female character, is given a trio of supportive servants to form a musical and romantic parallel for Aladdin's boy band. These servants are nameless and function only as backup singers for Jasmine's new song, 'These Palace Walls', and while one is portrayed by Marisha Wallace, a sonic and physical reminder of queer black women's music, she is never developed into a character beyond big black woman. Jasmine's maids' only musical moment outside of 'These Palace Walls' is an appearance at the end of 'High Adventure' that sets them up as heterosexual partners for Babkak, Omar and Kasim.

The absence of women allows for a greater presence of implied male queerness than even the film. Aladdin is unqueered by the inclusion of 'A Whole New World', the new love duet 'A Million Miles Away' and the insertion of Jasmine's 'Beyond These Palace Walls' into 'Babkak, Omar, Aladdin, Kasim' as underscoring for their silent, budding romance. Nevertheless, he also regains the character-defining ballad 'Proud of Your Boy', sung to his (absent) mother. As a classic 'I Want' song, rhythmically and thematically reminiscent of Ashman and Menken's 'Somewhere That's Green' and 'Part of Your World', 'Proud of Your Boy' demarcates Aladdin's main goal in life: pleasing mom. This goal differs sharply from the goals of most leading men and betrays a remnant of the childish sissy boy he once was.

The other characters, unburdened by romance, remain resolutely homosocial. Jafar (portrayed by Jonathan Freeman, who originated the role on film) is now paired with a human Iago (Don Darryl Rivera), their similar stature and inability to appear without the other making their characteristic bickering more that of a married couple than a wizard and his insolent familiar. Babkak, Omar and Kasim, despite their eventual pairing with Jasmine's nameless maids, spend the vast majority of their stage time interacting with one another, not even pretending to miss the company of women. The Genie, as in the film, is interested primarily in Aladdin, a relationship that could read as paternal but is resolutely queered by Iglehart's performance.

As in 'Arabian Nights', Iglehart, with the help of the writers, camps up the role of the Genie at every turn. He performs effeminacy in line with some of Robin Williams' drag turns in the film, despite his inability to shape shift into a woman as the animated Genie does. At the end of the first act, after Aladdin wishes to become a prince, Iglehart channels *Queer Eye for the Straight Guy* to critique Aladdin's outfit and becomes his personal stylist, vocally recalling the feminine enthusiasm of his exclamations during 'Arabian Nights' and his entrance number, 'Friend Like Me'.

Iglehart kicks off the second act with 'Prince Ali', his paean to the glories of Aladdin. In the film's version of 'Prince Ali', Robin Williams' Genie becomes what one reviewer called 'a butch harem girl' to sing the praises of Prince Ali's physique, counterpointed by a trio of significantly less butch girls singing the praises of his outfit. In the stage version, Iglehart's Genie instead sings the sartorial countermelody, as the male chorus gets 'weak at the knee' over 'that physique'. Iglehart is again the emcee of a gay choral spectacular.

The costuming in this number is less focused on displaying the bodies of the chorus men, as it instead focuses on quick changes between a variety of costumes – Iglehart explained in an interview that each chorus member starts the song wearing four layered costumes. The camp extravaganza of the number, as Genie and the mixed-gender chorus sing the praises of the muscular and toothily grinning Aladdin, recalls another Ashman camp tour de force, 'Gaston' from *Beauty and the Beast*. Like that number, 'Prince Ali' focuses the entire production's attention on the physical prowess and superhuman abilities of an idealized man, but here he is the hero, rather than the villain, an object of accepted desire, for lyricist and director, as well as for many audience members. 'Prince Ali' positions Genie as the admiring sidekick Le Fou, ringmaster of the circus of adoration, and indeed the original cast album includes a bonus track of Iglehart singing 'Gaston', among other Alan Menken Disney tunes.

This medley reflects a similar medley interpolated into the middle of 'Friend Like Me'. The choreographic and musical centre of the show, 'Friend Like Me' closes the first act, introduces by far the most important character (despite Aladdin's status as titular hero) and represented the show on the Tony Awards broadcast. A tour de force of stage magic and musical control by Iglehart's Genie, the song stops the show both in terms of not advancing the plot, and in the more traditional sense of a showstopper. Beyond these interruptions, the number also, in incorporating the medley of songs from other Disney musicals, explicitly steps outside of the fantasy time of the mystic Orient and jumps to the twenty-first century, further evidence of the Genie's Halberstamian queer temporality. Iglehart, in full diva mode, again camps the number, with a hand-on-hip sashay that accompanies his 'What will your pleasure be?' evocation of the 'strutting ... headwaiter of a Harlem nightclub' that Ashman envisioned for the role.

Beyond the high camp queer time of the number, however, Iglehart's evocation of Harlem brings me back to the troubling exoticization of blackness that marks this version of queer Orientalism. In the demo tape that Ashman and Menken sent to Disney in 1988, the score was loaded with deliberate references to blackness. Ashman's vocal performance was a clear attempt to indicate blackness to the listening executives, and his lyrics and asides included explicit mention of barbershop singing and tap dancing, both musical forms originating in black culture. The treatment mentions the use of saxophone, and the recording includes scatting and a gospel-style piano accompaniment in the numbers for Aladdin's gang. Most of these signifiers drop out in the stage show, leaving only the show's handful of black performers to somehow explain the dissonance of the jazzy American sound of Menken's score against the Arabian backdrop of Bob Crowley's set. This head-scratching conflict, while most prominently embodied in Iglehart's Genie, is perhaps best symbolized by the mighty Sultan of the fabled city of Agrabah – Clifton Davis, a black actor from Chicago who is also a minister and a former composer for Motown Records.

In classic Orientalist fashion, this exoticization is, of course, intended to paint blackness as desirable. Ashman's vision of the black Orient is complimentary, portraying what Boone describes as his 'willingness to open [him-]self up to up to unsuspected, multiple ways of being'. No matter the intention, however, the homoexotic depiction of blackness in *Aladdin* forms part of a larger pattern that serves to both foreclose 'normal' roles to black performers and open up marginal ones, both in terms of subject position and in terms of stage time. Nevertheless, at the same time, it provides an outlet for a star performer like Iglehart to wrest a show away from the white perspectives of its writers and into his own version of blackness that, while remaining queer, is far less exotic than his green makeup would suggest.

Conclusions

Ashman's brainchild never had much in the way of conclusion – his treatment finishes with a brief reprise that announces the not-really-an-ending: 'Come back soon / That's the end / 'Til another / Arabian Night', with an elaborate

Orientalist arabesque on the final syllable. The stage show takes that ending, though it tacks on a reprise of 'A Whole New World' to remind the audience of the heterosexual romance. Even then, however, the Genie takes over the melody, replacing Ashman's Orientalist ornamentation with his own gospel version, then interrupts with the spoken line, 'I just *love* a happy ending', his voice climbing to a falsetto squeal on 'love' that belies his investment in the inevitable marriage plot.

Iglehart's palpable pleasure in the role of the Genie prevents me from simply condemning *Aladdin* as a racist piece of entertainment. While it is clearly based in racist stereotypes, Ashman intended to satirize those stereotypes, and Iglehart undermines them with his virtuosic performance. Both the gay white writer and the straight black performer do their best to situate their work within a long history of racist entertainment and find the good in a history of racial oppression. That gesture, the rehabilitation of deeply problematic entertainment, is perhaps the queerest part of *Aladdin*, in all of its incarnations. In Ashman's words, 'an ethical mess / nonetheless, no one's very contrite'. That's the end, 'til another Arabian Night.

References

Batiste, Stephanie Leigh (2011). *Darkening Mirrors: Imperial Representation in Depression-Era African–American Performance*. Durham, NC: Duke University Press.

Boone, Joseph Allen (2014). *The Homoerotics of Orientalism*. New York: Columbia University Press.

Chauncey, George (1994). *Gay New York: Gender, Urban Culture, and the Making of the Gay Male World, 1890–1940*. New York: Basic.

Clum, John (1999). *Something for the Boys: Musical Theater and Gay Culture*. New York: Palgrave.

Davis, Angela Y. (1999). *Blues Legacies and Black Legacies and Black Feminism*. New York: Vintage Books.

Halberstam, Judith [Jack] (2005). *In a Queer Time and Place: Transgender Bodies, Subcultural Lives*. New York: New York University Press.

Knapp, Raymond (2006). *The American Musical and the Performance of Personal Identity* Princeton: Princeton University Press.

Miller, D. A. (1998). *Place for Us [Essay on the Broadway Musical]*. Cambridge, MA and London: Harvard University Press.

Sedgwick, Eve Kosofsky (1993). *Tendencies*. Series Q. Durham, NC: Duke University Press.

Wolf, Stacy (2011). 'Gender and Sexuality'. In Raymond Knapp, Mitchell Morris and Stacy Wolf (eds), *The Oxford Handbook of the American Musical*. Oxford and New York: Oxford University Press, 210–24.

'For the First Time in Forever': Locating *Frozen* as a Feminist Disney Musical

Sarah Whitfield

Disney princess musicals present a number of contradictions to a feminist audience. As a mother of young daughters, I struggle to try and reconcile some of these. On the one hand, my girls show an obvious delight in and connection with Disney princesses (even before they really have the concentration span to watch a full movie, they know which princess is which). On the other hand, my desire for my daughters to not be constrained by expectations about their gender leads to a sense of hesitation, to a sense of wanting an 'and' rather than an 'or' – princess *and* adventurer. Disney musicals can be seen as a formative precursor to what Elaine Aston calls in the Broadway musical 'women-centred, utopian pleasures' (Aston and Harris 2012: 117), though their audience is by no means limited to children or girls. So, the temptation is to stop the chapter here and say, yes, *Frozen* is feminist because we want and need it to be. As story arcs go, the Disney Corporation embracing feminism in *Frozen* would be an immensely satisfying conclusion as the studio approaches its upcoming centenary in 2023 (Buck and Lee 2013).

Frozen is progressive by the standards of its broader Hollywood context. It features two sisters as reasonably complex protagonists, unlike many films featuring two women, which present a good-one and an evil-one. Anna and Elsa overcome the death of their parents and the ensuing conflict together in order to reach their happy endings: they must 'sav[e] each other' rather than relying on any passing prince to intervene (Lee, in Solomon 2013: 14). To put this into context, Anna and Elsa's agency and screen time are depressingly rare: statistical analysis of a sample of 1,794 movies from 1970 to 2013 found 'that only half [have] at least one scene in which women talked to each other about something other than a man' (Hickey 2014). Women are present in *Frozen*'s creative team: Jennifer Lee is the first woman director at Disney animation; she wrote the screenplay and has co-writer credits for the story (she, along with co-directors Chris Buck and Peter Del Vecho, won the Oscar

Award for Best Animated Feature Film). Lyricist, Kristen Anderson-Lopez co-wrote the songs with composer Robert Lopez. While the balance is still 3–2, men to women, the presence of women in this team at all is notable in an industry in which during 2012 'women accounted for 4.1 per cent of directors, 12.2 per cent of writers and 20 per cent of producers' (Smith, in Hickey 2014).

Frozen enjoyed unprecedented financial success for an animation, eventually making almost $1.3 billion worldwide (IMDb 2014a), and sold '3.2 million Blu-ray and DVD discs in its first day of release' (Graser 2014). Predictably, plans for a sequel were announced in early 2015 at the Disney shareholder meeting; the annual report was effusive about the spectacular growth *Frozen* had delivered across multiple divisions. 'Consumer Products', for example, noted a 'record performance': 'During the holiday season *Frozen* outpaced previous sales records in several categories; the franchise is so powerful, one Elsa doll alone generated retail sales of $26 million in the U.S.' (The Walt Disney Company 2014). Plans for a Broadway stage musical adaptation were confirmed in February 2015 (Cox 2015).

Feminist film criticism has envisioned much more than 'better'; Annette Kuhn explains the fight to 'creat[e] awareness of the socially constructed nature of representations of women in films, and [offered] an impetus towards the creation of alternative representations' (1994: 6). In this chapter, then, I intend to consider the extent to which the film might offer any 'alternative representation'. I argue that in attempting to present 'better' representations of women, *Frozen* turns to the Broadway musical theatre, which, as Stacy Wolf has noted, manages 'to do double duty – to promote conservative values *and* to provide empowering representations of women, sometimes simultaneously' (2010: viii). In order to assess *Frozen*, this chapter explores the representation of women within the film through a particular focus on Elsa's transformation sequence and its place within the broader dramatic structure of the film. It pays attention to the conditions of production and reception that shape how meaning is produced.

Critical Responses to the Work: From 'Not Feminist Enough' to Female 'Superhero'

Initial reviews of *Frozen* were somewhat hesitant but tended to note its presentation of stronger women; *Variety*, though, saw the 'somewhat slack plotting and the generic nature of the main characters' (Foundas 2013). The *Guardian* praised the focus on Anna and Elsa: 'sisterhood feels like an abiding interest of the filmmakers and not a tacked-on afterthought' (Shone 2013). The *New Yorker* noted 'the chronic simperers, like Cinderella, have been superseded by tough dames' (Lane 2013). Since then, arguments over whether the film is or is not feminist, or even too feminist, have proliferated across mainstream journalism, blogs and fan communities. Some right-wing news hosts took it on themselves to warn potential viewers about *Frozen*'s 'nefarious plot to undermine American masculinity' (Krueger 2015). Much of the debate around the film's gender equality focuses on Elsa's anthem 'Let it Go', which was released first in a cover by pop star Demi Lovato, and then as Idina Menzel's own full-length version. Menzel's sold over 10 million copies (IFPI 2014) and the YouTube video has to date been watched over 554 million times (Walt Disney Animation Studios 2013).

Debate around Elsa has raged. Some have called her 'Disney's first emo princess' (Lynskey 2014) and 'the female equivalent of a superhero', noting that girls too 'want to emulate superheroes, not the demure and subservient princesses waiting for their prince to come' (Merrick 2015). Others felt 'Let it Go' was not feminist enough, citing a 'sense of deflation every time that pulse-racing song [...] culminates in a vision of female self-actualization as narrow and horizon-diminishing as a makeover' (Stevens 2014). Perhaps surprisingly, given Disney's traditionally conservative image, its fan communities have frequently provided rigorous intersectional analyses. The short description of the Feminist Disney Tumblr explains that the blog is 'an examination and documentation of the intersection of Disney and social issues. What is "Disney feminism"? It's using positive messages in Disney to turn the lens inward and examine what could be' (Rogers 2015). Rogers' review of *Frozen* addresses, among other things, the lack of queer representation in the film and subsequent queer readings, Anna and Elsa's active agency (as opposed to passively waiting princesses), racial exclusion and specifically the problematic representation of Saami people in the film. Other communities have worked to address the lack of ethnic diversity in films: Tumblr site Snow Queens and PoC (People of Colour) set out to encourage 'PoC and artists alike to try to re-imagine their own *Frozen* with people who look like or represent them' (Thiscouldhavebeenfrozen, 2014); others open up queer readings of the film, or highlight the suspicion about possibility of Elsa being intended to be gay, because of her anthem of self-acceptance (see Chrislove 2015; BBC News 2014). Queer readings of the film tend to focus on the limitations of Elsa: 'Elsa isn't the queer icon we DESERVE. Her queerness is simply an interpretation, a reading built on metaphor and subtext. She is not canonly queer [*sic*]. She does not give visibility and representation' (emphasis in original, ineffable-hufflepuff 2013).

The film was originally marketed in the US and UK as gender neutral (one imagines this will not be the case for its sequel). In these two regions, there was a clear attempt to mask the film's content in order to pass as a generic 'family film', thereby revealing a rather pernicious assumption that only girls would want to see a film about girls. Its vague title masks Anna and Elsa and their gender, as well as the original Hans Christian Anderson source material. This was not the case universally; many other countries, including France, Japan and several Spanish-speaking regions, explicitly reference *The Snow Queen* in the title (IMDb 2014b). This decision followed the rebranding of Rapunzel as *Tangled* (Greno and Howard 2011) after the slow box office takings for *The Princess and the Frog* (2009). Ed Catmull, President of Disney and Pixar Animation Studios, explained the reasoning behind this switch: 'Some people might assume it's a fairy tale for girls when it's not' (Chmielewski and Eller 2010). For *Frozen*, the US and the UK pre-launch advertising campaign could plausibly have been for a buddy movie between the loveable snowman Olaf and Sven, his reindeer sidekick. One TV spot ran under the vague tagline 'strange things happen when everything is Frozen' and avoided showing Anna and Elsa together in a single frame (MovieclipsComingSoon 2013). Some have assumed that the marketing strategy of masking the protagonists' gender worked in the US; one business article rather breathlessly reports the unprecedented financial success of the film by explaining that 'Disney lured in boys with a little white lie' (Gomez 2014). Others have presumed the character of Olaf exists to make the film 'safer for boys' (Brosch McKenna, in Lee 2014). In response to this, Jennifer Lee comments 'there was a point where there was that concern of [...] is there anything in it for the boys' (2014).

Realistically, the situation of women in Hollywood is so grim that being a 'more feminist' film is depressingly easy. Alison Bechdel's now well-known 'Bechdel–Wallace Test' only requires a movie to have the presence of two named women on screen, talking about something other than a man, in order to pass (Jusino 2015). *Frozen* not only passes, but goes as far as arguably to fail an imagined reversal, wherein two named men would need to be alone on screen talking about something other than a woman (see Lee 2014). Elsa is shown throughout the film without having or wanting any romantic attachment; her primary relationship could be considered either one of self-acceptance, or one of reconciliation with her sister. Anna does appear to be shown in relation to her 'Prince Charming' (Hans), and indeed instantly falls in love with him. Lee has said the story 'kind of turns some sort of fairytale things on its head, and yet those fairytale things allowed us to do things that we wouldn't have otherwise been able to do [...] her falling in love immediately, we buy it because it's a trope' (Lee 2014). Anna and Prince

Hans's love is soon revealed as a con on his part to steal Elsa's throne. The rewriting of such a potent trope as 'instant love, next day marriage' has been identified as an example of the delightfully named 'decon-recon', that is 'work which attempts to deconstruct a trope and then ends up reconstructing it in order to make the work function' (TVTropes 2015). Kristoff is Anna's true love after having known him only marginally longer than she knew Hans. Nonetheless, the act of 'true love' that saves Anna from her freezing to death is the sacrifice she makes for her sister. At this key point, Kristoff remains a spectator. Marriage is not the dramatic climax of the piece.

Significantly, *Frozen* is the first Disney film musical to feature a duet between two women – 'For the First Time in Forever (Reprise)' – who are physically singing in the same space. They are allowed, as Wolf puts it, to turn 'their attention toward one another' (2010: 18). There are precious few duets between women in Disney musicals at all: 'Oh Sing Sweet Nightingale' shows Cinderella cleaning the floor in harmony with her reflection in floating soap bubbles (*Cinderella* 1950). The straight-to-video *Little Mermaid 2* shows Ariel and her daughter Melody harmonising about the pleasures of the sea in 'For a Moment', but in different locations (*The Little Mermaid II: Return to the Sea*, 2000). Even the first version of 'For the First Time in Forever' has Anna and Elsa singing in separate parts of the castle. In a traditional Disney film musical three-act structure, Lee explains, 'there are no more songs after the end of the second act' (Lee 2014). The reprise of the duet is after this point, after 'Let it Go'. Though much of the duet is semi-recitative, the expansive lyrical section forms the dramatic climax of the musical: Anna tries to convince Elsa to return to the Arendelle, to sort out the 'deep, deep, deep, deep, snow' she has wrought (Buck and Lee 2013). As she furiously rejects Anna's help, Elsa accidentally mortally wounds her sister. All this, remember, is in a duet that has nothing to do with princes. The song is still limited: they at no point sing together in unison or in harmony, and it functions as a way to express conflict. Yet in terms of feminism, the duet, and more broadly the film, is – to misuse a Sondheim lyric – 'better than not' (1980).

Constructing and Enacting Gender

Disney princesses within their films

Anna and Elsa's apparent disruption of the trope of the traditional Disney princess reveals its ubiquity in Western culture. The original source of the Disney princess as cultural icon (the film) is intensified through extensive marketing and merchandise. I want to consider the film texts themselves first, and then later address the afterlife of the film and the particular impact this distribution has had on cultural ownership. In terms of the content of the film, Jennifer Lee's own account of her hiring as director reiterates this progress narrative: 'What's interesting for me as a woman coming in is, I was never treated like a woman coming in. The culture and storytelling are opening up: Women characters can be stronger and feistier and drive things' (Solomon 2013: 24). The de-gendering of her own experience (what would a 'woman coming in' actually have been treated like?) is coupled here with the problematic 'feisty', a word rarely used for anyone other than women and small dogs. *Frozen* is meant to challenge what Giroux has argued is Disney's view of women's agency in which a girl 'can only realize a gendered incarnation [...] by becoming the appendage, if not the property, of a man' (Giroux 2010: 108).

The actual films themselves are more complicated, as Amy Davis finds in her comprehensive exploration of the representation of women in Disney's output. She acknowledges that 'the reputation that Disney films are full of weak, passive women has gained a wide-spread, largely unquestioned acceptance' (2006: 10). She addresses the range of characters, with particular reference to Ariel, Jasmine and Pocahontas, noting they are by no means purely simpering stereotypes; they all retain agency in their own stories. As Davis notes, 'their motivation to do what they do is never solely romantic love' (2006: 9). Disney films have shifted away from implied marriage as being happily-ever-after; *Brave* (2012), though not a musical, shows arrow-wielding Merida attempting to repair her relationship with her mother in order to establish agency over her own life and choices). *Tangled* (2010) which is a musical, resolves with Rapunzel's reunion with her parents, with the love story being completed in the coda period. Davis identifies animated 'tough girl' characters outside of the musical catalogue, for example in *Lilo and Stitch* (2002), which also focuses on sisters and their relationship after being orphaned. In it, Lilo's older sister Nani becomes her guardian, trying to deal with an angry, grieving child while holding down a waitressing job. Davis suggests these characters 'leave audiences in no doubt that, far from needing (or even wanting) a man, these are women who can – and do – take care of themselves' (2006: 206). Despite the relative diversity of representations here, the Disney Princess that exists in the Western imagination is a far more controlled and closed type.

Embodying princess-ness: A physical trope

The Disney Princess that *Snow White* introduced has a specific physical archetype (*Snow White and the Seven Dwarfs*, 1938), refined over the decades to that of a post-pubescent yet petite woman with an extremely slim waist, large eyes and a small mouth. Some characters are already princesses at the beginning of the film, for example Jasmine in *Aladdin* (1993); others may have been introduced to us as a normal girl before experiencing some kind of transformation befitting their status, perhaps through a fairy godmother's intervention or with the help of their animal friends. However it is achieved, the Princesses' physical maturity is largely conservative and unthreatening. Unlike the portrayal of Jessica Rabbit in *Who Framed Roger Rabbit* (1988), theirs is not an exaggerated, voluptuous, pin-up style. Instead, this particular performance is of a clearly demarcated adult woman who maintains her 'innocence' while happening to have a neck circumference perilously close to being larger than her waist. This construction immediately calls to mind Judith Butler's classic critique of gender as explicitly performed, as operating through 'a sustained and repeated corporeal project' (1988: 522). However it is achieved, the Disney Princess as a gendered body matters because of its broader cultural influence; as a formative model of femininity for many children, it bears zero relation to how women will actually look.

The transformation sequence does not feature in every Disney film, but our pre-conception of it reinforces the visual delineation of the Princess. In *Beauty and the Beast* (1992) Belle's demure blue apron is switched in what Craven describes as 'semi-ritualized coming out as sexual debutante and possible wife for Beast [...] in a ball gown in the ballroom scene, a vignette unique to the Disney version' (2002: 130). Cinderella's bird-and-mouse-sewn ball gown is ruined by her jealous sisters, so her Fairy Godmother makes her a more magical (and mature) ball gown with bare shoulders and defined waist (*Cinderella* 1950). Such transformation also occurs in the studio's live-action films: *The Princess Diaries* shows the unwitting Princess Mia (Anne Hathaway) transformed in a distressing sequence – Mia's unruly hair is straightened, her glasses snapped in favour of contact lenses and her eyebrows named 'Frida and Kahlo' before being plucked into a proper fashion (*The Princess Diaries* 2001). At the end of the film, Mia resists: she is 'debuted' as a royal while wearing Doc Martens and a hoodie, but she swiftly changes back into the standard-issue ball gown and tiara. The recent furore over Kenneth Branagh's live-action *Cinderella* questioned the wisdom of showing a real life human corseted into the blue dress of a fantasy imagination (see Robertson 2015).

Such transition has also been parodied, most obviously in DreamWorks' *Shrek*. Fiona expects that when she experiences 'true love's kiss' she will take 'true love's form'. Indeed, at the crucial point, the dramatic music begins to play, lights flash and Fiona is left as an ogre (*Shrek* 2001). Disney's own *Enchanted* knowingly plays with the idea when Princess Giselle (Amy Adams) is expelled from her animated fairy tale world for a real-life New York (rats and all) and transforms from a ball gown-wearing figure to a human adult woman thanks to the magical powers of an American Express card (*Enchanted* 2007). Giselle's former true love, Prince Edward, is now left empty handed, so he instantly falls in love with Nancy (Idina Menzel); together, they go back to the magical kingdom, with Nancy now transformed in standard Disney-issue bridal clothes. Giselle adjusts to her less-than-fairy-tale reality, though she manages to end up with Robert (Patrick Dempsey), a reasonable swap for Prince Charming.

The Disney Company's dissemination of a story and its characters from a singular 'property' to a broader afterlife catapults Anna and Elsa across an unimaginably diverse range of media and products. Often these products offer the opportunity to transform one's self; children's princess play dresses facilitate their participation in the fantasy (see England et al. 2011). Indeed, the dress Elsa transforms into has been reported as being Disney's 'all-time best-selling costume'; a spokesperson for department store JC Penney said of the dolls and dresses 'You sell two Elsa's for every Anna' (Byron and Ziobro 2014). Beyond the dresses, it has for some time been possible to buy the experience of a 'real-life' transformation experience at Disney World's 'Bibbity Bobbity Boutique' (see Schweitzer and Bennett 2014 for an account of this). Characters can themselves be transformed outside the screen: arrow-wielding, wild-haired Merida (who survived *Brave* without any transformation) was radically reimagined in time for her 'coronation ceremony' at the theme park, now tidied up, slimmer and apparently 'sexier' (see Samakow 2013). The writer and ousted director of the film, Brenda Chapman, said that the makeover was 'a blatantly sexist marketing move based on money', noting that Merida was supposed to 'give young girls a better, stronger role model [...] not just a pretty face that waits around for romance' (Liberatore 2013).

The transformation fantasy is also pitched at an adult market, who can afford more than play dresses; Disney Weddings sell an Elsa-inspired gown, assuring potential brides that it 'capture[s] the essence of this strong and kind-hearted princess', ensuring them 'a perfect fairy tale ending' (Disney Weddings 2015). Koren-Kuik argues that Disney uniquely encourages its fans to engage with its products in order to develop 'the reciprocal relationship between fandom and a fictional world' (2014: 146). Disney merchandise, she suggests, acts as 'the connecting agent between content and media, fans and imaginary spaces […] it also encourages an engagement with narrative that is personal and free from temporal and spatial constraint' (2014: 148). Adult engagement with these characters has led to what Robertson calls the 'phenomenon of princess remixing', that is to say the taking apart of 'the old-fashioned values of the Disney princess franchise […] from many, many angles' (2015). Remixes often highlight the extreme nature of their physical characteristics – Robertson cites 'If Disney Princesses Had Realistic Waistlines' (Brantz 2014), and there are many more examples, including 'If Disney Princesses Were Proportioned Like Disney Princes' (Jones 2015) and the frankly terrifying 'We Got Photoshopped to Look Like Disney Princesses, and This is What Happened' (Bagg et al. 2015). Such articles serve to expose the hyperreal version of femininity that the Official Princess line performs. One women featured in the Photoshop article considered her transformation into Princess Tiana in the light of 'young girls' self-esteem', explaining: 'I'm an adult woman and when I see these two photos side by side I can't help but think how grotesque MY body looks' (Ibid., emphasis in original).

Elsa's Transformation: 'Looking Back'

Elsa's transformation sequence, however, has some radical differences to that of other Disney Princesses. Elsa chooses her isolation, accepts her own powers and physically transforms her own environment and her presentation of self to suit her own wishes. She changes her hair, shoes and outfit (albeit one with a waist so tightly corseted that a non-magical performer would have some serious issues producing the vocal-belt voice on which her anthem relies). She does this for her own benefit rather than for her wedding or for romance; it is for her own obvious pleasure. In this section, I consider Elsa's transformation in response to Judith Butler's argument that to 'become a woman' is to 'become a cultural sign, to materialize oneself in obedience to an historically delimited possibility, and to do this as a sustained and repeated corporeal project' (1988: 522).

It is also important to note that this sequence is the only moment in *Frozen* when the fourth wall is broken: Elsa is nominally looking out at Arendelle and closing the door to it, but the sequence of shots that frame her doing so (an extreme wide shot cutting to extreme close up) force us to see her as if looking directly at the viewer, when she delivers the line 'the cold never bothered me anyway' (see from 03:25 in *Frozen* 2013). Since Elsa's transition does not rely on any outside assistance, it has been seen as a profoundly feminist moment, resisting 'the fetishizing of young women for audience consumption' (Feder 2014). Others have questioned the limitations of the transformation: 'When you imagine a wardrobe change that represents empowerment and independence, do you really picture crystalline spikes right at your toe and heel joints?' (Colman 2014).

There is a clear tension between her independence and performance of agency, and Elsa's visual conformity to the image of the Disney Princess. When directly asked to explain Elsa's apparent sexiness, Lee points to the sheer number of collaborators involved in the film: 'There was a lot of pull of, I will say from the guys, of loving her as the – every man in the studio, and some of the women, were in love with Elsa [*sic*]' (Lee 2014). She explains the moment is about a private act: 'it was like you strut and you say nobody is looking […] I'm not going to be afraid of my sexuality. I'm not going to be afraid of who I am' (ibid.). The fact that we are looking summons the work of Laura Mulvey in establishing the concept of the male gaze in film. Mulvey's central arguments about women's 'to be looked-at-ness' lay out how a woman's 'visual presence' works against the 'development of a storyline' and '[freezes] the flow of action in moments of erotic contemplation' (1989: 19). Unlike the earlier example of Jessica Rabbit, we are not explicitly invited to contemplate Elsa erotically, but she certainly changes into 'sexier' clothes – a thigh-high split dress, slinky fabric and heels. Within the context of *Frozen*, this transition acts as a pause in which we undeniably invited to gaze at Elsa, but with music and lyrics serving to develop some kind of narrative at the same time. Butler's concept of the 'performative accomplishment' is helpful here (1988: 520), since it allows us to frame Elsa's transformation within the entire ice palace sequence, which is breathtaking in ambition and detail. We are invited through the weaving together of lyrics and screen imagery to marvel at what Elsa can construct: 'My soul is spiralling in frozen fractals all around' (Anderson-Lopez, in Walt Disney Animation Studios 2013).

Elsa's looking back at the audience could be seen as an invitation to spectators to 'notice the gaze and recognize their own involvement, through their desire, in what they see on the screen' (Gowan 2003: 29). It certainly develops the storyline, luxuriating in the telling of it. Kim Solga's discussion of Elin Diamond's work in setting out a potential gestic feminist criticism explains Diamond's idea that the feminist performer may 'return' the male gaze 'with a difference' (2015: 26) Performers may stage women's experiences in such a manner as to 'allow the contradictions shaping those experiences to become visible' (ibid.: 27). Women who 'bear such contradictions' are able to 'revel in them, looking back to the auditorium with an invitation to spectators to pay attention to the narrative's hidden feminist stories' (ibid.). Neither Diamond nor Solga are talking about the Disney musical, yet it suggests that the particular power of Elsa's 'looking back' warrants further unpicking. Elsa was originally intended to be an antagonist, and the song bears traces of the other kind of transformation sequence into which women in Disney films may enter.

Shape-shifting is characteristic of women antagonists in Disney animations, from *Snow White*'s Evil Queen (*Snow White and the Seven Dwarfs* 1938) to Ursula (half woman, half octopus) and her monstrous abilities in *The Little Mermaid* (1989) to Queen Narissa in *Enchanted* (2007). Some of Elsa's concept artwork shows a visual similarity to Cruella de Ville (Solomon 2013: 51). Disney villains have songs too, to manipulate others, as in 'Mother Knows Best' in *Tangled* (Greno and Howard 2011) and 'Poor Unfortunate Souls' in *Little Mermaid* (1989). These show-stopping numbers detail the lengths to which the villains will go to fulfil their nefarious ambitions: Scar's 'Be Prepared' in *The Lion King* (1994) shows him convincing the hyenas in Nazi-style military processions. Elsa's song could potentially have been very different indeed. Lee explains that when she joined the project 'we knew that Anna was going to save Elsa [...] And it was more of a redemption story at the time because Elsa was evil' (Lee 2014). In fact, the song Elsa sings during the scene came at a point when the creative team were struggling to make the dramaturgical structure of the story work. In Lee's words, it was 'the first song that landed in the film and was in the film'; Anderson-Lopez and Lopez presented the demo and it is 'exactly word-by-word the exact song' in the final film (ibid.). After hearing it, Lee jokes, 'I just went, "I have to rewrite the whole movie"' (ibid.). Elsa becomes trapped as a result of her powers rather than evil. 'Let it Go' won the Oscar for Best Original Song in 2014.

Borrowing from the Musical: Structural and Dramaturgical Considerations

'Let it Go' is an explicit turn to the Broadway musical; it belongs in what Stacy Wolf has identified as the 'act-1-finale-of-female-self-assertion [...] a conventional song type, repeated and reproduced in countless musicals' (2010: 4). Wolf considers this song type in reference to *Wicked*'s 'Defying Gravity' (Schwartz 2003), and there are clear similarities between the two numbers. Dramatically, both numbers portray a young woman making a key decision about her own life, and accepting their abilities and powers. The spectacular staging for *Wicked*, which sees Elphaba flying for the first time, is matched by the beautiful scenography of Elsa's ice palace. Both numbers are performed by Idina Menzel, and there are clear vocal connections between the two; both songs feature a stylistically identical jagged swoop at key moments – in 'Let it Go' when Elsa accidentally freezes Anna's heart, and in *Wicked* when Elphaba commits to her decision to go alone. This connection between one performer and her previous work has been called 'ghosting' by Marvin Carlson:

> The recycled body of an actor, already a complex bearer of semiotic messages, will almost inevitably in a new role evoke the ghost or ghosts of previous roles [...] a phenomenon that often colours and indeed may dominate the reception process. (2003: 8)

Wicked clearly demonstrates the possibilities for a musical about a relationship between two women, and for a central protagonist to act as quasi-antagonist. The stage musical's considerable financial success must have been reassuring for Disney in the prolonged filming process; *Wicked* is currently on track to reach \$4 billion in cumulative gross profits (Kramer 2015). One pre-release article in the *New York Times* noted the connection between the two, saying 'It can't be accidental [...] [that it has] a lot in common with that Broadway juggernaut and seems ready-made for theatrical adaptation' (Holden 2013).

Wolf has located the Broadway musical as 'a vehicle for female empowerment' (2010: 23). Broadway musicals have a legacy of women at the centre of their own story, something that *Frozen* moves to. At the beginning of this chapter, I noted Wolf's reading of the musical as doing 'double duty – to promote conservative values *and* to provide empowering representations of women, sometimes simultaneously' (ibid.: viii). This can be seen in the ambiguous nature of Elsa, particular in terms of queer readings. While a queer Disney protagonist seems almost unimaginable, *Frozen* is the first Disney film to openly present a gay family (albeit only for seconds). Eventually, inclusivity is just good business sense. When Anna stops at 'Wandering Oaken's Trading Post and Sauna', Oaken introduces his family to her – a handsome blond man and four children are shown waving hello. On being asked whether there is a gay family in the film, director Lee says 'We know what we made', adding 'But at the same time I feel like once we hand the film over it belongs to the world so I don't like to say anything, and let the fans talk. I think it's up to them' (Mackenzie 2014). *The Art of Frozen* book shows an early storyboard where an equally blond heteronormative family happen to be in the sauna (Chris Williams' design, in Solomon 2013: 24). The inclusion of a gay partner is deeply significant: when questioned about the decision, Lee explains: 'Disney films were made in different eras, different times, and we celebrate them all for different reasons but this one was made in 2013 and it's going to have a 2013 point of view' (Mackenzie 2014). This is plainly not the gay family anyone deserves, and yet is considerable progress from such a profoundly conservative cultural producer. Marina Warner has argued that fairy tales are explicitly shifty: 'We, the audience, you, the reader, are part of the story's future as well, its patterns are rising under the pressure of your palms, our fingers, too' (1995: 411). She notes: 'The faculty of wonder, like curiosity, can make things happen; it is time for wishful thinking to have its due' (ibid.: 418).

I want to locate *Frozen* as more than feminist wishful thinking and to argue that it reflects a certain progress in attempting to balance a similar double duty. It has achieved this by turning to the Broadway musical for a model that supports more comprehensive character development and permits women characters to enact the resolution to their own dramatic conflict. Wolf concludes her key text on musicals and feminism by noting the possibilities for reclaiming and repurposing musicals – they offer 'an ever-expanding archive of performance possibilities […] a living archive, a living, breathing, singing, and dancing archive. And because women are so central, active, and vocal, a future for feminist musical theatre is certain' (Wolf 2010: 243). Like fairy tales, musicals offer playful possibilities for encountering and rewriting the text in retelling, in re-performance.

Frozen may be a problematic feminist text, incomplete and unrepresentative, but it allows the hope of more. Perhaps its future iterations and expansions, whether that be the as-yet-untitled *Frozen 2* or its forthcoming adaptation into a Broadway stage musical, will have a third reprise in which two women in the same place sing together to and with one another about something other than a boy.

References

Aladdin (1993). Film. Burbank, CA: Walt Disney Feature Animation. Directed by Ron Clements and John Musker.

Aston, E. and G. Harris (2012). *A Good Night Out for the Girls: Popular Feminisms in Contemporary Theatre and Performance*. Basingstoke: Palgrave Macmillan.

Bagg, A., C. Lowry, K. King, K. Chirico, L. Parker, L. Brantz, M. J. Foronda and S. Watson (2015). 'We Got Photoshopped to Look Like Disney Princesses, and This is What Happened.' Available online: http://www.buzzfeed.com/kristinchirico/this-is-what-real-girls-would-look-like-as-disney-princesses#.toVbb42A4X (accessed 14 July 2015).

BBC News (2014). 'Disney's *Frozen* and the "gay agenda."' Available online:

http://www.bbc.co.uk/news/blogs-echochambers-26759342 (accessed 19 January 2016).

Beauty and the Beast (1992). Film. Burbank, CA: Walt Disney Feature Animation. Directed by Gary Trousdale and Kirk Wise.

Brantz, L. (2014). 'If Disney Princesses Had Realistic Waistlines.' Available online: http://www.buzzfeed.com/lorynbrantz/if-disney-princesses-had-realistic-waistlines#.mnrGGk2wke (accessed 14 July 2015).

Brave (2012). Film. Burbank, CA: Walt Disney Feature Animation. Directed by Mark Andrews and Brenda Chapman.

Butler, J. (1988). 'Performative Acts and Gender Constitution: An Essay in Phenomenology and Feminist Theory.' *Theatre Journal* 40 (4). doi: 10.2307/3207893.

Byron, E. and P. Ziobro (2014). 'Elsa Dominates Anna in "Frozen" Merchandise Sales.' Available online: http://www.wsj.com/articles/elsa-dominates-anna-in-frozen-merchandise-sales-1415131605 (accessed 8 July 2015).

Carlson, M. (2003). *The Haunted Stage: The Theatre as Memory Machine*. Michigan: Michigan University Press.

Chmielewski, D. C. and C. Eller (2010). 'Disney Restyles "Rapunzel" to Appeal to Boys.' *LA Times*, 9 March. Available online: http://articles.latimes.com/2010/mar/09/business/la-fi-ct-disney9-2010mar09 (accessed 19 January 2016).

Chrislove (2015). 'Top Comments: A Queer Perspective on Disney's *Frozen*.' Available online: http://www.dailykos.com/story/2014/02/21/1279401/-Top-Comments-A-Queer-Perspective-on-Disney-s-Frozen# (accessed 19 January 2016).

Cinderella (1950). Film. Burbank, CA: Walt Disney Feature Animation. Directed by Clyde Geronimi, Wilfred Jackson and Hamilton Luske.

Colman, D. (2014). 'The Problem with False Feminism – Disney and DreamWorks.' Available online: https://medium.com/disney-and-animation/the-problem-with-false-feminism-7c0bbc7252ef (accessed 22 July 2015).

Craven, A. (2002). 'Beauty and the Belles: Discourses of Feminism and Femininity in Disneyland.' *European Journal of Women's Studies* 9 (2): 123–42. doi: 10.1177/1350682002009002806.

Davis, M. Amy (2006). *Good Girls and Wicked Witches: Changing Representations of Women in Disney's Feature Animation*. New Barnet: Libbey.

Disney Weddings (2015). Elsa gown – collection 5 | Alfred Angelo bridal collection | Disney's fairy tale weddings & honeymoons. Available online: https://www.disneyweddings.com/disney-boutique/bridal-gowns/elsa-collection-5/ (accessed 3 January 2016).

Enchanted (2007). Film. Burbank, CA: Walt Disney Feature Animation. Directed by Kevin Lima.

England, D., L. Descartes and M. Collier-Meek (2011). 'Gender Role Portrayal and the Disney Princesses.' *Sex Roles* 64 (7–8): 555–67.

Feder, S. (2014). 'Slamming the Door: An Analysis of Elsa (*Frozen*).' Available online: http://www.thefeministwire.com/2014/10/slamming-door-analysis-elsa-frozen/ (accessed 22 July 2015).

Foundas, S. (2013). Film review: 'Frozen.' Available online: http://variety.com/2013/film/reviews/frozen-review-1200782020/ (accessed 19 January 2016).

Frozen (2013). Film. Burbank, CA: Walt Disney Animation Studios. Directed by Chris Buck and Jennifer Lee.

Giroux, H. A. and G. Pollock (2010). *The Mouse that Roared: Disney and the End of Innocence* 2nd edn Lanham, MD: Rowman & Littlefield.

Gomez, J. (2014). 'Why 'Frozen' Became The Biggest Animated Movie of All Time.' Available online: http://www.businessinsider.com/why-frozen-is-a-huge-success-2014-4?IR=T (accessed 2 July 2015).

Graser, M. (2014). '"Frozen" Sells 3.2 Million DVD, Blu-ray Discs in One Day.' Available online: at http://variety.com/2014/film/news/frozen-sells-3-2-million-dvd-blu-ray-discs-in-one-day-1201139509/ (accessed 19 January 2016).

Guilford, G. (2014). 'Big in Japan: Frozen's Feminist Rallying Cry.' Available online: http://www.theatlantic.com/entertainment/archive/2014/06/why-frozen-is-so-popular-in-japan/373714/ (accessed 19 January 2016).

Hickey, W. (2014). 'The Dollar-and-Cents Case against Hollywood's Exclusion of Women.' Available online: http://fivethirtyeight.com/features/the-dollar-and-cents-case-against-hollywoods-exclusion-of-women/ (accessed 19 January 2016).

Holden, S. (2013). 'Disney's "Frozen", a Makeover of "The Snow Queen."' Available online: http://www.nytimes.com/2013/11/27/movies/disneys-frozen-a-makeover-of-the-snow-queen.html?_r=0 (accessed 19 January 2016).

IFPI (2015). 'IFPI Publishes Digital Music Report 2015.' Available online: http://www.ifpi.org/news/Global-digital-music-revenues-match-physical-format-sales-for-first-time (accessed 19 January 2016).

IMDb (2014a). 'Box Office/Business for *Frozen*.' Available online: http://www.imdb.com/title/tt2294629/business?ref_=tt_dt_bus (accessed 19 January 2016).

IMDb (2014b). '*Frozen* (2013). Release Dates AKA Details.' Available online: http://www.imdb.com/title/tt2294629/releaseinfo?ref_=ttfc_ql_2#akas (accessed 30 October 2015).

ineffable-hufflepuff (2013). 'Be the Good Girl You Always Have to Be: Is …' Available online: http://fandomsandfeminism.tumblr.com/post/68687586103/be-the-good-girl-you-always-have-to-be-is (accessed 18 July 2015).

Jones, J. (2015). 'If Disney Princesses Were Proportioned Like Disney Princes.' Available online: http://www.buzzfeed.com/jamiejones/disney-reversed#.itVyyGnjGY (accessed 14 July 2015).

Jusino, T. (2015). 'Alison Bechdel Would Like You to Call it the "Bechdel-Wallace Test", ThankYouVeryMuch.' Available online: http://www.themarysue.com/bechdel-wallace-test-please-alison-bechdel/ (accessed 15 January 2016).

The Little Mermaid II: Return to the Sea (2000). DVD. Burbank, CA: Walt Disney Feature Animation. Directed by Jim Kammerud and Brian Smith.

Koren-Kuik, M. (2013). 'Desiring the Tangible: Disneyland, Fandom and Spatial Immersion'. In K. M. Barton and J. M. Lampley (eds), *Fan Culture: Essays on Participatory Fandom in the 21st Century*. Jefferson, NC: McFarland, 146–58.

Krueger, K. (2015). 'Fox Host Denounces Popular Movie *Frozen* for Anti-Male Propaganda.' *Guardian*, 4 February. Available online: http://www.theguardian.com/film/2015/feb/04/fox-host-denounces-popular-movie-frozen-anti-male-propaganda (accessed 19 January 2016).

Kuhn, A. (1994). *Women's Pictures: Feminism and Cinema*, 2nd edn. London: Verso.

LaPorte, N. (2014) 'How "Frozen" Director Jennifer Lee Reinvented the Story of The Snow Queen.' Available online: http://www.fastcompany.com/3027019/most-creative-people/how-frozen-director-jennifer-lee-reinvented-the-story-of-the-snow-queen (accessed 2 July 2015).

Lane, A. (2013). 'It's Cold Outside: "Inside Llewyn Davis" and "Frozen".' *New Yorker*, 9 Decmber. Available online: http://www.newyorker.com/magazine/2013/12/09/its-cold-outside (accessed 19 January 2016).

Lee, J. (2014). 'Scriptnotes, Ep 128: *Frozen* with Jennifer Lee – Transcript.' Interview with John August, Aline Brosh McKenna for JohnAugust.com, 1 February.

Liberatore, P. (2013). '"Brave" Creator Blasts Disney for "Blatant Sexism" in Princess Makeover'. Available online: http://www.marinij.com/article/ZZ/20130511/news/130519014 (accessed 28 October 2016).

Lilo & Stitch (2002). Film. Burbank, CA: Walt Disney Feature Animation. Directed by Dean DeBlois and Chris Sanders.

The Lion King (1994). Film. Burbank, CA: Walt Disney Animation Studios. Directed by Roger Allers and Rob Minkoff.

The Little Mermaid (1989). Film. Burbank, CA: Walt Disney Feature Animation. Directed by Ron Clements and John Musker.

Lynskey, D. (2014). 'Frozen-Mania: How Elsa, Anna and Olaf Conquered the World.' *Guardian*, 13 May. Available online: http://www.theguardian.com/film/2014/may/13/frozen-mania-elsa-anna-olaf-disney-emo-princess-let-it-go (accessed 19 January 2016).

Mackenzie, S. (2014). '*Frozen*: Disney's icebreaker.' Available online: http://www.bigissue.com/features/3593/frozen-disney-s-icebreaker (accessed 2 July 2015).

McGowan, T. (2003). 'Looking for the Gaze: Lacanian Film Theory and its Vicissitudes'. *Cinema Journal* 42 (3): 27–47. doi:10.1353/cj.2003.0009.

Merrick, J. (2015). 'Little Girls Dressing Up Like Elsa from "Frozen" are the Future of Feminism.' Available online: http://search.proquest.com/docview/1650730577?accountid=14685 (accessed 19 January 2016).

MovieclipsComingSoon (2013). 'Frozen TV SPOT – forecast (2013) – Kristen Bell Disney animated movie HD.' Available online: https://www.youtube.com/watch?v=mdjjYa2Gcms (accessed 18 January 2016).

Mulvey, L. (2009). *Visual and Other Pleasures*, 2nd edn. Houndsmills, Basingstoke: Palgrave Macmillan.

New York Cast Recording and S. Sondheim (2012). *Franklin Shepherd Inc – Merrily We Roll Along* [CD]. Encores! Orchestra.

The Princess and the Frog (2009). Film. Burbank, CA: Walt Disney Feature Animation. Directed by Ron Clements and John Musker.

The Princess Diaries (2001). Film. Burbank, CA: Walt Disney Feature Animation. Directed by Garry Marshall.

Robertson, E. (2015). 'Branagh's *Cinderella* Spits in the Face of Every Disney Princess "Remixer" on Tumblr.' *Guardian*, 25 March. Available online: http://www.theguardian.com/commentisfree/2015/mar/25/branaghs-cinderella-spits-at-every-disney-princess-remixer-tumblr (accessed 2 July 2015).

Rogers, M. (2015). 'Feminist Disney.' Available online: http://feministdisney.tumblr.com (accessed 2 July 2015).

Samakow, J. (2013). 'LOOK: Merida's Makeover Sparks Outrage and Petition.' Available online: http://www.huffingtonpost.com/2013/05/08/merida-brave-makeover_n_3238223.html (accessed 3 January 2016).

Schweitzer, M. and S. Bennett (2014). 'In the Window at Disney: A Lifetime of Brand Desire.' *The Drama Review* 58 (4) (T224): 23–31. doi: 10.1162/DRAM_a_00395.

Shone, T. (2013). '*Frozen*'s Celebration of Sisterhood Guaranteed to Melt the Coldest Heart.' *Guardian*, 29 November. Available online: http://www.theguardian.com/film/2013/nov/29/frozen-disney-pixar-film-criticism (accessed 19 January 2016).

Shrek (2001). Film. Universal City, CA: DreamWorks Animation. Directed by Andrew Adamson and Vicky Jenson.

Snow White and the Seven Dwarfs (1938). Film. Burbank, CA: Walt Disney Feature Animation. Directed by David Hand.

Solga, K. (2015). *Theatre and Feminism*. London: Palgrave.

Solomon, C. (2013). *The Art of Disney Frozen*. San Francisco, CA: Chronicle.

Stevens, D. (2014). 'That Weird Sexy-Makeover Moment at the Heart of *Frozen*'s "Let it Go" Leaves Me Cold.' Available online: http://www.slate.com/articles/arts/movies/2014/02/_let_it_go_idina_menzel_s_frozen_ballad_it_sends_the_wrong_message.html (accessed 19 January 2016).

Tangled (2010). Film. Burbank, CA: Walt Disney Feature Animation. Directed by Nathan Greno and Byron Howard.

thiscouldhavebeenfrozen (2014). 'Snow Queens and PoC.' Available online:

http://thiscouldhavebeenfrozen.tumblr.com/aboutthisblog (accessed 14 July 2015).

TV Tropes (2015). 'Decon-Recon Switch.' Available online: http://tvtropes.org/pmwiki/pmwiki.php/Main/DeconReconSwitch (accessed 22 July 2015).

Walt Disney Animation Studios (2013). 'Disney's *Frozen* "Let it Go" Sequence Performed by Idina Menzel.' Available online: https://www.youtube.com/watch?v=moSFlvxnbgk (accessed 15 November 2016).

The Walt Disney Company (2014). 'Fiscal Year 2014 Annual Report and Shareholder Letter'. Annual Shareholder's Report. Los Angeles, CA: Disney, 19 November. Available online: https://ditm-twdc-us.storage.googleapis.com/2015/10/2014-Annual-Report.pdf (accessed 22 July 2015).

Warner, M. (1995). *From the Beast to the Blonde: On Fairy Tales and Their Tellers*. London: Chatto & Windus.

Who Framed Roger Rabbit (1988). Film. Burbank, CA: Walt Disney Feature Animation. Directed by Robert Zemeckis.

Wicked (2006). Audio CD. New York: Decca Broadway.

Wolf, S. E. (2010). *Changed for Good: A Feminist History of the Broadway Musical*. New York: Oxford University Press.

Notes

Introduction

1   This can be seen on https://www.youtube.com/watch?v=ER4srD951bw
    (accessed 22 August 2016).
2   Thanks to Olaf Jubin for pointing out that although Disney is particularly
    powerful in the US and as a US brand, certain Disney musicals are even
    more successful abroad: in relation to the number of citizens, *Frozen* was
    most popular in Japan and Korea, and the stage versions of *Tarzan* and
    The Little Mermaid actually found an audience in Holland and Germany.

Chapter 1: Music and the Aura of Reality in Walt Disney's *Snow White and the Seven Dwarfs* (1937)

1   This chapter is based on a paper I delivered at the 2005 Society of
    American Music annual meeting in Eugene, Oregon. I am grateful to my
    UCLA colleague Raymond Knapp for his support of my work on this
    topic, and for his encouragement and help in bringing it to publication.
2   There are many books detailing the production of Disney films. For *Snow
    White* the most detailed is Kaufman (2012). The 'bible' for the animators'
    own view of their work is Thomas and Johnston (1981). Neal Gabler's
    extensive biography of Walt Disney discusses the film in Chapter 6, 'Folly',
    in Gabler (2006), 213–75. The earlier, authorized biography, Thomas
    (1994, 1st edn, 1976), discusses *Snow White* in Chapter 11, 129–42. Barrier
    (1999) discusses the film's production in Chapter 5, 'Disney, 1936–1938'.
    See also Canemaker (1999), 38–55.
3   The actual amount in 1937. Michael Barrier (1999: 229, 598) gives the
    figure as $1,488,422.74, citing a balance sheet submitted to RKO pictures
    during investment negotiations, dated 29 March 1947.
4   Famously the title of the sixth of a series of eight articles, 'My Dad, Walt
    Disney', by Diane Disney Miller, as told to Pete Martin (1956).
5   For descriptions of a sequence of three early stage versions of the tale, all
    with music (an 1856 German play and two American plays produced in
    New York City in 1905 and 1912), leading up to the silent 1916 film made
    in New York (interiors) and Georgia (exteriors) released by Paramount
    and starring Marguerite Clark, the star of the 1912 Broadway version, see
    Kaufman (2012), 12–24. Long considered lost, a print of the 1916 film seen

by Walt Disney in January of 1917 was rediscovered at the Nederlands Filmmuseum in Amsterdam in 1992 and restored by a team of film preservationists at George Eastman House in Rochester, New York, in 1994. Kaufman's descriptions are intended to show how plot and character details in the Disney film can be found in each successive theatrical version; while the presence of songs in the two American plays is called 'integral', little details about music itself is included. See also Allan (1999), 36–42.

6   From the advent of sound to the late 1930s, music and animation had been conceived as one thing. Wilfred Jackson, quoted by Thomas and Johnston, expressed the general feeling: 'I do not believe there was much thought given to the music as one thing and the animation as another. I believe we conceived of them as elements which we were trying to fuse into a whole new thing that would be more than simply movement plus sound.' Thomas and Johnston add: 'The effect of absolutely everything being related to the musical beat became so well developed that, in the musical world, "Mickeymousing" became the name for music that accented or echoed every action on the screen.' Thomas and Johnston (1981), 288.

7   For an extended analysis of *Snow White* as a musical, and Disney's contribution to the combination of fairy tales and musicals in the US, see Knapp (2006), 122–31.

8   Knapp noted only two 'nontrivial musical silences (lasting about half a minute each)' (2006: 125).

9   The numbering of sequences is drawn from Kaufman's Appendix A: Production Credits in Kaufman (2012), 286–94. Kaufman's sequence titles are given in all capitals; capitalization in this chart is mine, as are all comments in square brackets. Thomas and Johnston define the Disney use of 'sequence' to describe a section of animation:

> The term 'sequence' refers to a group of scenes all related to a single idea that make up a section of the story. They are like the divisions of an act in a play, in that the action usually occurs in one locale and has one overall mood. There can be an exciting sequence, a sad one, a musical one, a funny one; each is built to exploit the entertainment potential in the idea, and to give texture and a contrast to the other sequences around it. (Thomas and Johnston 1981: 539)

10   Knapp notes this kind of front-loading of songs in filmed musicals after *Snow White*, singling out *The Wizard of Oz* (1939) and *Meet Me in St. Louis* (1944) for discussion; see Knapp (2006), 94–5, 137. Knapp returns to those two films for a larger consideration of film musicals that 'stop being musicals' in Knapp (2012), 157–72.

11   Music and lyrics by Frank Churchill and Larry Morey. In the spring of 1937, sequence 2A was:

> one of the *last* sequences to be written, developed, and produced ...
> Walt recognized very early that this would be one of the most difficult

parts of the story for his artists to tackle. No slapstick action or gags, no cartoony characters ... the business of this sequence was to establish an absorbing, enchanting fairy-tale world on the screen, drawing in the audience with its charm and sincerity ...

Lyricist Larry Morey was responsible for the rhymed dialogue:

> as early as 1935 the multitalented Morey had combined his musical activities with story development ... In this position he could respond to Walt's request to 'weave [the music] into the story' – creating an animation equivalent of Rodgers and Hart's sophisticated scores for *Love Me Tonight* and *Hallelujah, I'm a Bum*, which had seamlessly interwoven dialogue, rhymed dialogue, and song. (Kaufman 2012: 104)

Lyricist Yip Harburg also followed Lorenz Hart in writing rhymed dialogue as a transition between speech and song for *The Wizard of Oz* (1939); his Munchkinland sequence is written entirely in rhyme. See Harmetz (1989), 67–8, 74–5, 85–9.

12 This sequence was the first to be animated. Interestingly, an early (October 1934) script has the dwarfs speaking in rhyme as well; this was changed – see Kaufman (2012), 144. Another scene in dialogue and rhyme for Snow White and the Prince between the songs 'I'm Wishing' and 'One Song' was planned and animated, but finally deemed unnecessary and cut in the summer of 1937 (ibid.: 106–9).

13 Paul Barber (1988) argues convincingly that European vampire and other monster legends were likely inspired by observation of human corpses.

14 For a discussion of the Uncanny Valley and computer graphics in films, see Pavlus (2011).

15 In enlarging the character's eyes to enhance the illusion of reality, Luske was anticipating psychological research by over seven decades. For a discussion of the ways in which humans perceive life in faces, and especially eyes, see Looser and Wheatley (2010).

16 This story that actual blush was used is corrected in Kaufman (2012), 87. The artist who specialized in applying the dye has been identified as Helen Ogger, see Johnson (1988).

17 'This opening scene was described as a "fade in from a long shot" on the final draft script of January 5, 1937. With the perfection of the multiplane camera later that year, it became a multiplane shot heightening the illusion of penetrating into the scene.' Krause and Witkowski (1995), 66–7.

18 Disney's multiplane camera was first used for the *Silly Symphony* short *The Old Mill* (1937). For the use of the multiplane camera and other technical details of the camera work in *Snow White*, see Kaufman (2012), 93–6 and Gabler (2006), 257–9.

19 On the use of colour in Snow White, see Gabler (2006), 255–7. Gabler quotes Walt Disney: 'Speaking of a Harman-Ising cartoon he had seen

recently, Walt told his layout men that he was striving for a more artistic effect.

> 'They got colors everywhere,' he said, 'and it looks cheap. There is nothing subtle about it at all. It's just poster-like. A lot of people think that's what a cartoon should have. I think we are trying to achieve something different here. We are not going after the comic supplement coloring. We have to strive for a certain depth and realism.' (255)

20   The Belgian cartoonist Hergé (1907–83) used this same combination of realistic, detailed backgrounds and stylized characters in his *Tintin* comics. For more on realism in comics, see McCloud (1993).

21   In a conference on Sequence 8A, 18 January 1936, Walt Disney specified what kind of contemporary music he did not want for the film: 'I don't like the Cab Calloway idea or too much OH DE OH DO … Audiences hear a lot of hot stuff. If we can keep this quaint, it will appeal more than the hot stuff.' Gabler (2006), 254.

22   Disney's live-action film *Enchanted* (2007) spoofs the identification of Disney heroines with singing established by Snow White: when Princess Giselle (Amy Adams) breaks into song in modern-day Manhattan, everyone around her joins in. Such is the power of Disney heroines!

23   Knapp (2005), 12. See also Knapp (2006), 7.

Chapter 2: Medieval 'Beauty' and Romantic 'Song' in Animated Technirama: Pageantry, Tableau and Action in Disney's *Sleeping Beauty*

1   Walt Disney's (2003) *Sleeping Beauty*. All subsequent quotations, timings and observations derive from this release. An earlier form of this essay was read at the 2015 National Meeting of the American Musicological Society (Louisville, KY, 12–15 November). I wish to thank Elizabeth Upton for our many valuable conversations about Disney animation, and about this film in particular. Thanks also to Rachel and Zelda Knapp and to Daniel Goldmark for their help at various stages of this chapter's development.

2   *Sleeping Beauty* was photographed using Super Technirama 70 widescreen process; Disney's *Lady and the Tramp* (1955) was also a widescreen release.

3   As Cari McDonnell (2015), 166–8 details. Regarding the background artwork in particular, see Chapter 14 of Canemaker (1996), 158–67.

4   Canemaker (1996) and Allan (1999); Canemaker provides striking illustrations of both Earle's tendency toward the overwrought (158–9) and the power of his early concept art (164–5); see also Allan's colour plate 81 (42).

5   Allan (1999), 233, 234, 236; Allan's comments echo many early

critiques of the film, some of which are excerpted in McDonnell (2015), 170–1.

6 I borrow this structural division between sight and sound – beauty and song – from the documentary '*Once Upon a Dream*': *The Making of Walt Disney's* Sleeping Beauty (filmed 1997), included on the bonus disc in the 2003 DVD release.

7 The Sleeping Beauty Storybook Gallery, included on the bonus disc in the 2003 DVD release.

8 The Tchaikovsky instrumental passages were recorded in Berlin by the Berlin Symphony Orchestra; George Bruns reportedly went to Berlin to take advantage of superior recording technology.

9 Aurora is an ironic choice for her name, given that it means the opposite of sleeping (as noted earlier). For Perrault's version, of course, that is the point of the name, since it is given to the sleeping beauty's first-born, after her awakening.

10 In *Enchanted*, the heroine, stranded in present-day Manhattan, searches for her betrothed there, only to find true love with a mortal. In *Frozen*, the 'act of true love' through which Princess Anna might be saved from the effects of a frozen heart, assumed by all to mean a kiss from her beloved, turns out to be, instead, an act of true love by the imperiled maiden, who in sacrificing herself for her sister Elsa actually saves herself. And *Maleficent* makes several related points: first that 'true love's kiss' may be betrayed, and later that more than one kind of love might be 'true', since Aurora is ultimately saved by a last, desperate kiss from the evil fairy herself, who had placed the curse in the belief that true love does not exist, but who has long since come to love the young princess.

11 Indeed, Aurora pricks her finger near the end of No. 8, during the reprise of the referential melody, just before Carrabosse reveals herself at the beginning of the Finale.

12 This music may arguably be said to belong to Maleficent as well, since the 'reveal' (the discovery of the Prince's cap in the cottage) points also to her as well as to him, and much of the music borrowed from Tchaikovsky ('E' in Table 2.1) is deployed in her lair, the Forbidden Mountain, and even during her reverie with her 'familiar' before she descends to the dungeon to taunt Prince Phillip. But, on balance, more of this music accompanies the good fairies than Maleficent, whereas her basic motive is taken over by Phillip during the ensuing action.

13 Maleficent's considerable camp appeal, based mainly on her theatrical costume and manner, is also enhanced by this choice for her characteristic music, especially for those who recognize its source in the ballet.

14 Table 2.1 is not complete. A few passages of background music, often generic and/or 'Mickey-Mousing' the film's action (even when derived from Tchaikovsky) are omitted, and several 'back-and-forth' passages, involving play between and among multiple leitmotivic sources, are

condensed. Nevertheless, Table 2.1 does give a representative account of the film's deployment of Tchaikovsky's music, embracing both the film's main sequences and all the borrowings that have seemed relevant to this discussion. All references here and in the following text to Tchaikovsky's score are from Tchaikovsky (1974).

15   I use 'musical comedy' here in the broad, generic sense. Cari McDonnell details discarded plans to turn Tchaikovsky's melodies more overtly toward musical comedy during the good fairies' cottage sequence, while noting that the film's only remaining comic song, 'The Skumps Song', does not use Tchaikovsky's music (2015: 169–70).

16   The subjunctive love song, of which Rodgers and Hammerstein's 'People Will Say We're in Love' and 'If I Loved You' are the quintessential examples, typically will change to a more definite declaration of love in its reprise. Here, however, the song starts and ends with definite claims despite its subjunctive basis ('I know you' and 'I know what you'll do, / You'll love me at once'). Moreover, despite the ways 'Once Upon a Dream' conforms to the type, it is never sung as an actual love duet, although, as McDonnell details (2015: 178–9), both the forest version and the final reprise were at one point intended to culminate with the lovers singing the song together.

17   Amanda responds to Elyot's 'Nasty insistent little tune' in Act I; the tune in question is Coward's own 'Someday I'll Find You', whose sentiment bears more than a passing resemblance to that of 'Once Upon a Dream'.

Chapter 5: Disney as Broadway *Auteur*: The Disney Versions of Broadway Musicals for Television in the Late 1990s and Early 2000s

1   Also, please see Daboo (2005), 330–7 on the controversy with casting non-Asian actors in *Bombay Dreams*.

2   Please also see the discussion on 'historical verisimilitude'. Available online: http://www.theguardian.com/commentisfree/2015/aug/17/trevor-nunn-war-roses-all-white-history (accessed 12 January 2017).

3   Here is Wilson speaking out against the above-mentioned *Death of the Salesman* production:

> To mount an all-black production of *Death of a Salesman* or any other play conceived for white actors as an investigation of the human condition through the specific of white culture is to deny us our own humanity, our own history, and the need to make our own investigations from the cultural ground on which we stand as black Americans. It is an assault on our presence, our difficult but

honourable history in America, and an insult to our intelligence, our playwrights, and our many and varied contributions to the society and the world at large. (1998: 499)

Chapter 6: *The Hunchback of Notre Dame* (1996): Too Far 'Out There'?

1   By far the most successful musical based on Hugo's masterpiece is the French 'spectacle musical' *Notre Dame de Paris* (1999) with music by Richard Cocciante and lyrics by Luc Plamondon.

2   This comic book adaptation stays very close to Hugo's original, merely deleting the Sister Gudule subplot.

3   Stephen Rebello here intentionally avoids the words 'love' or 'desire' as this would not tie in with the animators' aim to portray Quasimodo's feelings as 'puppy love'; this feature of the movie will be problematized later on.

4   Frollo has the former Captain of the Guard whipped. This happens off screen, but the lashes and the cries of pain can still be heard.

5   The filmmakers made it more evident that the apparition is fully clothed. Thompson (1996).

6   To give but two examples: Aurora in *Sleeping Beauty* (1959) imparts all her hopes for her future to the forest creatures who watch her singing in the woods, and Aladdin constantly explains his feelings and schemes to pet monkey Abu.

7   The film's directors, producers and animators describe him as having 'an innocent appeal' (Rebello, 1996: 52), as 'an abused child' (49) and 'a yearning, childlike guy' (62), while Tom Hulce was chosen to lend his voice to the character because it has 'this wonderful, innocent quality' (62).

8   In Britain, the film was awarded the 'Raspberry Ripple Award' for 'Worst Feature-Film Portrayal of a Person with Disability'. Norden (2013), 163–78.

9   The company, though, had no qualms selling 'Out There' T-shirts to its homosexual fan base on an unofficial 'gay day' at their Florida theme park resort Disney World in time for the film's release. Thompson (1996).

10 The film has a Rotten Tomatoes score of 73 per cent, with many reviewers pointing out that the film is decidedly uneven.

11 It was celebrated as 'the largest, most imposing score yet for an animated film', Tonkin (1996), 40; and as a 'true folk pop operetta', Gleiberman (1996), 43.

12 Another scene which hints at Frollo's sexual desire, 32 minutes into the movie, shows him lustfully sniffing Esmeralda's hair.

13 The latter record peaked at No. 30 in the 'US Hot 100' *Billboard* charts ('All-4-One'), while 'God Help the Outcasts' didn't chart at all.
14 Literally, *The Bell Ringer of Notre Dame.*
15 This is one of the reasons why Disney's *Beauty and the Beast* had already been a disappointment in Vienna and Stuttgart; in both cities it failed to turn into a major hit.
16 On a budget of $1 million it had box office receipts of $2.5 million. Anon. (1958), 30.
17 According to David Sterritt (1996b), it has 'largely faded from view'.
18 Ty Burr pans it as 'plain dull', although he praises Gina Lollobrigida's 'robustly sexual Esmeralda' (1997: 72).
19 While I was growing up in the 1970s and 1980s, the 1956 version was regularly shown on German television (at a time when there were only three channels, meaning that it regularly had huge ratings).
20 The very title of director Helmut Baumann's review speaks volumes: 'Gina, where are you when we need you?' Baumann (1999), 28.
21 Based on the exchange rate of 1999, that budget comes out as $21.6 million.
22 *Der Glöckner von Notre Dame* (1999).
23 I need to point out here that I saw neither the La Jolla nor the Papermill production. The following reflections and observations are therefore based on statements by the production team, on reviews and other sources.
24 Dom Claude Frollo was once again a cleric, the archdeacon of Notre Dame.
25 See the various statements at Anon. (2014).
26 For co-director Gary Trousdale, the judge represented 'unexamined, self-justifying evil incarnate'. Rebello (1996), 80.
27 Posted by 'Wicked Fanatic' on 29 October 2014. See Anon. (2014).
28 Comment by 'dave1606' on the message board of www.broadwayworld.com on 7 March 2015. Ibid.
29 Schwartz's staging reset the song 'Rest and Recreation' in a brothel and had Clopin mime sexual intercourse during 'Topsy Turvy', so perhaps this statement is to be taken with a grain of salt.
30 As one observer with the username 'Wildcard' put it on 10 November 2014: 'Disney makes more money licensing the shows than actually producing them. They wanted a production that can easily be recreated at the smallest level.' Anon. (2014).
31 The English writer has already been adapted by Disney, as their 1988 animated feature *Oliver & Company* is very loosely based on Dickens' *Oliver Twist.*

Chapter 7: *The Lion King*: A 'Blockbuster Feline' on Broadway and Beyond

1   Charles Isherwood used 'blockbuster feline' in his review of *Aladdin*, *New York Times*, 20 March 2014, http://www.nytimes.com/2014/03/21/theater/aladdin-tweaks-the-disney-formula-with-breezy-insouciance.html?partner=rss&emc=rss&_r=1 (accessed 30 March 2014).

2   'ABOUT *THE LION KING*,' Disney Theatrical Productions press release, current as of 17 January 2017. For additional information worldwide, visit www.lionking.com.

3   *The Lion King* (2003), 'Film Origins', Disc 2: Supplemental Features.

4   Ibid., Roger Allers, 'Story Origins'.

5   Ibid., Irene Mecchi.

6   Ibid., 'Production Research Trip.'

7   The voice belongs to South African singer and composer Lebohang Morake, known as Lebo M. *The Lion King* (2003), Disc 1: Feature.

8   Hans Zimmer, 'Scoring Emotion,' in *The Lion King* (2003), Disc 2.

9   Maslin (1994).

10 Ebert (1994).

11 Siskel (1994).

12 Michael Eisner, 'Reflections,' in *The Lion King* (2003), Disc 2.

13 This chapter will not include discussion of film sequels, television spinoffs or video games.

14 *Beauty and the Beast* enjoyed a thirteen-year run on Broadway, first at the Palace Theatre, then at the Lunt-Fontanne from November 1999 until July 2007.

15 Hardy also oversaw the renovation of the Victory Theatre, directly across the street. The city's oldest surviving theatre, it re-opened in December 1995 as the New Victory.

16 Donald Hahn, 'Stage: Musical Origins,' in *The Lion King* (2003), Disc 2.

17 Brantley (1997).

18 Julie Taymor, 'Stage: Musical Origins,' in *The Lion King* (2003), Disc 2.

19 Disney Theatrical Group (2010), II-4-18. I am grateful to Ken Cerniglia for giving me access to this script and for all his invaluable help.

20 There are six indigenous African languages spoken in the show, according to Disney Theatrical Productions (2016). The others are Swahili, Sotho and Congolese.

21 Every ensemble member plays both a hyena and a 'Grassland head'. Disney Theatrical Productions (2016).

22 Disney Theatrical Group (2010), II-4-19-20.

23 Ibid., II-1-7.

24 Disney Theatrical Productions (2016).

25 Mufasa's mask weighs 11 ounces, Scar's 7 ounces and Sarabi's just 4 ounces. Ibid.

26   Julie Taymor, 'Part 5: Discover the Costumes.' Disney on Broadway (2014),
     4 November 2009. Film clips from global productions of *The Lion King*,
     some authorized, others not, are widely available on YouTube.
27   The tallest are the four eighteen-foot giraffes in 'I Just Can't Wait to Be
     King.' Disney Theatrical Productions (2016).
28   Jack Galloway, Disney Theatrical Productions (2016).
29   On Broadway there are 142 people directly involved with the daily
     production of the show, including fifty-one cast members (eight of whom are
     South African) and twenty-four musicians. According to Disney Theatrical
     Productions (2016) the others are '19 wardrobe staff, 2 wig/hairdressers +
     3 make-up artists, 3 puppet craftspeople, 13 carpenters, 10 electricians, 3
     sound people, 4 props people, 6 creative associates, 5 stage managers + 2
     administrative/company managers, 1 child guardian, 1 physical therapist'.
30   Simon (1997).
31   Brantley (1997).
32   Miller (2007), 209. Miller also states that the demand for tickets was
     so 'overwhelming' initially that Disney considered opening a second
     production on Broadway.
33   Evans (1997).
34   Quotation from the *New York Times* on *The Lion King* website: www.
     lionking.com (accessed 30 January 2016).
35   Changes originally implemented for the 2009 Las Vegas production, 'The
     Morning Report' was dropped, 'The Madness of Scar' abbreviated, and the
     aerial ballet in 'I Just Can't Wait to Be King' cut except in Hamburg.
36   Disney Theatrical Productions (2016).
37   See www.lionkingexperience.com (accessed 22 July 2015).

Chapter 8: Not Only on Broadway: Disney JR. and Disney KIDS Across the USA

1   For their generosity in sharing resources and information about Disney's
    work for and with children, I want to thank Lisa Mitchell, Ken Cerniglia,
    Sarah Malone Kenny and David Scott from the Disney Theatrical
    Group, DTG President Thomas Schumacher for his inspiring talk at
    Princeton University, Paul Bogaev for inviting and publicly interviewing
    Schumacher, and Carol Edelson at MTI. In Nashville, my thanks go
    to Roberta Ciuffo West and Kristin Dare-Horsley for their generosity,
    graciousness and intelligence, and to Joseph Ashby, Josh Binkley, Lori
    Davis Howard, Kathy Hull, Nola Jones, Amy Kramer, Ginger Newman,
    Tonya Pewitt, Carole Pickett, Miya Robertson, Rachel Sumner, Stefanie
    Tinnell, Steve West and Laura Zuehsow, and to New York-based teaching
    artist Elizabeth Nestlerode for sharing their stories with me. Thanks to

Wendy Belcher, Jill Dolan, Judith Hamera and Tamsen Wolff for reading
previous drafts of this chapter. Finally, thanks to Katie Welsh for her
superb research help.

2   Thomas Schumacher, Public Interview with Paul Bogaev, Princeton
University, 7 April 2015. He said that on Broadway 80 per cent of shows
fail, but for Disney 80 per cent succeed because they invest so much
in 'R & D'. They can channel profits from big moneymakers like *The
Lion King* to fund new projects' extensive and long-term research and
development. This degree of preparation explains why they're surprised
when a show fails, like *The Little Mermaid* did.

3   See http://mtiblog.mtishows.com/category/conferences-festivals-and-
special-events/junior-theater-festival-2013/ (accessed 11 August 2015).

4   Musicians and musical training are, of course, not a part of this
programme. To be sure, students should be taught to play an instrument,
and, ideally, every performance would be accompanied by a live student
orchestra. For DMIS to enable young children as singers, dancers and
actors, professionally taped musical accompaniment is ideal.

5   DTG is well aware of this apparent contradiction. See Cerniglia and
Mitchell (2014), 142.

6   *The Lion King JR.* and *The Lion King KIDS* were added in January 2015.

7   See Music Theatre International Shows (2015).

8   DMIS resembles another successful NYC-based musical theatre outreach
program: Broadway Junior. Supported by the Shubert Foundation, Music
Theatre International and the New York City Department of Education,
Broadway Junior was the brainchild of MTI Cofounder and CEO Freddie
Gershon and supports the production of Broadway JR. titles, including
some Disney shows, at a handful of NYC public middle schools each year.

9   They cite Lisa Mitchell, 'Self-Efficacy and Theatre Production in Urban
Elementary Schools'. MS thesis, The City University of New York, 2011.

10 Referring to Israel (2009), 3.

11 Referring to Fiske (1999), 8.

12 Jones has a music background and has been instrumental (no pun
intended!) in growing music education in the Nashville public schools.
During my visit in May 2015 she was awarded a sizable NEA grant to
maintain 'Music Makes Us' in the schools. See http://mnpschildrenfirst.
com/2015/05/06/metro-schools-and-music-makes-us-win-100000-grant-
from-the-national-endowment-for-the-arts/ and http://musicmakesus.org/
about-us (accessed 17 August 2015).

13 See http://www.tpac.org/spotlight/country-duo-maddie-tae-to-host-
disney-musicals-in-schools-student-share-on-may-14-at-tpac/, 11 May
2015 (accessed 19 July 2015).

14 See http://www.lionkingexperience.com/inline/junior/sessions/1/
lesson-plan/Session%201%20-%20Lesson%20Plan.pdf (accessed 11 August
2015).

15   TPAC sponsors school visits to its theatres for kids to see a professional play, but some schools lack the resources to organize permission slips, bus rental and so on to get the children downtown (J. Ashby, personal communication, 7 May 2015).

16   TPAC got permission from Disney to expand their programme to include middle schools, which would perform JR. titles.

17   In conversations and interviews as well as the rehearsals and performances I observed, there were girls playing Baloo and Shere Khan but none playing Aladdin or Simba.

18   The charming production of *Alice in Wonderland JR.*, which I saw at Wright Middle School, boasted a cast of forty kids, almost all of them Latino/a, Kurdish or African-American. For a spectator accustomed to a depressingly white Broadway, seeing so many children of colour in a musical is nothing short of revolutionary.

Chapter 9: Dancing toward Masculinity: *Newsies*, Gender and Desire

1   The film began rolling in April 1991. This oft-repeated story is ubiquitous in press about the show. See Cerniglia (2013).

2   See Scheck (2011), 36; J. Dziemianowicz (2011), 37; Sommers (2011), 53.

3   The original audition notice for the Paper Mill run was for ages 18 and up. See also Cerniglia and Mitchell (2014), 144. According to Gattelli, for the (union) tour the 'singing/acting/dance ensemble is actually younger, on average, than we had in New York. We've got guys as young as 16, and an average age of 20–1.' See Takiff (2014).

4   Suskin's mention of *West Side Story* here is notable primarily because of the absence of such references in other reviews. *West Side*, famously a show about 'juvenile delinquency', was populated almost entirely with actors in their twenties. See Herrera (2012).

5   I am grateful to *Newsies'* dance captain Michael Fatica for his assistance with my descriptions of the dancing in *Newsies*. Michael is a dear friend and also generously volunteered his time as a reviewer of this chapter in draft.

6   The other leads for the show remained white, but producers also added more people of colour to the dancing chorus when the show moved to Broadway.

Chapter 10: 'We're All in This Together': Being Girls and Boys in *High School Musical* (2006)

1   Sport, and especially team sport, is an area that can offer a particularly benign image of male virility, physicality and power. On the other hand, the gender segregation of much sporting competition can and has led to entrenched and debasing attitudes, particularly in aggressive misogyny and homophobia towards women and gay men. See for example Sanday (1999).

2   There are cheerleaders in *High School Musical*, though these are sidelined in favour of a more post-feminist presentation of women who have brains (the 'Brainiacs').

3   The guide also suggests that 'Teachers may also wish to adapt the material for Key Stage 2, as the production is also recommended for this age range [ages 7–11]' (2).

4   See Sheila Whiteley's 'Madonna, Eroticism, Auto-eroticism and Desire' in Whiteley (2000), 136–51. For further examples of the sort of visual language shown here see Leona Lewis's 'Bleeding Love' (2007), Christina Aguilera's 'You Lost Me' (2010) or Beyoncé's 'Best Thing I Never Had' (2011).

5   See Sells (1995), 181.

Chapter 11: 'I Wanna Be Like You': Negotiating Race, Racism and Orientalism in *The Jungle Book* on Stage

1   Original production dates.

2   Consider the similar casting practices of the black best friend in the Broadway musical versions of *The Little Mermaid*, *Tarzan* and *Shrek*, J. Brater et al. (2010).

3   In *Broadway: The American Musical* (2004), *The Lion King* director Julie Taymor positions this animal-human-race slippage as inspirational: 'Imagine, a young, African-American child going and seeing a king who's black.'

4   Although Zimmerman claimed to be taken out of context, the Executive Editor of *Chicago* denied this (Isaacs 2013).

Chapter 12: Ashman's *Aladdin* Archive: Queer Orientalism in the Disney Renaissance

1   Envelope, Box 8, Howard Ashman Papers, Music Division, Library of Congress, Washington, DC (hereafter Ashman Papers).
2   Ashman had Mrs Potts refer to Lumière and Cogsworth as 'you pansies' (Notes, Box 3, Ashman Papers).
3   *Aladdin* Treatment, 12 January 1988, Box 1, Ashman Papers.
4   Ibid.
5   See also relevant endnotes in Knapp's *The American Musical* for an elaboration of the subtext in *Singin' in the Rain*.
6   Inter-office communication from Charlie Fink to Howard Ashman, 19 January 1988, Box 1, Ashman Papers.
7   Here the parrot is named Sinbad, in keeping with the Arabian Nights theme, rather than the Shakespearean Iago.
8   Ashman's treatment and Clements and Musker's draft scripts from 1988 through 1990 contain annotations from Katzenberg explaining what he liked and didn't like (mostly what he didn't like) as well as penciled responses from Ashman, some of them quite tart.
9   See also Angela Y. Davis, *Blues Legacies and Black Feminism*, especially pp. 141–2.
10 Menken, quoted in David Morgan's 'Two Wishes for Aladdin', *The Hollywood Reporter*, 25 August 1992, S-25.
11 Iglehart, quoted in Harry Haun, 'The Hardest Working Genie in Show Business', in the Playbill for *Hedwig and the Angry Inch* on 19 July 2014.

Index